Criminal Justice
Recent Scholarship

Edited by
Marilyn McShane and Frank P. Williams III

A Series from LFB Scholarly

Felony Disenfranchisement in America
Historical Origins, Institutional Racism, and Modern Consequences

Katherine Irene Pettus

LFB Scholarly Publishing LLC
New York 2005

Library of Congress Cataloging-in-Publication Data

Pettus, Katherine Irene, 1956-
  Felony disenfranchisement in America : historical origins,
institutional racism, and modern consequences / Katherine Irene Pettus.
     p. cm. -- (Criminal justice)
  Includes bibliographical references and index.
  ISBN 1-59332-061-2 (alk. paper)
  1. Suffrage--United States. 2. Prisoners--Suffrage--United States. 3.
Criminal justice, Administration of--United States. I. Title. II. Series:
Criminal justice (LFB Scholarly Publishing LLC)
  JK1846.P48 2005
  324.6'2'0869270973--dc22

2004019388

ISBN 1-59332-061-2

Printed on acid-free 250-year-life paper.

Manufactured in the United States of America.

To all the missing and disappeared from the American polity since its inception.

Table of Contents

Acknowledgments

I would like to thank Professors Nadia Urbinati and Robert Amdur of Columbia University, and J. Phillip Thompson, and Ester Fuchs of Barnard, for their encouragement and help in developing and finishing the dissertation that was the foundation of this book. I would also like to thank Professors Robert Shapiro, David Johnston, and Jean Cohen of Columbia University for their assistance over the many years it took to complete my degree. I am grateful to Marc Mauer and The Sentencing Project for bringing the problem of felon disenfranchisement to my attention many years ago and for the ongoing data and policy reports provided by that organization. On a personal level, I could not have completed any of this work without the support of my partner, Andy Romero, and my sons, Pablo, Orlando, and Noah, as well as the friendship of Aysen, Mary and Sue.

Without the gracious technical and editorial assistance of Kay Hessemer, this work would not have gone to press.

No man is an island, entire of itself;
Every man is a piece of the continent, a part of the main.
If a clod be washed away by the sea, Europe is the less,
As well as if a promontory were, as well as if a manor of thy friend's
Or of thine own were: Any man's death diminishes me,
Because I am involved in mankind,
And therefore never send to know for whom the bell tolls;
It tolls for thee.

John Donne, Meditation XVII

If a constitution is to survive, all the elements of the state must join in
willing its existence and continuance.... Those constitutions which
consider only the personal interest of the rulers are all *wrong* constitutions, or *perversions* of the right form. Such perverted forms are despotic
[i.e. calculated on the model of the rule of the master, or 'depotes' over
slaves], whereas the polis is an association of freemen.

Aristotle, *Politics,* II, ix 1270b; III.vi. 1279a

Introduction

Classical political theory since Plato has asked the question, "what is the nature of the regime?" in a particular polity. Theorists such as Aristotle answered the question by looking at who is a citizen "in the full sense of the term." This book uses this classical standard of citizenship to interrogate the American claim that the United States is a democracy. I take this position because the modern American practice of felon disenfranchisement (state enforced but federally sanctioned) had its origins in the classical conception of citizenship invented and practiced in Athens more than two millennia ago. The first chapter of the book establishes this genealogy.

The red thread connecting Athens to Alabama, so to speak, is the fact both were slave societies, both considered themselves democracies, and both disenfranchised convicted felons for life. In 2004, approximately four million United States citizens are denied the right to vote in both state and federal elections because they have been disenfranchised by their states for felony (see Table 1).[1] Coincidentally, this is the same number of slaves who became "Americans" after the Civil War. This study is motivated by a curiosity about the fact that a disproportionate number of the criminally disenfranchised are non-White relative to their populations in the citizenry as a whole, although "criminality" is distributed relatively proportionally throughout the population.

The classic question of the identity of the regime has been largely ignored by the contemporary theoretical discourse on disenfranchisement, which looks at the constitutionality of the modern practice, its effect on minority voting rights, and partisan politics. All these aspects of the practice are important and deserve scholarly attention, but the question of the identity of the regime frames the bigger picture. Unquestionably, the United States qualifies as a democracy for the majority of its citizens, and felon disenfranchisement is constitutional, if only in terms of the particular version of citizenship that prevailed at the time of the First Founding.

Table 1. Categories of Felons Disenfranchised Under State Law

State	Prison	Probation	Parole	Ex-Felons All*	Ex-Felons Partial
Alabama	X	X	X	X	
Alaska	X	X	X		
Arizona	X	X	X		X (2nd felony)
Arkansas	X	X	X		
California	X		X		
Colorado	X		X		
Connecticut	X		X		
Delaware	X	X	X		X (5 years)
District of Columbia	X				
Florida	X	X	X	X	
Georgia	X	X	X		
Hawaii	X				
Idaho	X	X	X		
Illinois	X				
Indiana	X				
Iowa	X	X	X	X	
Kansas	X	X	X		
Kentucky	X	X	X	X	
Louisiana	X	X	X		
Maine					
Maryland	X	X	X		X (2nd felony, 3 years)
Massachusetts	X				
Michigan	X				
Minnesota	X	X	X		
Mississippi	X	X	X	X	
Missouri	X	X	X		
Montana	X				
Nebraska	X	X	X	X	

State					
Nevada	X		X		X (except first-time nonviolent)
New Hampshire	X				
New Jersey	X	X	X		
New Mexico	X	X	X		
New York	X	X	X		
North Carolina	X	X	X		
North Dakota	X				
Ohio	X				
Oklahoma	X		X		
Oregon	X				
Pennsylvania	X				
Rhode Island	X	X	X		
South Carolina	X	X	X		
South Dakota	X				
Tennessee	X	X	X		X (pre-1986)
Texas	X	X	X		
Utah	X				
Vermont					
Virginia	X	X	X	X	
Washington	X	X	X		X (pre-1984)
West Virginia	X	X	X		
Wisconsin	X	X	X		
Wyoming	X	X	X		X (5 years)
U.S. Total	**49**	**31**	**35**	**7**	**7**

* While these states disenfranchise all persons with a felony conviction and provide no automatic process for restoration of rights, several (Alabama, Kentucky, and Virginia) have adopted legislation in recent years that streamlines the restoration process.

Source: Jamie Fellner and Marc Mauer, *Losing the Vote: The Impact of Felony Disenfranchisement Laws in the United States*, Human Rights Watch and The Sentencing Project, October 1998, and updated by The Sentencing Project. 05/04

The fact that it is still constitutional and still relegates a portion of the citizenry to what Nora Demleitner calls "internal exile" raises the question of the consistency and integrity of the contemporary version of American democracy for the polity as a whole, not just a part.

Twentieth (and no doubt 21st) century students of political theory are taught Plato's, Aristotle's, and Polybius' theories of regimes in the context of the history of pre-modern political thought, rather than in the context of critical theory. Contemporary normative political theory analyzes and critiques liberal, republican, and democratic discourses of citizenship, [2] but ignores regime classification as such because it takes for granted the status of universal, *jus solis* citizenship. I believe this is a mistake. A polity such as the United States that claims democratic legitimacy in terms of a universal citizenship regime needs to ensure that claim is consistent in terms of all the citizens' political rights.

My search for the genesis of the contemporary American practice of felon disenfranchisement began with an examination of Aristotle's political theory, which studies citizenship regimes and identifies regimes in terms of their "conception of justice." A regime's conception of justice, in turn, determines who is and who is not a citizen, and therefore reveals what constitutes citizenship for those who qualify. The practice of disenfranchising or, less anachronistically, "dishonoring" citizens for transgressions of the requirements of the status began and was institutionalized as *atimia* in classical Athens, and was discussed by Aristotle in *The Politics*.

An Aristotelian analysis of the contemporary American citizenship regime brings the practice of felon disenfranchisement into theoretical perspective, since in The Philosopher's lexicon the disenfranchised are not citizens "in the proper sense of the term." Nonetheless, they "share" a polity in which citizenship is universally ascribed by birth. In the post-14th-Amendment American polity all persons born and naturalized in the United States are citizens both of the nation and of the state in which they live. Therefore, the presence in those polities (states and nation) of citizens without political rights raises the core Aristotelian questions of the nature of (American) citizenship and the identification, as well as the "justice" of the regime.

Although this study focuses primarily on the institutional issues outlined above, it is motivated by more than clinical curiosity to classify the contemporary American citizenship regime in terms of a modern taxonomy. The Aristotelian perspective, while superficially clinical, is deeply normative: the "end and purpose of the *polis* is the good life, and the institutions of social life are a means to that end." The ordering of those institutions in the political associations reveals their "justice," and "justice consists in what tends to promote the common interest." The weakly normative argument of the book is therefore that lifetime felon disenfranchisement, as it is institutionalized and legitimized in the United States today, is an unjust institution because it does not tend to promote the common interest. The genealogical enterprise of the book is to trace the origins of the contemporary injustice to its institutional root, which, empirically speaking is racial slavery, and philosophically speaking, is the absence of a normative framework within which Americans can judge, or adjudicate, the claims of the victims of slavery. The result is a deficit of justice that is expressed via the *criminal* justice system, as a failure of democracy. Permanent felon disenfranchisement is a contemporary (constitutional) American practice that explicitly contravenes the twin democratic promises of the anonymity and universality of political rights.

My claim that felon disenfranchisement is an unjust institution because it does not promote the common interest does not imply the existence of any predetermined notion of the "common interest" that can be discerned and implemented by particular citizens or rulers possessed of vision and skill. It is agnostic about the substance of the common interest, which I understand as something that can only be determined only by means of a fully inclusionary collective undertaking on the part of free citizens whose basic rights to participate in the political process are protected by fundamental law. It is agnostic because it denies that any group of citizens, no matter how morally "worthy" their qualifications may be in that they have never been convicted for crime, can discern the "common interest" if they exclude any portion of the citizenry from their deliberations.

The modern American practice of disenfranchising felons, particularly ex-offenders who have been released from prison into the polity of free enfranchised citizens, is a structural impediment to the fully inclusionary undertaking of discerning the common interest. This undertaking, in my view, is a precondition for the formulation of public policy that serves the good of the whole rather than the good of the part. Democracy is not simply a good in itself; it is not a political form that must be achieved and perfected for its own sake: its conception of justice as political equality is *functional*. Its purpose is to include all citizens on equal terms because only through inclusion can the potential of all individuals to develop and learn and therefore contribute to the whole be maximized.

This can also be put negatively: to the extent that free citizens are legally excluded or marginalized from the polity through institutions such as felon disenfranchisement, the polity (in John Donne's words) "is the less." The disenfranchised are America's "missing," our "disappeared," and the cumulative impact of their exclusion for as long as disenfranchisement laws have been in effect in the polity is incalculable. It has created an epistemological deficit in that the demos can never know what it has missed by fencing them out of the democratic process. Modern democracy is an ideally inclusive form: it is no longer the classical "rule of the poor," and the democratic political unit defined as "the whole" must justify political exclusions in terms of its own universal criteria in order to claim legitimacy.

I argue that the contemporary American practice of disenfranchising felons is predicated upon a (usually unarticulated) ideological, rather than deeply moral belief that "they" are importantly different from "us," and are therefore unworthy of political rights. The modern practice is structurally implicated in what was historically, and continues to be, a citizenship regime based on status honor that serves only the good of the part. As long as it continues to serve the good of the part, it is unjust and dysfunctional when the goal of today's democracy must be the good of the whole.

I say this because I believe, as all political theorists throughout the ages have believed, that we live in very critical times, particularly with regard to the condition of the planet and the future of life on earth. The United States, as the "most powerful nation on earth," the largest consumer of the world's resources, and "the leader of the free world," has a particular moral obligation to all the other inhabitants of the planet to organize its political society to serve the common interest. In that it is organized as a democracy, its citizens have the responsibility to develop the best public policies they can; by definition these require the collective wisdom of the demos, which cannot know in advance which voices to exclude, which will not be "worth" listening to.

The interesting question is why the ancient practice of disenfranchising citizens for crime is not only federally legitimized, but actively functions at historically unprecedented rates in a modern constitutional democracy such as the United States despite heroic and often successful grassroots efforts to change state laws.[3] The answer has several parts: constitutional, political, legal, and social. Constitutional law and federal jurisprudence positively sanction the practice; elected representatives allow historically enacted provisions to stand (political); offenses classified as felonies automatically trigger disenfranchisement upon conviction (legal); and law enforcement officials tend to profile and arrest suspects who can be charged, convicted and disenfranchised (social). The practice is both formally and informally sanctioned by officials of the criminal justice system, from the arresting officer to the

Supreme Court justice. It continues in the twenty-first century because a disproportionate number of those incarcerated and disenfranchised for crime are poor and minority citizens. To run the counterfactual, were the criminal laws applied generally, such that those incarcerated and disenfranchised for crime members were (proportionally) members of the political majority, white middle class or suburban citizens (voters) before their arrests, it is fair to speculate that the practice might have been abolished by now.

Felon disenfranchisement statutes have been on the books, in most states, since their incorporation into the Union, whether as former colonies, new states, or "reconstructed" states. As long as incarceration rates were stable in the U.S., and crime was not a publicly salient issue, the somewhat archaic requirement that convicted felons be disenfranchised did not appear to be either politically or normatively significant.[4] As incarceration rates began to rise exponentially in the second half of the twentieth century, and as public and scholarly attention began to focus on the negative or collateral consequences of the war on drugs, the issue of disenfranchisement became a "live" one for scholars and critics with concerns about American democracy. Formally speaking, disenfranchisement rates are tied to conviction and incarceration rates, which must be distinguished from crime and victimization rates. Socially and politically speaking, though, arrest, conviction and incarceration rates are institutionally inseparable from the American history of democracy, which is rooted in slavery and the institutionalized racism that has been legitimized by electoral majorities and constitutional jurisprudence since the Founding.

State felon disenfranchisement practices are a tool that can be used to deconstruct the "positive face" of the status of American citizenship. They reveal the "negative face," those citizens who are permanently exiled from the polity. The federalism that perpetuates felon disenfranchisement creates a double citizenship identity, which can be described as follows: American citizens cannot, despite their national citizenship status, vote in federal elections if they have been disenfranchised for felony by the *state* in which they are a citizen. Yet Americans must, and do have the constitutional right to vote for their national officers: President, Vice-President, and Members of Congress, those who represent them in virtue of their American, rather than state citizenship.

Insofar as American citizens disenfranchised by their state laws do not have this right, American policy, including foreign policy, lacks democratic legitimacy. Furthermore, American citizenship, according to the language of the Fourteenth Amendment, and the legislative history of its framing and passage, is lexically prior to state citizenship, yet in states that disenfranchise felons, that priority is reversed such that state citizenship trumps national citizenship on Election Day. The public policy corollary of this argument is that, although state law may disqualify a convicted felon from voting for local and state officers, federal law should allow her to vote for the federal officers who will represent her in virtue of her American citizenship.[5]

In the American states that disenfranchise felons today, in contrast with the premodern societies that disenfranchised citizens for what was essentially political misconduct, all convictions for offenses classified as "felonies," which range from trivial to serious, result in disenfranchisement. The American category of "infamous" crimes has expanded the original, highly serious meaning of "infamy," which was applied to capital crimes such as treason, to the point that the words "infamy" and "infamous" are now politically (as opposed to juridically) meaningless. Cesare Beccaria, the Enlightenment philosopher of punishment, made this point more than two centuries ago: "The punishment of infamy should not be too frequent, for the power of opinion grows weaker by repetition, nor should it be inflicted on a number of persons at the same time, for the infamy of many resolves itself into the infamy of none."

I argue throughout the book that just as the use of the penalty of felon disenfranchisement to exclude citizens from political rights creates double citizenship, it institutionalizes a fractionalized polity. The first polity—the numerator so to speak—comprises fully enfranchised, politically equal citizens who are entitled to participate in the representative system of "democratic" rule. Members of this polity, an internally democratic citizenship regime, take turns "ruling over" one another, but rule permanently over members of the second polity, constituted by the disenfranchised "free" citizens.[6] Members of the numerator polity have a positive political identity, members of the denominator polity a negative one.

My conclusion, after surveying the history of disenfranchisement, American criminal justice policy, and the jurisprudence regarding the practice, is that the American political "doubleness" structured by felon disenfranchisement configures a neo-colonial regime comprising a metropolis of "citizens proper" and a periphery of subjects. I believe the perspective of post-colonial theory, together with the immanent critique of liberalism articulated in the concept of the "racial contract" (Mills 1997) most accurately accounts for the racial bias in the American criminal justice system and the rates of disenfranchisement that "dilute" the minority vote. The identification of the regime as neo-colonial demystifies, de-"moralizes" the criminal justice policies that result in the incarceration and disenfranchisement of large numbers of poor and minority citizens. Revealing those policies and practices as the cumulative institutional expression of a multi-century pattern of racialized group domination (colonial) rather than the aggregated statistical expression of individual or personal moral failure (liberal/ republican) opens the way for political—democratic—conversation and action to alter those practices.

My argument is based upon the fact that the United States, as a post-colonial nation, constitutionalized the practice of African slavery institutionalized under English rule and structured the norms of white supremacy into its particular conception of republican citizenship. The Union victory in the Civil War and the ascendancy of the Republican Party during the Reconstruction Congresses that constitutionally abolished slavery, represented neither national rejection of those norms, nor an accounting for slavery insofar as it was a crime, and comprehended many "crimes." Never having developed a normative framework of retributive justice sufficient to evaluate such a domestic crime—as the Allies did in Nuremberg—the legacy of two and a half centuries of legalized slavery has gone unrepaired.

According to Hegel's theory of retributive justice, the harm wrought by a crime continues if it is left unpunished, and I argue in the final chapter that the national failure to address the federal crimes of slavery has damaged, and continues to damage both the polity as a whole and the democratic conception of justice that legitimizes it. Until it is addressed democratically, through the issue of reparations for slavery, the legacy of the original crime will continue to manifest itself by means of the structural racism that configures such institutions as the criminal justice system. The democratic "memory-justice" (Booth 2001) type of conversation called for will put the issue of felon disenfranchisement front and center, since according to the theory of democracy described in Chapter Two, all free members of the polity must be included or the reasons for their exclusion legitimately justified. Distortions in the national citizenship regime wrought by felon disenfranchisement and law enforcement practices could become apparent to American citizens by means of a democratic "memory-justice" conversation. Only then do I believe Americans will reject both the practice of permanent ex-felon disenfranchisement, as well as cumulative impact of discriminatory law enforcement policies that result in chronic offender disenfranchisement, and accept that democratic conversation will teach us how much we still have to learn from one another.

CHAPTER ONE

Citizenship and Status Honor: Pre-modern Origins of the Contemporary American Practice of Felon Disenfranchisement

INTRODUCTION

This chapter explores the classical, medieval and Early American genealogy of the modern American practice of felon disenfranchisement. It identifies *atimia,*[1] *infamia,*[2] outlawry, attainder,[3] and (contemporary) felon disenfranchisement as the negative juridical aspects of the positive (juridical) status of citizenship in the family of regimes where that status was an honorific one for a designated, bounded section of the community. It argues that *atimia* was consistent with the Athenian democracy, *infamia* with the Roman republic, outlawry and civil death with the medieval fiefdoms, and felon disenfranchisement with the colonial American and pre-Reconstruction slavocracy[4] because all bestowed (honorific) citizenship *non*-universally. The chapter looks at what was common to the Athenian, Roman, feudal, and colonial variations of felon disenfranchisement in order to lay the groundwork for an analysis of its "postmodern" legitimation in the modern American polity.

The chapter begins by reviewing the concept of status honor developed by Max Weber, whose theory describes what I believe is common to all the citizenship regimes that have, historically, institutionalized various versions of felon disenfranchisement. Status, which is instantiated both negatively and positively in reciprocal social, economic, and political relations, controlled the distribution of honor among defined groups of citizens (and "non-citizens") in classical and pre-modern regimes. Section 2 examines how status honor was

11

institutionalized in the classical "republican" concept of citizenship, and how it structured the "dual system of law" in the Athenian, Roman, and ante-bellum American regimes. Insofar as a core dimension of all those citizenship regimes was their interpretation of honor, only *citizens* were punished for infractions of collective honor by complete or partial withdrawal of their citizen rights. Slaves, women, and non-citizens whose lower status did not confer the property of honor were punished differently. Honor was the positive valence of citizenship in societies based on status, whose negative institutional counterpart was disenfranchisement for the *dis*honor incurred by offending the demos, which by definition was an elite, juridically distinct status group. The antithesis of the protected status of citizenship was the existential vulnerability of the disenfranchised, which reciprocally conferred impunity upon enfranchised citizens who could legally violate the person, household members and property of the convicted member of the demos.

Because the Athenian citizenship regime was the original political organization that institutionalized both citizenship and the penalty of disenfranchisement, or *atimia*—literally "dishonor," Section 3 looks closely at the Athenian practice, the offenses that triggered disenfranchisement, and the legalized vulnerability of the disenfranchised. Section 4 glances at the associated Roman concept of *infamia*, and at the European penalties of attainder and civil death, which continued the genealogy of disenfranchisement in the post-Roman world. Section 5 reviews the modern instantiation of that genealogy, the "felonies" and "infamous crimes" that warrant disenfranchisement in the contemporary United States. It also looks at what was *not* punished as a felony in order to establish my claim that, until slavery was abolished, the U.S., like the classical polities, operated under a "dual legal system" based on status honor.

The purpose of this brief excursus into historical institutionalism is to lay the groundwork for the jurisprudential argument of this book. In that felon disenfranchisement was once a "just" institution in the context of particular, premodern citizenship regimes based on status honor, it is dysfunctional in a high modern political context legitimated by universal citizenship rights. Its "injustice" can be described in terms of the social and political pathologies it generates, which contradict the conception of justice articulated by the regime. Ironically, the normative theoretical framework I am using to distinguish between citizenship regimes— Aristotle's—is quintessentially classical, in that its institutional configuration supported *atimia*.

1. MAX WEBER'S CONCEPT OF STATUS HONOR

Weber defines the "status order" as "the way social honor is distributed in a community between typical groups participating in this distribution." He distinguishes the status order from the social, economic, and legal orders, but claims that there is a strong reciprocal influence between the economic and status orders. "All are phenomena of the distribution of power within a community," but what distinguishes "status groups" or *Stände,* from economic classes is their often "amorphous" nature, and the fact that they are determined by "a specific, positive or negative, social estimation of *honor.*" Weber does not define the criteria of honor, which vary according to the particular societies, but says that honor "may be connected with *any quality shared by a plurality.*" The status group with the most power, therefore, defines the criteria of honor and dishonor: normatively acceptable acts and omissions that the legislator, in Aristotle's definition of political ethics, may reward and punish. Status honor, according to Weber can "of course (...) be knit to a class situation: class distinctions are linked in the most varied ways with status distinctions. Property as such is not always recognized as a status qualification, but in the long run it is, and with extraordinary regularity."

Status groups can come into being through a variety of ways, but for the purpose of analyzing citizenship regimes, the most important one is "through monopolistic appropriation of political or hierocratic powers." This emergence, in turn, can be linked to power over land and what Weber calls "special law," which was founded on status derived from certain social relationships related to material objects (such as land—a "copyhold or a manor.") In other words, the privilege of a status group, such as the voting rights of Athenian citizens, originally coincided with land ownership of adult males registered in the demes and enrolled in the military association of a phratry.

Status honor is linked to "maintenance of a specific style of life," which is expected of all those who wish to belong to the circle, and marriage is an important link between all members of the circle. Thus in almost all societies where status honor is distributed, there are legal and customary restrictions on social intercourse that may "lead to completely endogamous closure" between groups. This closure becomes particularly important in societies where status honor is distributed on the basis of ethnicity and ethnic segregation has evolved into a system of caste. Weber calls "ethnic groups"

> Those human groups that entertain a subjective belief in their common descent because of similarities of physical type or of customs or both, or because of memories of colonization and

migration; this belief must be important for the propagation of group formation; conversely, it does not matter whether or not an objective blood relationship exists... It is primarily the political community, no matter how artificially organized, that inspires the belief in common ethnicity. (389)

Status distinctions based on ethnic consciousness that have hardened into caste hierarchies are then guaranteed not merely by conventions and laws, but also by religious sanctions. "This occurs in such a way that every physical contact with a member of any caste that is considered to be lower by the members of a higher caste is considered as making for a ritualistic impurity and a stigma which must be expiated by a religious act." Caste segregation is the "normal form in which ethnic communities that believe in blood relationship and exclude exogamous marriage and social intercourse usually interact with one another." In societies where status honor has fossilized into caste hierarchies, laws against intermarriage or sexual relations between ethnic groups are strictly enforced.[5]

To sum up the relation between the concepts of status groups, ethnic groups, political communities, legal privilege, and honor, we might say that a particular ethnic group with its own sense of honor appropriates and monopolizes political power and legal privilege. It then can define itself in the social, legal and political terms of what is theoretically called a "status group." Weber is clear that status groups can be "positive" and "negative" and that "the road to legal privilege, positive or negative, is easily traveled as soon as a certain stratification of the social order has in fact been "lived in" and has achieved stability by virtue of a stable distribution of economic power." Moreover, law does not just protect economic interests, "but rather the most diverse interests ranging from the most elementary one of protection and personal security to such purely ideal goods as personal honor or honor of the divine powers. Above all, it guarantees political (...) and other positions of authority." This relation between law, status honor, and citizenship converged clearly in the Athenian, Roman, and antebellum American *poleis*. Its negative instantiations were the punishments of *atimia, infamia,* outlawry, and disenfranchisement, which literally entailed that a citizen be deprived of his honor, and existentially of his safety, should he transgress the norms of citizenship.

2. STATUS HONOR INSTITUTIONALIZED: CITIZENSHIP IN THE "REPUBLICAN" TRADITION

In what is called the civic republican tradition, the *practice* of citizenship as political participation reflected collective agreement among the select few who enjoyed the status of citizenship as defined by the laws of their particular polity about a particular set of values. In the Athenian polity that status was literally, etymologically, related to the possession of honor, or *timē*. Honor was

> a concept used to designate a specific political or legal status assigned to the different classes in the city such as slaves, metics and citizens. To have political rights was to be *epitimos*; to have none—or to be deprived of some—was to be *atimos*. To hold office was to be *entimos*. Demosthenes called citizens the class (*taxis*) in which the greatest amount of honor (*timē*) is present (*taxis en hei pleistes an tungchaoi timēs*) and so we can say that full *timē* was for male citizens; demi-*timē* for female citizens; certain bits of *timē* for metics; while nearly none was available for slaves. All citizens were equal before the law and thus had the same level of honor in this one sense. But every public competition gave an Athenian citizen a chance to increase (or risk) the honor that he received due to his personal characteristics and thereby to raise his status-role in the community. The manipulation of honor thus allowed for rank and distinction within the citizenry despite the equality of citizens and allowed the Athenians to establish and maintain social hierarchies. The competitive ethos in Athens was fueled by the construction of honor, which provided simultaneously for equality and rank. (Allen 2000, 60)

In the civic republican tradition the honor of the "good citizen" derived from his publicly displayed love of liberty and the laws over his private interests. Since the legal status of citizenship denoted equality before the law and under the law, it acted symbolically on citizens to produce love of country—*pietas, caridad:* the desire to serve all who shared the territory (Viroli 1998, 77). Montesquieu reformulated the classical "spirit of citizenship" for the moderns as "a love of the laws and the common good, even when it conflicts with particular interests." [6]

The political equality between citizens that obtained in republican polities and served as the foundation of the ideal of republican honor and virtue *cannot*, and this is the key point, be equated with the political equality that obtains in modern liberal democracies where citizenship is a birthright status distributed by the state. This is because the citizenry in the classical republican polities was a distinct status group that was not identified with the population of the polity as a whole, as it is in the modern nation-state. The legal structure defining the equal citizenship that obtained between members of the status group was embedded within a larger structure characterized by political and legal *in*equality.[7] Citizens were a select group of persons identified primarily by descent and distinguished by law from those co-inhabitants of the polity who did not possess the requisite genealogical or material qualifications of citizenship and were thus identified with negative status groups.[8] The laws and liberties virtuous citizens were required to love and defend *included* those that distinguished them from non-citizens and maintained their privileged status in civil and criminal law. Again, according to Aristotle, the particular concept of justice obtaining in a regime was linked to the particular concept of equality:

> [Political justice] consists chiefly in equality; for the citizens are associates of a sort, and tend to be peers by nature, though they differ in their habits. But there does not seem to be any justice between a son and his father, or a servant and his master—any more than one can speak of justice between my foot and me, or my hand, and so on for each of my limbs. For a son is, as it were, a part (*meros*) of his father, until he attains the rank (*taxin*) of manhood and is separated from him. Then he is in a relationship of equality and parity with the father. This is what citizens are like. In the same way and for the same reason there is no justice between master and servant. For a servant is something of his master's... Political justice seems to consist in equality and parity. [*Magna Moralia* 1194b5-23][9]

Where one expression of political justice in modern liberal-democratic states is a single legal system based on the civil equality of all citizens, political justice in classical or republican polities was based on a "dual," or two-tiered system of justice. This "distribution" in Weber's sense reflected the distribution of honor inscribed in the distinct legal status of citizens (*polites* in Athens, *honestiores* in Rome, and whites in the ante-bellum U.S.) and non-citizens (women, slaves, *metics*, and *humiliores*). The citizens in these polities enjoyed membership in what Weber calls special "law communities" where "all law appeared as the privilege of particular individuals or objects or of particular constellations of individuals or objects." As Hansen (1976) points out in his detailed discussion of punishment in Athens, there was a marked difference between the way *atimoi* and *kakourgoi* were punished.

Kakourgoi were typically first offenders executed without trial if they confessed and only brought before jurors if they pleaded not guilty when arrested and handed over to the Eleven. *Atimoi* on the other hand, were persons guilty of a previous offense for which they had incurred a loss of rights—procedures could only be employed against them if they committed a second offense by not respecting the *atimia*. With the exception of homicides and adulterers, *kakourgoi* invariably belonged to the lower classes. They were thieves, cutpurses, burglars and robbers who, if they failed in their crime, were usually caught in the act and summarily executed…. The largest group of *atimoi* was undoubtedly state debtors, who were mostly public officials who had administered public funds, wealthy citizens who had farmed one of the public revenues or discharged a *leiturgia,* and prominent Athenians who, in a public action, had incurred a heavy fine which they could not pay.

Moreover, in the economy of citizenship the life of a citizen commanded the highest price. The murderer of a citizen (or his Athenian wife or daughter) was tried before the court of the Areopagos, and could receive the death sentence; the murderer of a *metoikos* or *doulos* went before a lesser court, the Palladion, and was liable only to exile. "Athenian law held Athenian life dearer and maintained a firm separation between members and non-members of the polis." (Manville 1990,12)

Since the murderer of a citizen had deprived the polis of a portion of its collective honor, he was punished more severely than the man who killed someone without honor. In discussing the dual legal system of the Roman republic, Patterson (1982) relates status honor to legal privilege:

The privileged were tried in a different court, and the penalties they received differed from those meted out to the non-privileged who had committed the same offense. There were several channels of privilege; these included birth, Roman citizenship, wealth, and proximity to power. However, the main channel of legal privilege was the possession of *honor* or *dignitas,* which derived from character, birth, office, and wealth. (89)

In the United States, before the abolition of slavery, when ethnic status (in the Weberian sense) was defined and regulated by law, slaveholders (most of whom were citizens) were granted entirely different legal protections than were slaves and freedmen. As in the classical republics, the law also gave men and women—members of different (gender) status groups within the same ethnic group—entirely different sets of rights under civil and criminal law.[10] Moreover, the dual system of law was institutionalized throughout the several states as well as nationally by means of such laws as the Fugitive Slave Act.[11] As Fredrickson (1988) points out, "The South wanted slavery and blacks—it was committed to a hierarchical biracial society—and the North wanted neither—the popular preference was for white homogeneity. In one case ethnic status was based on direct domination and in the other on exclusion." (225)

Members of the citizen body of republican polities were not only "passively" qualified for their privileged status by ascertainable descent and/or property ownership, they were also required to embody the specific values that constituted the substantive "virtue" or "honor" of being a citizen. These included serving in the military (with valor), marrying within the citizen status group, and respecting the constitution. Evident possession and exercise of citizen virtue in Athens was rewarded with "honors" and offices (*timē*), while a deficit was penalized with "dishonor" or disenfranchisement (*atimia*). Aristotle's conflation of the two uses of *timē* as both "office" and "honors" in the following passage nicely illustrates the civic meaning of *timē*, which can be understood as both an institutional and evaluative concept:

> There are several different kinds of citizen, and the name of citizen is particularly applicable to those who share in the offices and honors of the state. Homer accordingly speaks in the *Iliad* of a man being treated
>
> Like an alien man, *without honor*
>
> And it is true that those who do not share in the offices and honors of the state are just like resident aliens. (*Politics* 1278a)[12]

As Ward (2001) argues, honor was a "fundamental political phenomenon" for Aristotle's political science, since it provides a bridge between moral virtue, which is not necessarily political, and necessity, which can be morally and politically vacuous. Honor, because it is socially constituted, depends on the judgment of others—citizen peers— and honors are distributed by the legislator. As

> the active moral principle of the citizen soldier, [honor] links the individual and the community in a way not possible in the perspective dominated by the extremes of nobility and necessity. One is publicly honored both for one's own merit and for service to the political community. In describing honor as "something noble" Aristotle defines the relation between the two as that between the particular and the universal (*NE*

1116a28). The noble transcends any particular, and honor operates as a particular manifestation of the noble expressed through public and private rewards. (80)

Since a citizen in a classical polity was a man who participated in "ruling and being ruled in turn," who had a "share in the polis," he naturally, *natally,* possessed the property of honor that was distributed to his status group of citizens. The theoretical propositions, like many of Aristotle's, are tautological and descriptive, since someone who did not share in the polis (was not a citizen)—a woman, a slave or a metic, by definition had no honor and therefore, of course, could not be *dis-honored*—could not be *atimos*. They were natally dishonored and natally vulnerable to the violence of their husbands, masters, and fellow citizens. They could not *dis*honor the polis by their actions. Yet when a citizen dishonored him*self* by an individual act or omission, he dishonored the polis as a whole and therefore lost his civic rights. He forfeited his share in the polis, either temporarily or permanently, depending on the nature of his transgression. He became one of the "Others"—members of status groups who "naturally" had a negative share in the distribution of honor and were physically, existentially vulnerable in a way enfranchised citizens were not. The citizenship/honor/protection—disenfranchisement/dishonor/vulnerability syllogism implies that citizenship status is synonymous with safety and protection. The classical theorists called a constitution or regime based on an economy of honor a "timocracy."[13] His political equals assessed an individual citizen's honor by comparing his personal attributes with those of their peers. Honor was a social and *public* property: men established their own worth by monitoring their standing vis-à-vis other men in their status group. In such a polity, "social relations define themselves through a politics of reputation, and the currency of that politics is honor, together with the social virtues which constitute it." (Cohen, 1995, 63)

Patterson (1982), citing the work of John Hope Franklin (1964) calls the ante-bellum South a timocracy, because Franklin "correctly emphasizes the notion of honor—not romanticism—as the central articulating principle of southern life and culture."[14]

Franklin shows how the notion of honor diffused down to all free members of the society from its ruling-class origins. Third, and most important, he demonstrates the direct causal link between the southern ruling class's excessively developed sense of honor and the institution of slavery. More specifically, he shows how the master's sense of honor was derived directly from the degradation of his slave. (95)

Drawing on Aristotle's discussion of honor in the *Rhetoric,* Cohen (1991) notes that "The man who confines his activities to the private sphere in the narrowest sense, the house, loses his honor, for such self-confinement is woman-like...To win honor, a man must live his life in public. Honor exists only in the evaluation of the community and requires openness and publicity." (80) Hence the inverse of honor (*timē*) —the punishment of *atimia*—demanded that punished citizens refrain from appearing in public, and confine themselves to the private sphere like women and slaves. Except that, unlike women and slaves whose "head of household" was *not atimos,* women and slaves who were therefore protected to a certain extent by *his* (the master's) untainted citizenship, the *atimos* was *un*protected, as were the members of his household.

Josiah Ober (1996) distinguishes between honor in an oligarchic citizenship regime—aristocratic honor—and in a democratic regime— citizen dignity—the former being a scarce resource in a zero-sum game, the latter "a collective possession of the demos" created by the power of collective action. (102) Ober argues that where aristocratic honor was personal, the "most precious possession of the ordinary Athenian citizen was, for want of a better term, the dignity he enjoyed because he was a citizen." (101) Citizen dignity, according to Ober, is a composite of individual freedom, political equality, and security. It is won through collective action of the demos, and because it is "a collective possession of the demos" can only be defended by collective action. [15] Hence stripping an individual citizen of his rights, making him *atimos,* disenfranchised, was an act of self-defense on the part of the demos. In Ober's theoretical framework, it was self-defense against pretensions of the oligarchy, rather than against either fellow citizens, or the "Others" of the polity, against whom no defense was necessary. No defense was necessary because the "Others" were not *and could never be* political equals with whom citizens would be called to compete for social honor. Post-bellum and contemporary American felon disenfranchisement turns the Athenian practice on its head, because as we will see in Chapter Four, it was the American "oligarchy" that was defending itself (and its honor) against the "pretensions" of the (reconstituted) demos. (The former slaves—during Reconstruction—and their descendents who clamored for their citizenship rights.)[16] This fits Aristotle's analysis of the causes of *stasis.* Stasis is an existential condition of the polity in which all citizens are vulnerable to violence and loss of livelihood, but particularly those who feel that their *honor* is threatened by those who aspire to equality.[17] This is because democratic equality displaces the aristocratic notion of honor, which as the *sine qua non* of the aristocratic citizenship identity cannot be relinquished without loss of that identity and the protections it confers.

Here Bourdieu's (1980) analysis of the fundamental principle of "equality in honor" is helpful, since the "exchange of honor" is always addressed to a man capable of playing the "game of honor." Bourdieu stresses the principle of "reciprocity" in honor, noting that "only a challenge issued by a man equal in honor deserves to be taken up." Conversely, a man who enters into an exchange of honor with someone who is not his equal in honor *dishonors* himself. Bourdieu argues that this is a "fundamental principle" in the universe of practices really observed that "impress both by their inexhaustible diversity and apparent necessity." Thus when a citizen dishonored his citizenship status and by extension his polity by transgressing certain norms, and was punished for doing so, he was forced into exile in the private realm. In that realm, where honor has no currency, the boundary between the public and private worlds defines the meaning—the positive valence—of citizenship. We now turn to the negative valence, the inverse of the citizenship regime, as it was expressed in the practice of disenfranchisement.

3. THE PUNISHMENT OF ATIMIA IN ATHENS AND SPARTA

The most common Greek word for punishment was *timoria*, another cognate of *timē*, or honor, while "to punish" was *timoreisthai*, which we might translate as "to assess and to distribute honor." (Allen 2000, 61) Punishment of citizens that resulted in *atimia* was a form of collective "forgetting" of an individual: it required that the citizen "disappear" from the polity so that his act would cease to pollute its collective honor. Thus *atimia* can be construed as a *negative distribution of honor*, in terms of Weber's spatialized framework. Unless, however, the *atimos* (dishonored citizen) chose exile, he did not disappear from the polity at all, he faded into the ranks of metics, slaves and women whose negative status prevented them from appearing at the Assembly or the law courts, and only rarely at the temples. Therefore, when citizens punished one of their own, they redistributed equality—or justice, in the Aristotelian definition given above—such that the *atimos* forfeited both his honor and his political equality. As Hedrick points out

> None of the rights and privileges of Athenian citizenship are "essential" qualities; they are only defining characteristics of the citizen insofar as they are not allowed to non-citizens. If both "citizens" and "non-citizens" were commonly permitted to vote, for instance, then the franchise would not be a quality of the

citizen, nor would it be any more significant or deserving of mention in a discussion of citizenship than say breathing or the ability to walk, or any of the other qualities and characteristics that humanity shares. (297) ... Boundaries, in other words, are made apparent and concrete by those excluded, not by some abstract, intrinsic, positive qualities possessed by those living within the edges. (295)

What was most "apparent and concrete" about those excluded was that they were socially, physically, legally and economically vulnerable in ways that *non-dishonored* citizens *were not.* So long as a citizen retained his honor, he retained his personal and psychic safety, his existential sense of intactness, which insofar as it was *politically* conferred by the demos, could be withdrawn or withheld by the demos.

Judith Shklar (1991) made this same point about status in her study of American citizenship, emphasizing the value of citizenship to white men as long as women and slaves were *un*enfranchised, but did not connect it to safety:

The value of citizenship was derived primarily from its denial to slaves, to some white men, and to all women (16) (...) The civil standing that these creatures could *not* have, defined its importance for the white male, because it distinguished him from the majority of his degraded inferiors. (49)

It was the very legally codified *existence* and negative status of those Shklar called "degraded inferiors" that conferred honor and distinction on the citizen class in a status-based regime. Yet in her compelling 1991 study of American citizenship, which emphasizes the centrality of voting and earning, Shklar misses the existential *function* of status. This could not simply have been the "feeling" of superiority, but was a very visceral sense of safety, of immunity (from random violence), and even of impunity (for the commission of random violence). That was the sense slaves, women, and the *atimos,* lacked as the victims, rather than the perpetrators of legalized violence.

And as Patterson (1982) emphasized in his discussion of honor and slavery in the U.S. South, honor and degradation were reciprocal properties: "the master's sense of honor was derived directly from the degradation of his slave." Thus the punishments of *atimia* or *infamia,* which involved the citizen's degradation and relegation to the ranks of the civilly dishonored served to sharpen and clarify the boundaries and principles of justice that defined the honorific qualities of the citizen status group. *Atimia* comprised a defensive tactic on the part of the demos that allowed it to identify itself against the non-citizen class by expelling those that had dishonored the demos. In doing so, however, the demos created a "dangerous class:" it wielded a double-edged sword that simultaneously made the *atimos* existentially vulnerable individually—endangered by potential attack—and itself, *the demos,* vulnerable, in danger of attack or subversion from those outside the citizen body, "for a state with a body of disenfranchised citizens who are numerous and poor must necessarily be a state which is full of enemies" (*Politics* III, xi., 1281b).

The ethical "contents" of the honorific core of citizenship, the virtues that constituted it, were specified in both law and custom. When those virtues were evidently absent, or violated through particular proscribed behavior, it fell to a citizen (as prosecutor) to bring the deficit to the attention of a citizen jury, which (unless the *atimia* was automatic) would convict and sentence their fellow citizen if they found him guilty. According to Hansen (1976) *atimia* was used as a penalty for not complying with an injunction, rather than for defying a prohibition. Thus it could be imposed for *not* appearing when called up for military service, for not obeying the general's order, or for desertion. Similarly, it could be imposed for cowardice, for abstaining from a naval battle, or for desertion from the navy. Failing to serve as an arbitrator in one's sixtieth year, for taking care of elderly parents, for dropping a public action, or for non-payment of debts to the state or to the gods all could result in *atimia.*

When *atimia* was imposed for an act—rather than for an omission or failure to act—it was usually either a punishment for a second or subsequent offense or an additional penalty. *Atimia* for a second or subsequent offense was inflicted on persons convicted for the third time of the crime of giving false evidence, making unconstitutional proposals to the Assembly, and habitual idleness. These were clearly political offenses against the *demos* itself, which had the direct responsibility of ruling Athens and funding the Athenian wars. Since most of the revenue of the state came from court fees and fines, and leases of state property such as mines, rather than taxes, private debt had serious public implications, rendering debt a political offense that resulted in temporary, and possibly permanent disenfranchisement:[18]

> The largest group of *atimoi* was undoubtedly state debtors, who were mostly public officials who had administered public funds, wealthy citizens who had farmed one of the public revenues or discharged a *leiturgia,* and prominent Athenians who, in a public action, had incurred a heavy fine which they could not pay. *Atimia* may be described as the typical penalty for failure

to perform civil duties or abuse of civil rights. Accordingly, politicians especially were in constant danger of incurring *atimia*. (Hansen, 1976, 54)

Atimia meant that the citizen lost his *timē*, because his status honor as a citizen consisted in his right to go to the assembly and vote, to serve on a jury, worship at the temple, bring any type of civil or criminal prosecution, fight in the army, appear in public places, or receive any of the material benefits of citizenship such as grain distributions. Some of these rights were also obligations to the polity, and included the obligation to marry a female citizen, or *asta*. A male citizen could be *atimos* if he married a female alien after 451/50. If someone gave an alien woman in marriage to a male citizen as if she were a woman of his family, he suffered loss of civic rights, his property was confiscated, and a third of it was assigned to the prosecutor. Any Athenian could open suit against him before the *thesmothetai*, as in the procedure against an alien who poses as a citizen. (Sealey, 1990) In his discussion of ethnic honor, Weber emphasized the point that marriage was a key element in the preservation of the status group.[19] As Garner (1987) points out, an hereditary *atimia* could be imposed for refusing to divorce a foreigner, marrying of a foreigner, and adopting a descendent of an *atimos*. These were all instances of trespassing the laws by which citizen rights were reserved for legitimate Athenians.[20]

Other crimes that triggered hereditary *atimia* were treason, attempts to overthrow the democratic constitution, bribery, theft of public property, and proposals to abolish certain laws. The descendants of state debtors did not inherit the *atimia* until the debtor died, unlike the descendants of traitors and thieves, who suffered it immediately. Anyone adopting heirs of someone convicted of such crimes were subject to *atimia*. (See also Garner [1987] on hereditary *atimia*.) Another distinction was made between *atimia* that was automatic and that which was imposed by sentence.[21]

Thus we have automatic *atimia* in all cases where a person had committed an offense for which he immediately incurred *atimia* prescribed by law or decree. The sanction took effect automatically without trial, and if the person did not respect the *atimia*, he could be prosecuted and incur a penalty more severe than the original *atimia*.

If the offender ventured to appear in public after the conviction he could be prosecuted anew, and could then be given a sentence more severe than the original *atimia* (66-67). *Atimia* was never a penalty directly imposed by jurors, and not prescribed by law. Hansen is unclear, though, about which crimes require *atimia* by sentence.

It is remarkable, and a significant contrast to the contemporary American system, as Hansen (1976) points out, that *atimia* was never inflicted on persons guilty of acts of violence (homicide, assault, rape etc.) or offenses against property (theft, burglary, robbery, etc.). As such, he concludes: "*atimia* was the penalty *par excellence* which an Athenian might incur in his capacity of a citizen, but not for offenses he had committed as a private individual." This did not mean, however, that *atimia* was a purely symbolic or abstract penalty, without potentially harmful consequences for the individual who suffered it. First of all, what to moderns might be considered a peripheral right or even a burden, the right to appear in the Assembly or to vote was a core *privilege* for Athenians. Moreover, since prosecutions for crimes such as assault or rape (of household members, for instance) were not brought by the state as they are today, but by the individual citizen affected by the crime, the *atimos* was potentially vulnerable to all manner of assaults against his person and his property, including members of his household, since total *atimia* included the loss of the right to prosecute in public as well as in private actions. Since this right to prosecute, to resort to self-help, was the only legal defense Athenians had against infringements of their personal rights, to lose it meant that all other, ostensibly "private" rights (to enforce contracts, for instance) were compromised.[22]

Although there was a difference between archaic and classical *atimia*, Hansen comments that the contrast with classical and archaic is not so great as it initially appeared. In archaic times, the *atimos,* like the outlaw in later European law, could be killed with impunity: "it must have been almost a civil duty," Hansen says, whereas in classical times it was only a possibility.[23] Aside from the inability to implement the essential "self-help" mechanisms of Athenian justice, the *atimos* lost the right to receive food during public distributions to citizens, such as the grain given by an African prince in 445 BC. This particular distribution led to a purge of the citizen roster because some non-citizens, falsely inscribed as citizens, were claiming a privilege to which they were not entitled (Finley, 82). Moreover, during periods of *stasis,* when the *diapsephismos* of 510 took place, the contrast between those who were "truly" citizens ("without defect" in Aristotle's words) and those who were vulnerable to *atimia* is dramatically described by Manville (1990):

> This "scrutiny" was not an orderly or parliamentary review of citizen lists. It was a reign of terror, caught up in the bitter civil war among aristocrats, ruthless leaders striving for political

power. (...) During 510/9 for the many men who were not aristocrats—and the many others who were—exile and "disenfranchisement" (and with it uncertainty about one's very life) were to be feared as much as anything they had ever known. It is against this background of the *diapsephismos*—a reign of terror in which "true" citizenship was a man's only defense—that the enormous popularity of Kleisthenes' reforms (which regularized the status of citizenship and the appropriate records) can be appreciated.[24]

Finally, turning briefly to Sparta, where *atimia* was a humiliating and defamatory penalty according to Xenophon, the link between status honor and citizenship was decisive. (ix. 6.) *Atimia* involved both loss of personal and public honor, as well as civil rights. MacDowell (1986, 61) attributes the more total nature of Spartan *atimia* to the link between citizenship and the Spartan "way of life."[25] He says that "it was a fundamental principle of the 'laws of Lykourgos' that a man lost his status as a citizen if he failed to keep to the Spartiates' way of life," translating this as "the life of honor." "It included both toils and privileges, and a man who deviated from it ceased to be a Spartiate peer." (42) For instance, a citizen who did not belong to a mess or who engaged in menial work or crafts for money could be disenfranchised. Just as in Athens, citizens could be condemned for a serious offense like treason or cowardice in battle. "Thuciydides, describing the action taken against the Spartans who surrendered at Sphakteria, after they returned home, clearly uses *atimia* to mean a loss of specific rights." The *atimia* seems to have been temporary, though, since they were later re-enfranchised.[26] MacDowell says that although we don't know much about it, it is reasonable to assume that "the life of honor" was central to being a Spartan citizen.

4. THE ROMAN INFAMIA

In Rome, whose citizen body was vastly larger than Athens, the formal divisions between citizen classes, divisions that did not obtain in Athens, are revealed by the different kinds of punishments each received for the same crime. In other words, differences in citizen status delineated the different degrees of physical and psychic violence the various classes were subjected to. The primary citizen division was between the plebeians (*humiliores*) and higher status citizens (*honestiores*). In Athens, all citizens received the same punishment under the democracy, and their punishments were distinguished, as we saw, from those of slaves and *metics*, by being non-corporal. In Rome, by contrast, lower class citizens could receive all sorts of corporal punishments, as well as gruesome capital punishments, which in many ways mitigated the distinction between citizen and slave.[27]

The Roman instantiation of Athenian *atimia* was *infamia*, which applied differently to different types of citizens because the Roman polity comprehended a spectrum of citizenships based, broadly speaking, upon property and status. Roman *infamia* struck directly at the civic honor (*existimatio*) of the high status citizen,[28] who either held or aspired to hold a public position.[29] Standards of citizen conduct were conformable to rank, to the notion of *dignitas* peculiar to the *public* position held by the citizen. Therefore, the notion of *existimatio* was not

> A simple and universal conception, attaching to *honores* in general, or to *jura publica* in general, but attaching to a class, or *ordo,* which is presumed to have a lifelong tenure of its position, and to which necessarily but few of the citizens can belong.... *Infamia* could not have been a uniform procedure if *existimatio* was not a uniform conception. (Greenridge 1894, 10-11)

During the heyday of the Roman Republic, *infamia* was a penalty that carried serious civic and political consequences. As political participation waned, though, and power of the Ceasars predominated, the force of *infamia* was proportionally reduced, and became virtually meaningless.[30]

The penalty of *infamia* applied when a man was awaiting trial, and followed him after conviction and into exile, if that was the penalty (only available to citizens) he claimed. If he returned to Rome after exile, he could be killed on sight, with impunity. His property was confiscated upon conviction, and he was without political or civil rights. Some people chose exile over trial, even, because they did not want the shame of even temporary *infamia*. It seems as though the severity of punishment in Rome made *infamia* a weaker penalty than the Greek *atimia*: in Athens, *atimia* and fines were really the only elite punishments available, whereas in Rome, execution, exile, the mines, and confiscation were the primary punishments of the elite. Execution and exile seem to make *infamia* irrelevant.[31]

A Roman citizen could suffer the penalty of *infamia* if he acted in bad faith under the law of what we might call today private contract, or mandate in Roman law. Under the Emperor Julianus, *infamia* was incurred upon dishonorable discharge from the army, as well as for conviction of theft, robbery, *injuria*, or fraud. Citizens who engaged in certain professions, such acting or procuring, were declared *infamis*, as were false accusers in criminal actions. A citizen who was derelict in his duties as a guardian of more vulnerable citizens, suffered *infamia*. For instance, if he was convicted of failing in his duty of guardianship, *mandatum*, or *depositum*; or if he married off a widow under his paternal authority before she had legally completed her period of mourning; or who married a widow before such completion; and other marriage "crimes."[32] While from the modern perspective the above, partial list may appear to comprehend a spectrum of unrelated offenses, a "grab bag" so to speak having no internal consistency, the common thread lies in the "injury to reputation" (*laesa existimatio*) incurred by the citizen who committed any of those offenses:

> The questions to which [special disqualifications based on an injury to reputation] give rise are partly moral, partly juristic: since the institution (*infamia*) itself depended on the theory that a moral taint involved a civic disability. It was this civic disability, conceived consciously as based on a moral imperfection, that was generally spoken of by the Romans as *infamia*. (Greenridge 1894, 13)

The earlier Roman *Infamia* was imposed by censors at their discretion,[33] and although in the later Republic offenses giving rise to *infamia* were codified, there is no necessary connection between the pronouncement of a convicted offender as *infamis* and exclusion from political rights. Greenridge's (1894) exhaustive study concludes:

> It is obvious... that the criminal law of Rome knew of no one perpetual disqualification attendant on a *minutio existimationis* brought about by conviction. Above all, loss of the most distinctive right of citizenship—the *suffragium*—is never mentioned in these cases. Sometimes these laws disqualify from *honores* and from the Senate, sometimes from the *album judicum*, sometimes they go so far as to inhibit the evidence of the condemned; but nowhere do they imply the loss of all political privileges. (33)

The later practice of *infamia* saw a marked change as a result of "the transference of law-making from the judges and the interpreting jurisconsults to the sole person of the Emperor. The infamia no longer has a natural growth: it almost loses its moral significance. It is employed merely as a very powerful weapon in the hands of the Emperor to check the evils of administration as they arose." (Greenridge, 144-145) This most interesting contrast with the American practice of felon disenfranchisement, instead of punishing petty criminals, brought the full wrath of the state down on negligent, corrupt and abusive judges, lawyers, and prosecutors. Suppression of documentary evidence necessary for the full solution of disputes, toleration of harsh treatment of prisoners, and failure to punish guardians of prisoners guilty of such treatment could all render administrators and judges *infamis*.[34] Treason, of course, was a crime that conferred infamy, and for the first time the penalty was made hereditary, and citizens who refused to fill the offices of their native places, to be Senators, suffered the penalty of *infamia*. Heretics, under the later Empire, were *infamis,* although pagans, interestingly enough were not.

In conclusion, the Roman *infamia,* like Greek *atimia,* rendered the citizen vulnerable to private and public attack, since the *infamis* could not resort to the "self-help" system of prosecution and protection. He could not bring criminal accusations, testify in court, or protect his family's honor by slaying an adulterer. Greenridge calls this a "serious disability" attendant on the pronouncement of *infamia*. As I will argue in Chapter Three, below, once the modern office of the public prosecutor, the representative of "the People," replaced the classical "self-help" systems, in which private citizens were the protagonist of criminal trials, the punishment of the *atimia* and *infamia* became institutionally superfluous and unjust.

5. Infamy, Civil Death, Attainder, and "Felony" in European and American Law

Since eleven American states disenfranchise offenders for "infamous crimes,"[35] and four states—Idaho, New York, Rhode Island, and Mississippi—have "civil death" statutes on the books, we will briefly investigate the medieval and feudal practices of outlawry, civil death, and attainder, which were punishments for "infamous" crimes. It will be noted that the "citizen's" franchise (*jus suffragim*) was not at stake during this historical juncture, as it was both in the *polis* and at Rome, since "citizenship" and the privileges and obligations that attached thereto, was not an institution associated with the medieval tribes or feudal fiefdoms. What was at stake for subjects were their lives and property, their existential safety, and that of their descendants.

Subjects could be declared civilly dead for serious crimes such as "treason against the community," homicide, severe wounding, and heresy. According to Itzkowitz and Oldak (1973), after the fall of the Roman Empire, the Germanic tribes if Europe and England used outlawry to punish those who committed particular crimes involving serious harms to society and to compel wrongdoers to comply with orders of the court. The offender was expelled from the community and completely deprived of his civil rights and society's protection. Thus the consequences of outlawry were severe: resulting in a denouncement as "infamous," the deprivation of all rights, confiscation of property, exposure to injury and even to death, since the outlaw could be killed with impunity by anyone.[36]

> Civic death means the absolute loss of all civil rights (…) it sunders completely every bond between society and the man who has incurred it; he has ceased to be a citizen,[37] but cannot be looked upon as an alien, for he is without a country; he does not exist save as a human being, and this, by a sort of commiseration which has no source in law." (von Bar 1916, 272, quoting Guyot, "Repertoire" "*mort civile*")

Civil death implied absolute vulnerability, since it "closed the doors to most of the honest occupations, and the frequent banishments from the cities and the country districts made the offenders homeless and deprived them of means of livelihood. In addition to this a deplorable part was played by confiscations (partial or total) of property."[38] The beneficiaries of the confiscations were the feudal lords and judges, to whom the traitors' lands reverted upon conviction. "Closely akin to confiscation is the other consequence of capital punishments, namely *civic death*. It is derived, in part from the rules of the feudal law regarding the loss of "*respons en cour*" in part from the Roman law notions of "*infamia*" and the "*dominatio in metallum*."[39]

While the sanctions of outlawry, civil death and infamy evolved in continental Europe, England developed its own method of imposing civil disabilities: attainder. Under the English system, a person pronounced "attainted" after conviction for a felony or the crime of treason was subject to three penalties: forfeiture, corruption of the blood, and loss of . civil rights (Itzkowitz and Oldak, 724, citing Blackstone, *Commentaries* 381-89).[40] As they colonized North America, the English settlers transplanted much of their common law heritage, including the imposition of civil disabilities and forfeiture of property that resulted from the procedure of attainder.[41] In some colonies, the concepts of infamy and outlawry were introduced into their criminal codes.[42] Following the American Revolution, the newly independent states rejected some of their inherited legal tradition, specifically prohibiting in the United States Constitution ex-post facto laws and bills of attainder,[43] as well as forfeiture and corruption of blood except during the life of a person convicted of treason.[44] Nonetheless, eleven states retained civil disabilities in their constitutions adopted between 1776 and 1821, denying voting rights to convicted felons or authorizing their state legislatures to do so.[45] Before the Civil War, 19 of the 34 states in the Union excluded serious offenders from the franchise.

A random survey of Table A.7 "Suffrage Exclusions for Criminal Offenses: 1790-1857" in Keyssar (2000) describes the constitutional exclusions. California: "persons convicted of any infamous crime;" Connecticut: "Those convicted of bribery, forgery, perjury, dueling, fraudulent bankruptcy, theft, or other offenses for which an infamous punishment is inflicted;" Iowa: "those convicted of any infamous crime;" Maryland: "Persons convicted of larceny or other infamous crime;" New Jersey: "those convicted of felonies;" Minnesota: "those convicted of treason or felony." The language in at least twenty of the constitutionally authorized state statutes restricting the franchise lists conviction for "high crimes and misdemeanors," along with "bribery, perjury, forgery," and "infamous" crimes as causes for disqualification.

Under American law, the term "infamous" may signify the mode of criminal punishment inflicted, or may refer to the fact that one is disqualified from testifying in a court of justice.[46]

> It is in this latter sense that our law is similar to the Roman Law concerning *infamia*. In our law, it is only crime that works infamy and renders the criminal incompetent as a witness. The crimes that so result are treason, felony, and every species of *crimen falsi*, such as forgery, perjury, subordination of perjury, false pretenses, public cheating, and any other similar offense which involves falsehood and affects the public administration of justice.[47]

Since "felony" is one of the classes of crimes which, along with treason, result in infamy, and still, in seven American states, lifetime (ex-offender) disenfranchisement, it is worth reviewing the origin of the word. The Oxford English Dictionary traces the etymology of "felony" to the Old French *vil*, meaning "treachery, ill will, misdeed" from *villein*, which translates as "villain," or "rogue," and from the Middle English *vilein*, or *villain*, "of base or depraved character: wicked, dastardly; of common birth or origin." A "felony" is defined as

1. An act on the part of a vassal involving the forfeiture of his fee or an act of a lord involving the forfeiture of his lordship in feudal law.

2. A grave crime (as murder, mayhem, manslaughter, rape, robbery, larceny, burglary, arson, rescue of a felon, some types of prison breach, some offenses for which benefit of clergy was abolished, and sometimes treason) declared

expressly as distinguished from a misdemeanor in English common law and resulting in outlawry if the offender fled and until the Forfeiture Act of 1870 resulting upon conviction in the offender's loss of his goods or lands or both and sometimes in punishment by loss of a member, whipping, death, or imprisonment.

It is interesting that the root of the word felony is associated with low status members of the polity, but that those attainted for felony were invariably high status members. The association must have been that their behavior, their offense, was worthy only of low status persons, therefore warranting the attainder.

The foregoing thumbnail sketch of two millennia of the legal history of civil disabilities should have clarified at least two key points: first, those rendered *atimos, infamis*, attainted, or outlawed by the sovereign, were members of high status groups according to Weber's theory described in Section 1 of this chapter. They were either citizens, possessed of political rights, or later, subjects who owned property, or had status honor, that could be forfeited to the sovereign. Slaves, serfs, and peasants by (status) definition could not be dishonored, rendered "infamous" or forfeit property. The punishments they were subject to were corporal, and usually capital. So all these penalties and disabilities applied only to an elite. Second, the crimes that triggered the disabilities under discussion were very serious ones, usually capital crimes such as treason or murder, or crimes such as bribery, forgery, or perjury, which compromised the integrity of the legal and political system and prevented citizens/subjects from serving as witnesses or public officials.

I shall now briefly note a few examples of what was and was *not* considered a felony under the "dual legal system" that was institutionalized in the colonies and the United States before the Civil War and Reconstruction. The relevance of this empirical excursus will not become theoretically apparent until the discussion of impunity in Chapter Five of this book. For instance, Higginbotham (1978, 121) cites a 1705 New York statute that declares that runaway slaves could be "convicted of a felony and executed." It was a capital offense for a slave to try to obtain his or her freedom in New York and in many other states. Nonetheless, killing a slave was *not* a felony. A master could kill his slave with impunity. The Virginia Act of 1699 stated:

> "*Be it enacted and declared by this grand assembly,* if any slave resist his master... and by the extremity of the correction should chance to die, that his death shall not be accompted Felony, but the master (or that other person appointed by the master to

punish him) be acquit from molestation, since it cannot be presumed that propensed malice (which alone makes murther Felony) should induce any man to destroy his own estate." (*ibid.* p. 36)[48]

Higginbotham claims that slaveholders didn't want criminal laws to apply to slaves because such application would result in economic losses, so they applied "private punishment," which usually involved what would in modern terms be called "assault and battery" that could result in the death of the slave.[49] "Masters' prerogative of ownership was rarely the subject of judicial or legislative scrutiny," so scrutiny and punishment were largely confined to the conduct of slaves, free blacks, the "dangerous classes" in general, and those whites who fraternized with blacks. As we have seen throughout this chapter, the status honor conferred by citizenship has always had a protective function so long as citizens remained within its written and unwritten legal parameters: a citizen *dis*honored by a felony conviction loses the protection of society and becomes economically and physically vulnerable.[50] As an Athenian *atimos* or Roman *infamis,* he couldn't file suit against an assailant or robber, serve as a witness or as a juror, and in many cases he forfeited his property. In the contemporary United States, the civil disabilities attendant upon conviction reach far beyond disenfranchisement, in many cases inhibiting the right to be married, have custody of children, own property, serve as a juror, own a firearm, and hold public employment.[51] The ultimate existential vulnerability is, of course, life in the "ghetto" and in prison.[52]

The same vulnerability that followed a citizen dishonored by a conviction under formal, written law implicitly attached by virtue of "unwritten law," which Aristotle considered more authoritative, to those (not convicted) citizens whom the original citizen body considered "dishonorable" or natally unworthy of citizenship.[53] In the American case, although political majorities did not consider the recently emancipated slaves worthy of full citizenship, the Reconstruction Amendments dismantled the dual legal system that had operated since colonial times, and decreed that blacks were citizens. My claim is that the portion of the dual legal system that had formerly applied to non- or sub-citizens, and that had been *formally* superceded by the constitutional amendments of the Radical Reconstruction, was reconstituted in the realms of both 'unwritten' and statute criminal law. By the turn of the century, the Southern (and some Northern) states were able to 're-constitutionalize' black exclusion via jim crow laws.[54]

The vulnerability of free blacks (and Southern Republicans) under "unwritten law" and the terror perpetrated with impunity by the Ku Klux Klan[55] of the turn of the 20th century was graphically described by Ida Wells-Barnett in 1900. Despite the fact that they were formally "citizens" in the terms of the Fourteenth Amendment, they had (existentially speaking) the *status* of "outlaws," in the legal terms described in this chapter. Yet, under the terms of formal law, the codes of criminal procedure that are legitimate in a unitary, rather than dual legal system, it was the enfranchised citizens who were acting as "outlaws" in the received sense of the term. The terror inflicted on black citizens was

> ...[t]he work of the 'unwritten law' about which so much is said, and in whose behest butchery is made a pastime and national savagery condoned. The first statute of this 'unwritten law' was written in the blood of thousands of brave men who thought that a government that was good enough to create a citizenship was strong enough to protect it. Under the authority of a national law that gave every citizen the right to vote, the newly-made citizens chose to exercise their suffrage. But the reign of national law was short-lived and illusionary. Hardly had the sentences dried upon the statute books before one Southern State after another raised the cry against 'negro domination' and proclaimed there was an 'unwritten law' that justified any means to resist it. (Wells-Barnett 1900, 71)

In somewhat different terms Cesare Beccaria (1766, 1983), the Enlightenment theorist of punishment, states that actions taken in the name of honor (honor being the central property of timocratic citizenship) put offenders outside the realm of written law:

> [H]onor, being produced after the formation of society, could not be a part of the common deposit, and therefore, whilst we act under its influence, we return, for that instant to the state of nature *and withdraw ourselves from the laws,* which in this case, are insufficient for our protection.

In my reading of American history, this means that when political majorities—those who are actually protected by formal rights of citizenship—enforce the written and unwritten codes of honor that were the genesis of their political society, they reproduce the structural *dis*honor of non-citizen vulnerability. Kant (1797, 1991) also claimed that the laws of honor (re-)place us in a state of nature and clash with civil law (the categorical imperative); he asserted that when civil law trumps honor, those who are punished for acting in its name will perceive the state as illegitimate. (159) That is exactly how the "reconstructed" Democratic South perceived the federal government until the passage of the civil rights laws in the mid-twentieth century, when it began to transform itself into the Republican South, in an attempt to control the federal government.[56]

What happened after the American Civil War, following Radical Reconstruction and the re-admission of the former Confederate states into the Union, was that many states[57] added phrases such as "confinement in the penitentiary" to the relevant articles in their constitutions that enumerated the causes for disenfranchisement. In other words, conviction for *any* crime that carried a prison sentence could result in disenfranchisement for a specified period (up to life), depending on statutory provisions for pardon or release from the disability, if such provisions existed.[58] Thus disenfranchisement became contingent upon both the criminal code of the particular state, as enacted by the legislature—which crimes carried prison sentences—as well as upon the proclivities of judge and jury to convict and sentence in each particular case.[59] Moreover, some states enumerated "new" crimes (apart from "infamous" crimes, perjury, and bribery) that triggered disenfranchisement.

These included (in the case of Alabama, 1901) such offenses as "embezzlement, larceny, receiving stolen property, obtaining money or property under false pretenses, assault and battery on the wife, bigamy, miscegenation, crime against nature or crime involving moral turpitude; also any person convicted as a vagrant or tramp, or election fraud."[60] Georgia's (1877) constitution included a "moral turpitude" disenfranchising clause, and South Carolina's included "bigamy, wife beating, housebreaking, receiving stolen goods, breach of trust with fraudulent intent, fornication, sodomy, assault with intent to ravish, miscegenation, larceny, or any offense against election laws." During the infamous "disenfranchising conventions" when these constitutions were drafted, delegates were explicit that their intention was to disenfranchise the newly emancipated (male) slaves, whose enfranchisement "except for participation in rebellion or other crime" was mandated by Section 2 of the Fourteenth Amendment. Former Confederate elites used the political process to transform the practice of felon disenfranchisement from a rarely used provision that applied only to a relatively tiny part of the population (enfranchised white males)[61] for a restricted number of "high crimes," into a practice that was applied to a relatively large part of the population (newly enfranchised male former slaves) for a virtually unlimited number of petty crimes.

In the states today, popularly elected legislatures and/or Attorneys General enumerate and define disenfranchising felonies. The most recent and greatest expansion since Reconstruction in the definition of felonies and crimes warranting imprisonment in the penitentiary has taken place in the contexts of the "wars" on crime and drugs. The medieval punishment of forfeiture has returned, as those charged with "drug crimes" are required to surrender their property to the state, and disenfranchisement for felony and the definition of "infamy" has tracked the historically unprecedented incarceration rates associated with the war on drugs.[62]

CONCLUSION

The brief survey of ancient and premodern citizenship regimes, which constitute the "positive" institutional genesis (the DNA) of the modern practice of American felon disenfranchisement, suggests that a core component of the identity of the pre-modern citizen was the symbolic and material property of honor. The premodern citizen enjoyed the social and legal privileges of positive "status honor," which distinguished him from those "Others" in the polity whose status honor, according to Weber's scheme, was negative. This scheme implies the existence of a publicly recognized *quantum* of honor, whose attributes were determined by the political elite, and whose configuration constituted the "justice" of the polity in Aristotle's terms. When a citizen violated the legal code of honor that defined his citizenship and set him apart from those who were *not* citizens, his peers "punished" him by depriving him of honors, or citizen rights. This punishment of *atimia,* the negative cognate of *timē,* literally the honor that denoted the property of citizenship, cast the transgressor into the state of legal and material vulnerability of the non-citizen: foreigner (migrant), woman ("welfare queen"), or slave ("drug addict/dealer/prisoner"). The very existence of this caste of non-citizens who lacked the property of honor, and who did not share in the equality enjoyed by citizens, defined both the value of citizenship and the degree of protection it conferred on its legal "honorees."

Before the Civil War and the passage of the 13th, 14th, and 15th Amendments, the United States as a federal polity, and the several states as individual polities, represented citizenship regimes that were legally—constitutionally—based on status honor. The American founders articulated the dialectical relationship between honor/freedom, and slavery/infamy in the following passage justifying their "right to revolution against Great Britain:"

> We have counted the cost of this contest…and find nothing so dreadful as voluntary *slavery. Honor,* justice, and humanity forbid us tamely to surrender that freedom which received from

our gallant ancestors, and which our innocent posterity have a right to receive from us. We cannot endure the *infamy* and guilt of resigning succeeding generations to that wretchedness which inevitably awaits them, if we basely entail hereditary bondage upon them.[63] (Italics added)

As countless commentators have pointed out, the founders saw nothing ironic in declaiming *their* "voluntary slavery" and proclaiming *their* "right" to be "free" while maintaining a system of "involuntary" slavery (an oxymoron) that conferred hereditary dishonor and infamy on its victims and their descendants.[64]

As I hope to demonstrate in the following chapters, under the post-14th-Amendment American citizenship regimes, felon disenfranchisement in the (formally) biracial, post-slavery electorate became a partisan weapon aimed at (racial) group, rather than individual, political exclusion. The structural imperatives of representative government, party competition, and majoritarian elections in the context of the social imperatives of *herrenvolk* democracy made it so.[65] Insofar as that is the case, twenty-first century felon disenfranchisement, particularly ex-offender disenfranchisement, is *not* the same institution as that codified in Section 2 of the Fourteenth Amendment, to which Chief Justice Rehnquist deferred when he declared that the Constitution had given "affirmative sanction" to the state practice alluded to in 1865.[66] Ex-offender felon disenfranchisement, a classical and later medieval remedy for individual elite crimes against the ("democratic," "republican" or feudal) elite sovereign, renders the American federal *jus solis* citizenship regime undemocratic.

CHAPTER TWO

Felon Disenfranchisement and the Problem of Double Citizenship

Since the institutional identity of the disenfranchised felon is the "negative" of the citizen endowed with political rights, and negativity is notoriously hard to describe save in terms of the positive, I analyze the practice of felon disenfranchisement as an aspect of citizenship. My perspective is explicitly Aristotelian, in that I interpret citizenship as an institution and a practice that directly corresponds with distinct constitutions, or "regimes" (*politeis*). This chapter approaches the issue of felon disenfranchisement in the American states from this perspective of regimes. In order to orient the reader to this perspective, I am supplying a glossary of the terms used throughout the chapter. All are from *The Politics* (trans. Barker):

> **Regime**: A polity or constitution [or regime] may be defined as 'an organization of offices in a state, by which the method of their distribution is fixed, the sovereign authority is determined, and the nature of the end to be pursued by the association and all its members is prescribed. (1289a)

> A constitution (or polity) may be defined as 'the organization of a *polis*, in respect of its offices generally, but especially in respect of that particular office which is sovereign in all issues. The civic body, [the *politeuma*, or body of persons established in power by the polity] is everywhere the sovereign of the state; in fact the civic body is the polity (or constitution) itself. In democratic states...the people [or *demos*] is sovereign. (1278b)

> Regimes differ from one another in kind...hence the citizen must necessarily differ in the case of each sort of regime." (1275b) "Citizens, in the common sense of the term, are all who share in the civic life of ruling and being ruled in turn. In the

particular sense of the term, they vary from constitution
[regime] to constitution.

Citizenship: A polis or state belongs to the order of
'compounds' ... a state is a compound made up of citizens...
the nature of citizenship, like that of the state, is a question
which is often disputed: there is no general agreement on a
single definition: the man who is a citizen in a democracy is
often not one in an oligarchy. (1275a)

Citizenship belongs to a particular class of things where (1)
there are different bases on which the thing may depend, (2)
these bases are of different kinds and different qualities—one of
them standing first, another second, and so on down the series.
Things belonging to this particular class, when considered
purely as so belonging, have no common denominator
whatever. (1275a)

Justice: Justice, which is a determination of what is just, is an
ordering of the political association," (1253a) "The good in the
sphere of politics is justice; and justice consists in what tends to
promote the common interest. General opinion makes it consist
in some sort of equality...it holds that justice involves two
factors—things, and the persons to whom things are assigned—
and it considers that persons who are equal should have
assigned to them equal things. But here there arises a question
which must not be overlooked. Equal and unequals—yes; but
equals and unequals in what? (1282b)

Both oligarchs and democrats have a hold on a sort of
conception of justice...in oligarchies, inequality in the
distribution of office is considered to be just; and indeed it is—
but only for those who are unequal, and not for all... Justice is
relative to persons, and a just distribution is one in which the
relative values of the things given correspond to those of the
persons receiving. (1279b)

Justice is a ground which is usually pleaded in establishing any
form of constitution—be it aristocracy or oligarchy, or be it,
again, democracy. In all forms alike the claim is made that
justice demands the recognition of some sort of superiority,
though the sort for which the claim is made varies from one
form to another. (1288)

INTRODUCTION: THE SCHOLARLY CRITIQUE

The literature on the American practice of felon disenfranchisement, almost all of which is found in law review articles, unanimously condemns the practice as "irrational and discriminatory behavior of the states" (Fletcher 2001 148), a "violation of equal protection," (Reback, 1973, 845), a racially discriminatory practice that results in minority vote dilution (Shapiro, 1993, Harvey 1994, Hench 1998), and an anachronistic and counterproductive form of punishment (Itzkowitz and Oldak, 1973; Tims, 1975).[1] Jesse Furman (1997) says the modern Supreme Court's failure to overrule state laws disenfranchising felons reflects "an ambivalence deep within modern liberalism's normative ideals," and a 1989 Harvard Law Review Note calls felon disenfranchisement "a prop in the communal act of self-delusion [that] absolves the community of any complicity in the creation of crime and rationalizes harsh punishment of offenders." (1311) I have found no scholarly literature that unequivocally defends the practice, particularly that of ex-felon disenfranchisement. Only Jean Hampton (1998) argues that offenders incarcerated for violent crimes, particularly crimes against women, should be disenfranchised.[2]

All the authors problematize the contemporary practice of felon disenfranchisement in the context of the national trend since Reconstruction to broaden and federalize the franchise. Increased judicial scrutiny of voting rights in the states since the 1960s apportionment cases, they argue, make the persistence of ex-offender disenfranchisement in the face of a series of legal challenges, an anomaly. Most discuss the theoretical and constitutional justifications for the practice—most famously the "purity of the ballot box" argument adduced by the states—in the light of modern philosophies of punishment, and claim that ex-felon disenfranchisement is a contradiction and an anachronism in a modern liberal democracy. Shapiro, Harvey, and Hench in particular argue that the disproportionate incarceration of minority males in the recent decades of "sentencing reform" interacts with felon disenfranchisement laws to impermissibly dilute the black vote under the Section 2 of the Voting Rights Act. None of the authors cited believe that the practice should withstand the modern Supreme Court's standard of "strict scrutiny" of state abridgments of the franchise. All the authors criticize felon disenfranchisement from the perspective of citizenship in a unitary democratic nation-state where it is entirely appropriate for the federal judiciary to put an end to what they perceive as unconstitutional abridgments of citizens' political rights.[3]

Indeed, the convincing empirical evidence and legal arguments these scholars bring to their critiques of felon disenfranchisement beg the question, how has the practice withstood the constitutional challenges it has faced in many states, and in the Supreme Court, in the past few decades? The very short legal answer, whose theoretical underpinnings will occupy us in this chapter, is federalism, and "Guarantee Clause"[4] of the Constitution. The guarantee of a "republican form of government" in the federal system means that the states, within the "negative strategy"[5] of the 14th, 15th, 19th, 24th and 26th Amendments, have plenary power to regulate both the "police power"[6] and the electoral franchise within their boundaries.[7] The explicit constitutional basis of felon disenfranchisement, affirmed in 1974 in the governing case, *Richardson v Ramirez,*[8] is Section 2 of the Fourteenth Amendment, which mentions the traditional state practice and in (then) Justice Rehnquist's words, "is of controlling significance."[9]

Rehnquist considered the modern arguments against felon disenfranchisement adduced by the respondents in the California case,[10] and the impassioned dissent by Justice Marshall arguing that the practice should be overruled by the federal judiciary, but stated (I believe correctly) that

> We would by no means discount these arguments if addressed to the legislative forum which may properly weight and balance them against those advanced in support of California's present constitutional provisions. But it is not for us to choose one set of values over the other. If respondents are correct, and the view which they advocate is indeed the more enlightened and sensible one, presumably the people of the State of California will ultimately come around to that view. And if they do not do so, their failure is some evidence, at least, of the fact that there are two sides to the argument. (56)

As such, Rehnquist was taking the position that a state's choice to disenfranchise convicted felons was a *political* matter, an issue for the citizens of the state, the demos, to decide as they think fit who shall have the right to vote.[11] This is the essence, as we shall see below, of "republican" government. When the Supreme Court decides *for* the people who—beyond the limits imposed by the Congress in the Amendments otherwise forbidding the states from abridging the franchise—may or may not be included in its definition of "the people," it acts improperly. In the second Justice Harlan's words, quoted from his dissents in the apportionment cases decided by the Warren Court, it "judges constitutional questions on the basis of abstract "justice" unleashed from the limiting principles that go with our constitutional system."[12] Such judgments spring from "impatience with the slow workings of the political process." In Harlan's view, "the vitality of our political system" is weakened by "reliance on the judiciary for political reform" with the result that in time "a complacent body politic" may develop.[13]

The problem with leaving the question of felon disenfranchisement to popular majorities in the states, while constitutionally as well as politically "correct" in terms of republican theory and practice, is that the same persons whom the states qualify to elect state and local officials are also those who elect *federal* officers. This means that, institutionally speaking, the state citizen's right to *national* representation is compromised by his state identity if he is disenfranchised under the law of his state. Multiple (unconstitutional) inequalities in national citizenship, which will be explored in the next chapter, flow from the diversity of state laws regulating the franchise of felons. It is this structural situation, the compromised identity of the *federal* citizenship of each individual member of the polity, which calls for the intervention of the federal judiciary, and the disaggregation of state and federal voting rights. In other words, although a convicted felon may be disqualified by state law from voting for local and state officers, she *should*—in a unitary national democracy—be qualified by federal law to vote for the *national* officers, such as Congressperson, Senator, President, and Vice-President, who will represent her in virtue of her American citizenship.[14] Notwithstanding the fact that the U.S. is a federal nation-state, the concept of *American* citizenship, as Michael Walzer (1996) has argued, is compelling:

> The United States is not a literal "nation of nationalities" or a "social union of social unions." At least, the singular nation or union is not constituted by, it is not a combination or fastening together of, the plural nationalities or unions. In some sense, it includes them; it provides a framework for their coexistence; but they are not its parts. Nor are the individual states, in any significant sense, the parts that make up the United States. The parts are individual men and women. The United States is an association of citizens. Its "anonymity" consists in the fact that these citizens don't transfer their collective name to the association. It never happened that a group of people called Americans came together to form a political society called America. The people are Americans only by virtue of having come together. (27)[15]

Moreover, the Supreme Court itself has declared that "The citizenry is the country and the country is its citizenry."[16] Yet American citizens who are convicted of crimes are deprived of all political rights if the laws of their state of residence disenfranchise for felony convictions. There is, as I noted above, no "federal" electorate apart from the aggregated, and politically splintered, state electorates that can remedy this situation by means of a "democratic" debate and decision about national voting rights.[17]

What the scholarly legal literature on felon disenfranchisement fails to analyze is the political theory of citizenship and constitutions that configures this federal structure and the conception of democracy that results from aggregating the residual "republican" polities of the states into a national polity. Outright prohibition of the state practice of felon disenfranchisement, recommended by the majority of scholars, would result in effective abandonment—or radical redefinition—of the guarantee of republican government to the states, and a reconfiguration of the conception of justice of the national, federal polity. The prevailing "double citizenship" regime historically entailed by federalism and consistently reaffirmed by Supreme Court decisions, despite the federalization of voting rights since Reconstruction, actually creates and maintains a "double polity" that contradicts the constitutionally inscribed conception of democratic justice all the scholars assume obtains in the modern national polity. They critique the practice of felon disenfranchisement in terms of that "discursive" or "textual" conception of modern democratic justice, but do not acknowledge or theorize the normative implications of its structural emptiness.

The state right to disenfranchise felons is the cipher that can be used to decode the double polity, and reveal the structural "injustice" buried in the national citizenship regime as a result of the multiple citizenship regimes extant in the states. In other words, felon disenfranchisement is not an anomaly in an otherwise just or democratic national citizenship regime that can simply be adjusted to eliminate it. It is an essential part of the deep structure of modern American citizenship. As such, only an alternative vision of democracy, a moral vision, along the lines traced by American idealists such as Whitman and Dewey, can provide a perspective that will allow American citizens to criticize and overcome— in the political realm—the institutionally structured inequality that currently defines their national identity. This is because the moral vision of democracy is based on a conception of the person that is relational— inter-subjective—and that demands universal political inclusion in order to maximize individual *and* collective development and security. A society envisioned democratically by its members "shoots itself in the foot" so to speak when it permanently excludes members of the citizen body from political rights. A moral or normative vision of democratic citizenship demands an "internal" or subjective political identity as well as an external, or structural set of democratic procedures that secure universal political rights. This vision will be taken up in the third section of the chapter.

1. THE PROBLEM OF DOUBLE CITIZENSHIP IN THE UNITED STATES

In the modern United States, the apparent sovereignty of the national government and the lexical priority of national over state citizenship[18] belie the fact that multiple citizenship regimes based on different conceptions of justice and configured by different distributions of political rights co-exist in the same body politic. As James Madison pointed out in Federalist 45:

> The State governments may be regarded as constituent and essential parts of the federal government... Without the intervention of the State legislatures, the President of the United States cannot be elected at all. The Senate will be elected absolutely and exclusively by the State legislatures. Even the House of Representatives, though drawn immediately from the people, will be chosen very under the influence of that class of men whose influence over the people obtains for themselves an election into the State legislatures. Thus, each of the principal branches of the federal government will owe its existence more or less to the favor of the State governments, and must consequently feel a dependence, which is much more likely to beget a disposition too obsequious than too overbearing towards them.

While U.S. Senators are no longer selected by state legislatures but elected directly by the voters in each state, the federal structure of the national franchise remains much as Madison described it. Officers of the sovereign national state are elected by the citizens of the several states, not by citizens who are members of a national electorate governed by uniform rules. This federal structure poses a question of the identity of the political regime or constitution and its associated conception of justice: what is the identity of the American state if its sovereign body is elected by the citizens of the several states, each of which has a distinct political identity and allocates political rights among its citizens differently? The political identity of the American nation-state is not what it appears to be—a unitary democratic republic based on national membership—since no political rights inhere in the ascribed status of American citizenship.[19]

> [Voting] is not a privilege springing from citizenship of the United States... It may not be refused on account of race, color or previous condition of servitude, but it does not follow from mere citizenship of the United States. In other words, the privilege to vote in a State is within the jurisdiction of the State itself, to be exercised as the State may direct, and upon such terms as to it may seem proper, provided, of course, no discrimination is made between individuals in violation of the Federal Constitution [obviously referring to the Fifteenth and not the Fourteenth Amendment]...the question whether the conditions prescribed by the State might be regarded by others as reasonable or unreasonable is not a federal one." *Pope v Williams*, 193 U.S. 621 cited by Harlan, J. in his dissent in *Carrington v Rash* 380 U.S. 89 (1965)

In order to ascertain the identity of a regime, Aristotle suggested that his students begin by identifying the citizens. Acknowledging that "there is no general agreement on a single definition: the man who is a citizen in a democracy is often not one in an oligarchy," he takes a Wittgenstinean turn and refers students to linguistic usage:

> Citizens, in *the common sense of the term*, are *all* who share in the civic life of ruling and being ruled in turn. In *the particular sense of the term*, they vary from constitution [regime] to constitution." (1275a,b) (Emphasis added.)

In the United States, the first sentence of Section 1 of the Fourteenth Amendment apparently answers the question "who is a citizen?" in the particular sense of the term, referring to the American constitution. Moreover, the language of the amendment itself implies a conception of justice based on equality. Logically, if "*All* persons born or naturalized in the United States, and subject to the jurisdiction thereof, are citizens of the United States and of the State wherein they reside," then all are equal in virtue of that status. This sentence of the Constitution ushered in a new national citizenship regime of *jus soli* equality where what had existed before was a citizenship regime based on the birthright *in*equality of slave and free status. It expressed the "refounding" of the Republic, in Professor Ackerman's words. No provisions for "ruling and being ruled in turn" appeared in the constitutional language of the *re*founded constitutional regime. American citizens cannot be identified as such in "the common sense of the term" (of ruling and being ruled) because definitions of political rights still vary according to the constitution, criminal codes and felon disenfranchisement provisions of each state.

Prior to the Civil War Amendments, "the status of national citizenship remained at best vague. The Constitution mentioned it without defining what it was."[20] What had existed before was a federal compact between the states, which had been free to define citizenship and qualify electors for state and national office on their own terms. The post-bellum citizenship regime, whose genesis was the Union's military victory, proclaimed a new right of national membership but did not abolish the states' control over political rights of those members. The first sentence of the Fourteenth Amendment contains all the complex implications of this contradiction by affirmatively defining the compound nature of the polity: Americans are citizens of the nation *and* of the state in which they reside. So what took place in 1866 was not a complete *change* of citizenship regimes in the sense of transformation: what actually happened was that a new national citizenship regime of status equality was superimposed by constitutional amendment onto the old "republican" state regimes, which retained both their ante-bellum status distinctions and control over citizens' political rights.

This "superimposition" of a national citizenship regime onto the state regimes settled only the legal status of the former slaves. As such, it raised questions of "justice" that before the war had not been salient political questions for elected majorities in the South, since neither slaves nor freedmen were included in the civic body.[21] Those questions of justice were never democratically settled or accepted by the *politeuma* as a whole. The constitution was amended by the victors of the military contest, who held electoral majorities in the Reconstruction Congresses, but national mores didn't change along with it, even after a devastating civil war:[22]

> A more serious difficulty [with regard to identifying who is a citizen] is perhaps raised by the case of those who have acquired constitutional rights as the result of a revolutionary change in the constitution. We may take as an example the action of Cleisthenes at Athens, when after the expulsion of the tyrants he enrolled in the tribes a number of foreigners and a number of resident aliens belonging to the slave class. The question raised by such an addition to the civic body is not the question of fact, 'Who is actually a citizen?' It is the question of justice, 'Are men [who are actually citizens] rightly or wrongly such? (*Politics* 1275b)

Elected majorities in the states, considering the men who were actually citizens under the new regime to be "wrongly such" used the constitutional means at their disposal to strip former slaves of their citizenship status and restore the "right" conception of justice. The states "reserved" this right in the system of American federalism that guaranteed them a "republican" form of government. They could not deny or abridge the right to vote "on account of race, color or previous condition of servitude," according to the Fifteenth Amendment, but they could do so—and did—on account of illiteracy, failure to pay a poll tax, or conviction for felony.[23] They used constitutional and extra-constitutional (terroristic) means to institutionalize state citizenship regimes that corresponded with their particular conception of justice.[24] Nonetheless, the conception of justice associated with the "refounded" *national* citizenship regime was, and remained, "democratic" because "the people" are sovereign,[25] and the citizens who *do* have political rights are equal.

> The democratic conception of justice is based on the enjoyment of arithmetical equality, and not the enjoyment of proportionate equality on the basis of desert. On this arithmetical conception of justice the masses must necessarily be sovereign; the will of the majority must be ultimate and must be the expression of justice. The argument is that each citizen should be on an equality with the rest. (*Politics* 1317b)

The U.S. Supreme Court reaffirmed this ancient democratic conception of justice in a series of cases during the early 1960s:

> The concept of 'we the people' under the Constitution visualizes no preferred class of voters but equality among those who meet the basic qualifications.

> The conception of political equality from the Declaration of Independence, to Lincoln's Gettysburg Address, to the Fifteenth, Seventeenth and Nineteenth Amendments can mean only one thing—one person, one vote. Douglas J., ruling in *Gray v Sanders,* 372 U.S. 368.

There is a fault line running through this apparently uniform "arithmetic" conception of democratic justice based on equality, though. Justice Douglas's allusion to "those who meet the basic qualifications" in his *Gray* ruling implies that there are citizens who do *not* meet the basic qualifications, and who are therefore *not* equal (in terms of their political rights) to their fellow citizens who are qualified voters. The existence of a set of "unqualified" citizens suggests that there is "equality for equals" (among the set of natural citizens and the subset of qualified voters) and "inequality for unequals," (among the subset of unqualified voters and qualified voters in the set of national citizens). In terms of political rights, therefore, it can be said that there is "proportionate equality" (1279b) in the national citizenship regime.

So there is a problem of political identity for those members of the polity who are free American citizens but who, as a result of their state identity, are not "qualified voters" for the purposes of national elections. As such, they are absent from the *politeuma,* or civic body, of the United States. The fact that "unqualified" citizens exist within the civic body and are therefore logically outside the democratic polity of the United States, indicates that another constitution, one that may be conceived of as a parallel one that accounts for their negative status, exists within the nation-state. The obvious answer, that they live in the same "democracy" as their fellow American citizens, who as a matter of law have decided to exclude these citizens from the electorate, will not do, since there is no such thing as an "American electorate" or demos, governed by uniform laws that can "decide" anything. What appears as an "American electorate" represented by federal officers is actually an aggregation of the state electorates, each of which comprises a distinct citizenship regime in its own right.

Disenfranchisement for crime is the primary source of ongoing citizen exclusion from modern state electorates, and therefore from the (aggregated) national electorate or *politeuma.* The duration of the exclusion, from none whatsoever in two states, to lifetime exclusion in seven states, varies according to the constitutions and statutes of each state.[26] Unlike the "passive," uniform exclusions from the citizen electorate of minors and the insane, which are based on (relatively) objective criteria, felon disenfranchisement is a non-uniform, "active" form of exclusion based on majoritarian state laws and varied, subjective criteria.[27] The central point for the present purposes is to distinguish the political exclusion of felons and ex-felons from that of children and the mentally incompetent, about which there is widespread national and international consensus. The argument may be restated in the following terms:

1. Citizenship regimes in the states, which co-exist on equal (sub-sovereign) terms in such national institutions as the Senate and the Electoral College, give otherwise equal (national) citizens different sets of political rights, i.e. create different types of citizens in the national citizen body;

2. No national electorate corresponds with the national citizen body;

3. The nominally "national electorate" that chooses federal officers such as President and Vice-President is an actually an aggregate electorate comprising all the sets of "qualified voters" in the several states. It is therefore a "splintered" rather than "unitary" national electorate.

4. The existence of a "parallel" or "shadow" citizenship regime comprising citizens of the national body without political rights in the national electorate can be hypothesized.

Although the juridical status of these citizens without political rights and the identity of the polity to which they belong are empirical questions, the normative question has to do with the legitimacy of the national "democratic" regime and its relationship to the "shadow" or parallel regime comprising the "unqualified" citizens.

Hyland's definition of democracy as "a system of decision-making in which all those who are subject to the decisions made have equally effective power to determine the political outcomes of the decision-making" reinforces the analytical link between democracy and participation in the formation of legislation to which citizens are subject. (1995, 81) All those who are "subject to the decisions made," and who have "equally effective power to determine (...) outcomes," enjoy full citizenship in a democracy. This *fact* of equal political freedom reveals the normative *function* of democratic citizenship, which is the creation of legitimate sovereignty. The method associated with the creation of legitimate sovereignty is "democratic" when it includes competitive and "free" elections of representatives, conditions of full information and so on.[28] If these conditions are defective, then the legitimacy of the sovereign regime can be called into question. The central structural "defect," I shall argue in this chapter, arises from the variation in qualifications of voters who comprise the electorate that chooses the representatives of the nation.

The defect results from each American citizen's "double identity." The constitutional sovereignty of the national government should mean, logically, that the national citizenship identity of Americans should also be sovereign. Yet national birthright citizenship, which identifies the citizens who are members of "the People," does not automatically confer national political rights on those individual members:

> The right to vote, per se, is not a constitutionally protected right, and the constitution does not compel a fixed method of choosing state or local officers or representatives. *Rodriguez v Popular Democratic Party* 457 U.S. 1[29]

Even though,

> The political franchise of voting [is] a fundamental political right, because preservative of all rights. *Yick Wo v Hopkins*, 118 U.S. 356 (1886).

And

> Undoubtedly, the right of suffrage is a fundamental matter in a free and democratic society. Especially since the right to exercise the franchise in a free and unimpaired manner is preservative of all other basic civil and political rights, any alleged infringement of the right of citizens to vote must be carefully and meticulously scrutinized. *Reynolds v Simms* 377 U.S. 533 (1964)

The apparent "contradictions" in these rulings point to the fact that, as Aristotle taught, not only can the polity contain different kinds of citizens, the person can embody different kinds of citizenship. Since Americans are citizens of their states and of their nation, and each state is entitled to a "Republican form of government,"[30] each state defines the political rights of its citizens differently. Equal citizenship status in the sovereign nation is not matched by equal citizenship rights of national political representation. The Guarantee Clause is the root of this structural disjunction. As Justice Black commented in *Oregon v Mitchell,*

> No function is more essential to the separate and independent existence of the States and their governments than the power to determine within the limits of the Constitution the qualifications of their own voters for state, county, and municipal offices...

But his list of the offices for which states qualify their voters is too short. Elections for national offices—President, Vice-President, and Congress—are also run within each state, and citizens who vote for those offices must have the same qualifications as those who vote for the local offices on Black's list. A person who is qualified to vote for President in New York may not be qualified to vote for President in Mississippi or Wyoming. Thus they are represented differently, if at all, in the sovereign citizen body, the *politeuma*.

To my knowledge, no classical or contemporary political theory examines the tension that results from the co-existence of institutionally unequal rights to political representation in the citizen body of a modern democratic nation-state. Classical political theory analyzes the citizenship identities that correspond to different (unitary) political regimes such as monarchy, democracy, oligarchy, and aristocracy, as well as the cycles of regimes and the different configurations of citizen rights and obligations that result from the transformation of one regime into another. Aristotle even tackles the "compound" polity, which may combine elements of the citizenship regimes of aristocracy, and democracy. Politically speaking, though, the classical "composite" citizenship regime comprised only citizens who enjoyed political rights, but who were assigned different functions: i.e. deliberative or judicial, and "Others." The existence of slaves, disenfranchised citizens (*atimos*), and colonial subjects who were "Others" without political rights was a given in Aristotle's compound polity.

> Modern state citizenship differs sharply in this respect from citizenship in the ancient Greek polis or in medieval towns. There it was axiomatic that some persons ought *not* to be citizens of any city. Persons lacking citizenship were not placeless; their status was not anomalous. Rather, they did not form part of the self-governing or otherwise privileged civic corporation. (Brubaker 1992, 31)

Recent American political theory assumes the structural sovereignty of national citizenship and denies the (axiomatic) presence of "others" (besides "aliens" or "illegals") in the polity now that blacks, women, and formerly shunned immigrant groups have been enfranchised by constitutional amendment. Contemporary debates focus on whether the United States is a "republican" or "liberal" polity in terms of the theoretical lineages of its founding, and the extent to which democratic political rights either are or can be equitably distributed among individual members or designated groups. Normative theoretical analysis of the fact that the federal structure of the United States as it has evolved has configured structures of dual citizenship for all members of the polity, including enfranchised members, is startlingly lacking. How the plethora of distinct and in some cases irreconcilable rights and privileges entailed and implied by those citizenships implicates a normative theory of democracy, is unexplored ground.

I will use the institution of felon disenfranchisement to decode this tangle of citizenships; its very negativity can be dialectically contrasted with more inclusive democratic practices—or with a "democratic way of life" in John Dewey's words. The following two sections review the theoretical underpinnings of the "compound" structure of American citizenship, and the meaning of the "republican" or Guarantee Clause as it applies to state citizenship. The final section presents a normative American democratic theory—George Kateb's notion of democratic individuality, based on Emersonian idealist philosophy, and John Dewey's distinctively "moral" concept of the "democratic way of life."

This more lengthy analysis will serve as a basis for my critique in Chapter Three of the contemporary judicial interpretations of the political rights of American citizenship and the apparent anomaly of felon disenfranchisement.

2. COMPOUND CITIZENSHIP: THEORETICAL PERSPECTIVES

The modern federal polity of the United States is a "compound republic" on many levels: institutionally speaking power is divided among the different branches of government and exercised concurrently by political subdivisions within the nation and within the states. A standard definition is Riker's (1964, 11):

> A constitution is federal if (1) two levels of government rule the same land and people, (2) each level has at least some area in which it is autonomous, and (3) there is some guarantee (even though merely a statement in a constitution) of the autonomy of government in its own sphere.

In terms of political identities, the United States is also a "compound republic" in the sense that some of its citizens exist within a political limbo because they are un- or differently represented, having been disenfranchised for crime, whereas their fellow citizens enjoy political rights and representation. Conceiving of citizenship as an identity opens up two different perspectives on the apparent anomaly of felon disenfranchisement in a modern liberal democracy that is also a federal republic. The first identity to consider is the "administrative" or juridical identity of national citizenship, which is defined in terms of natural, status equality. This identity is ascriptive, and based on the imperative of territorial closure in a world of nation states. It is

> regulated by formally articulated norms and enforced by specialized agents employing formal identification routines... Thus the development of citizenship proceeds *pari passu* with that of an administrative apparatus of classification and surveillance (in the broadest sense) and a corresponding body of administrative knowledge. (Brubaker 1992, 30)

The citizen is identified and defined as

> a member of a state, an enfranchised inhabitant of a country, as opposed to an alien; in U.S., a person, native or naturalized, who has the privilege of voting for public offices, and is entitled to full protection in the exercise of private rights.[31]

In a modern "liberal-democratic" polity, where citizenship is distributed on the criteria of *jus soli:* the "personal values or merits" of an individual are irrelevant to his status as a citizen. As Aristotle says, "in democracies, justice is considered to mean equality. It does mean equality, but equality for those who are equal, not for all." In the post-14th-Amendment U.S. polity, Aristotle's democratic "equality" is modernized to include all those born or naturalized on U.S. soil, who are co-"equal" citizens simply in virtue of their natality. This administrative conception of the identity of citizenship entails a vertical relationship between the state and every individual citizen: it does not entail any intersubjective, or horizontal relationship between the individual citizens who comprise the citizen body of the nation.

The administrative definition of citizenship, though, begs the question: who is a *dis*enfranchised member who has "served his time," paid his "debt to society" and yet now lives within the citizen body as a "free" person?[32] What is *his* political identity, and what is the nature of the civic bond between enfranchised and disenfranchised individuals, both of whom are identified as "citizens," who inhabit the same polity? The generic definition of "citizen", although correct from the juridical perspective of the nation, misses the intersubjective, or "political" aspect of citizenship, which brings the practice, or relationship, of (dis)-enfranchisement into view. The "political" is what Hannah Pitkin (1993), following Sheldon Wolin, calls the "we," the collectivity, the shared public interest, which is developed by means of discourse and requires a plurality of viewpoints.[33] Those who are equal citizens in status from the administrative perspective of the nation may be *un*equal from the political perspective of the demos in a "republican" polity constituted by one of the several states. It is this perspective that demands a dynamic, intersubjective definition of citizenship.

Charles Tilly (1996, 5-7) insists on this intersubjective element in the definition of citizenship, which he identifies as a "tie," "a continuing series of transactions to which participants attach shared understandings, memories, forecasts, rights and obligations." The participants share an identity, which is located in "connections among individuals and groups rather than in the minds of particular persons or whole populations."

As such, the identity of modern citizenship can be described theoretically as a compound: a pair of at minimum, two relationships. There is a "political" relationship that obtains between members of a polity, and a juridical one that obtains between the state and the individual. The relationships are asymmetrical, though, since the political is "prior" to the legal: the intersubjective tie that constitutes the sovereign ultimately determines who does, or does not, enjoy the legal status of citizenship. Furthermore, as the practice of felon disenfranchisement shows, even if citizens enjoy the birthright citizenship according to the legal criteria of the national sovereign, the state demos may still decide to deprive that person of the privilege of political rights. This is what Aristotle meant when he said that the polis is "prior" to the individual or the family, because the "whole is necessarily prior to the part." (*Politics* I, ii, 13)

The conception of citizenship as an "intersubjective tie" can be described in terms of the Aristotelian concept of "justice."

> Justice is relative to persons; and a just distribution is one in which the relative values of the things given correspond to those of the persons receiving. It follows that a just distribution of offices among a number of different persons will involve a consideration of the personal values, or merits of each of those persons. (*Politics* III, ix, §3)

In republican polities such as those represented by the several states, elected majorities determine "a just distribution of offices [and political rights] among a number of different persons," since it is the prerogative of the states to set the criminal justice codes and the rules of elections for local, state, *and* federal office. This conception of justice can both originate in and result in *in*equality, since the original, self-appointed demos in the republican polity may erect institutions, and enact laws and regulations that subsequent elected majorities perpetuate. As Tilly points out, this type of identity is cultural, and historical, in

> calling attention to the path-dependent accretion of memories, understanding and means of action within particular identities. (...) Thus scholars have come to think of citizenship as a set of mutual, contested claims between agents of states and members of socially-constructed categories: genders, races, nationalities and others.

The concept of "path-dependence" Tilly employs is useful for such an understanding of citizenship as an "intersubjective tie" that is born in, and continues to generate inequality. Path dependence is analytically related to the concept of increasing returns processes, which may also be described as self-reinforcing, or positive feedback processes. (Pierson, 2000, 251) Originally a concept used in the study of economics, path dependence can be usefully applied to political phenomena.

> Indeed, factors such as the prominence of collective activity in politics, the central role of formal, change-resistant institutions, the possibilities for employing political authority to magnify

power asymmetries, and the great ambiguity of many political processes and outcomes make this a domain of social life that is especially prone to increasing returns processes. (*ibid*.252)

The political relationships between citizens in a "republican" polity that distributes political privileges on the basis of status honor, and historical institutions and practices such as felon disenfranchisement are easily assimilated to this model. Theories of path-dependence and increasing returns are particularly interesting when applied to such political problems as the difficulty of implementing norms of racial justice in an institutionally modern polity such as the United States. According to the theory, even when practices become "inefficient" in economic terms, or "unjust" in normative terms, they remain "locked in" to a path-dependent process because "the costs of exit—of switching to some previously plausible alternative—rise" as rules and norms are institutionalized by collectivities. A "status-quo bias" results from the difficulty of overturning change-resistant public policies and institutions that are *designed* to be difficult to overturn for two broad reasons:

> First, those who design institutions and policies may wish to bind their successors... Unlike economic actors, political actors must anticipate that their political rivals may soon control the reins of government. To protect themselves, they may create rules that make preexisting arrangements hard to reverse. As Moe (1990, 125) puts it, designers [owing to political uncertainty] "do not want 'their' agencies to fall under the control of opponents. And given the way public authority is allocated and exercised in a democracy, they often can only shut out their opponents by shutting themselves out too. In many cases, then, they purposely create structures that even they cannot control themselves. Second, in many cases, political actors are also compelled to bind themselves"... To constrain themselves and others, designers create large obstacles to institutional change. (262)

Path-dependent arguments in studies of politics focus on historical junctures, or "critical moments" that trigger the formation of durable institutions, practices, and lawmaking.[34] In terms of the study of American citizenship and felon disenfranchisement, the critical historical juncture is the Reconstruction period, particularly the passage of the Fourteenth Amendment. (This historical juncture and its impact on American citizenship will be analyzed in Section 1 of the following chapter.) As noted earlier, the new regime was superimposed on the "old regime" of republican citizenship that prevailed in the states. The following two sections will review normative dimensions of republican and democratic citizenship theory insofar as they pertain to the "compound polity."

3. REPUBLICAN CITIZENSHIP

The genesis of American constitutionalism and the immediate post-revolutionary citizenship regime was the colonial experience of British subjecthood. This experience provided the Founders with both a heritage of political theory and law, including the laws of slavery, as well as an object lesson in how *not* to construct a polity if the goal was to protect individual freedom. The revolutionaries who founded the new regime viewed the colonial regime as a corrupt tyranny, and sought to construct a polity that embodied the principles of republican self-government for those considered capable of exercising political rights. Their reaction against tyranny was based on an ideal of the free citizen who elected representatives to a government divided in such a way that the various branches checked and balanced one another to ensure that no one branch could dominate.[35]

What distinguished the American citizen from the British subject was his "freedom" *from* tyrannical, monarchical rule of the Old World, and his freedom *to* chose who would represent him in the legislative assembly. Moreover, as an American citizen whose rights were protected by the constitution, he was free to pursue his private interests and "happiness," which may indeed be "public happiness,"[36] without government interference. The American citizen enjoyed what Isaiah Berlin was later to call both positive and negative liberties within his chosen community.

In actuality, there was no one American "citizenship regime," between the post-revolutionary and antebellum periods, but a succession, as Rogers Smith (1997) has convincingly demonstrated in *Civic Ideals*. The construction of what Smith calls a "civic identity" was an ongoing political process that began with what was originally a self-appointed elite citizen body of white male property (which included slaves) owners[37] and was transformed by white manhood suffrage by the time of the Civil War. Like the Athenian regimes two thousand years earlier, it evolved from oligarchy to participatory democracy. Nonetheless, for the purpose of my argument, all the citizenship regimes that developed out of the experience of British subjecthood between the post-Revolutionary and ante-bellum period were hierarchical and explicitly excluded significant ascriptive groups, such as slaves, free blacks, "Orientals," Native Americans, women, and some European immigrants from political rights. Indeed, according to Smith, a primary cause of American colonial discontent was that Native American tribes and free blacks were included as British subjects and therefore protected by the Crown against the violence and territorial incursions of the colonists.

It is beyond the scope of this book, let alone this chapter, to analyze the extent and meaning of all these exclusions, and more economical to focus on the "positive" citizenship profile produced by the sum total of the exclusions: "whiteness" as defined by law, and maleness. Moreover, beyond the material ascriptive "negativities" rejected in the ideal of American citizenship, early theorists also rejected the custom of political subordination to what they considered "undemocratically" constituted, or tyrannical, authority.

Like citizens of the classical republics we discussed in the previous chapter, the enfranchised citizen of an American state enjoyed his freedom and the right to protect himself as a member of a privileged status group. He was part of an elite that was legally distinct from the population of slaves, freemen, women, Indians and propertyless whites who lacked the essential material pre-requisites of fully-fledged American citizenship, and whose rights to protect themselves against the violence of white citizens were either non-existent or strictly curtailed. The key qualification for enjoyment of the political rights of early American citizenship was property ownership, which was thought to establish the foundation of virtue necessary for the responsible exercise of those rights.[38] As the democratic revolution progressed during the eighteenth and nineteenth centuries, ownership of real property ceased to be a primary qualification for the franchise in most states, and the properties of whiteness and maleness became central.[39]

> The Constitutional period marks the beginning of an experimental reorganization and extension of whiteness to manhood through national incorporation (an incorporation that would alternately identify its fraternally "equal" subject through the terms of competitive individualism and market exchange-ability.) This incorporation promised to manage the potentially divisive effects of interpersonal, interclass, and interregional masculine competition by relocating them in a symbolically fraternal, reassuringly "common" manhood. One index to that new, more explicitly harnessed equation of national manhood with white manhood becomes manifest in the projection of cultural fears about dependence and rivalry onto groups of people who were excluded from that category. (Nelson, 37)

In the ante-bellum American citizenship regime, which was considered "democratic" in the Jacksonian period, status honor in the form of voting rights was distributed freely among adult male citizens who possessed the property of whiteness.[40] This "democracy" of free and equally "qualified" voters was not a contradiction to the "slavocracy" of the South, or indeed, of the nation.[41]

> By sharing in the collective honor of the master class, *all free persons legitimized the principle of honor* and thereby recognized the master class as those most adorned with honor and glory (...) A truly vibrant slave culture, if it is to avoid the crisis of honor and recognition, must have a substantial free population. (Patterson 1982, 99,100) (My italics).

Race was a legally constructed category that determined an individual's position in the status hierarchy, and whether he *was* property or owned it.[42] The "justice" of the citizenship regime, in Aristotle's terms, was relative to the color of a person's skin, and

> The value of citizenship was derived primarily from its denial to slaves, to some white men, and to all women. (...) The civil standing that these creatures could *not* have, defined its importance for the white male, because it distinguished him from the majority of his degraded inferiors. (Shklar 1991, 16, 49)

According to Merritt (1988) widespread agreement exists among scholars and jurists about the core meaning of "republican government." Since at least the eighteenth century, political thinkers have stressed that a republican government is one in which the people control their rulers.[43] That control, moreover, is exerted principally—although not exclusively—through majoritarian processes.[44] A republic, James Madison wrote, is "a government which derives all its powers directly or indirectly from the great body of the people."[45] Alexander Hamilton agreed that the "fundamental maxim of republican government...requires that the sense of the majority should prevail."[46] Charles Pinckney told the members of South Carolina's ratifying convention that a republic was a form of government in which "the people at large either collectively or by representation, form the legislature."[47] And Thomas Jefferson assured Congress during his first inaugural address that "absolute acquiescence in the decisions of the majority" is "the vital principle of republics."[48]

Nor, according to Merritt, has the twentieth century altered our conception of a republic. "The first principle inherent in our republican form of government," one federal judge concluded in 1966, "is that individual citizens submit to rule by legislative fiat enacted by a majority of a popularly elected legislative body working within a constitutional framework."[49] "A distinguishing feature of this form of government," the Kansas Supreme Court concurred, "is that the people . . . have the right to choose their own officials for governmental affairs and enact their own laws pursuant to the legislative power reposed in representative bodies."[50] Political theorists, famously Madison in Federalist Ten, frequently identify republican government with representative government. That is, the citizens of a republic elect representatives who enact laws; they do not govern through popular referenda. The use of representatives, however, does not undermine the fundamental point that all governmental power in a republic derives from the people. The normative link between representative republicanism and *atimia,* or felon disenfranchisement, which takes on a completely different aspect in a polity "ruled" by representatives rather than by the citizens themselves, will be explored in Chapter Three.

People, or groups, with the power to control the franchise control the mechanism that regulates the distribution of all social goods:

> Politics is always the most direct path to dominance, and political power (rather than the means of production) is probably the most important, and certainly the most dangerous good in human history. Footnote: political power is the regulative agency for social goods generally. It is used to defend the boundaries of all the distributive spheres, including its own, and to enforce the common understandings of what goods are and what they are for. (But it can also be used, obviously, to invade the different spheres and to override those understandings.) In this second sense, we might say, indeed, that political power is always dominant—at the boundaries, but not within them. The central problem of political life is to maintain that crucial distinction between "at" and "in." (Walzer 1983, 15)

Control over the franchise by the citizen body, an originally self-appointed *politeuma,* which axiomatically constitutionalizes the survival of its own criteria of political virtue along the lines suggested by the theorists of path-dependence, is a hallmark of republican government.

Montesquieu observed that "it is as important to regulate in a republic, in what manner, by whom, to whom, and concerning what suffrages are to be given, as it is in a monarchy to know who is the prince, and after what manner he ought to govern."[51] James Madison echoed this thought, declaring in The Federalist that "[t]he definition of the right of suffrage is very justly regarded as a fundamental article of republican government."[52] In order to establish a government responsive to its electorate, a state must first define that electorate. The power to define the franchise for state and local elections, therefore, is one of the powers that the Guarantee Clause originally reserved to the states.

The modern Supreme Court has recognized that control over the franchise is an essential component of state sovereignty under the Guarantee Clause. In *Lassiter v. Northampton County Board of Elections*,[53] the Court firmly rejected the claim that a state-imposed literacy test for voters violated the Fourteenth Amendment. Justice Douglas, writing for a unanimous court, observed that "[t]he States have long been held to have broad powers to determine the conditions under which the right of suffrage may be exercised."[54] In particular, he suggested, states have authority to deny the franchise based on residence, age, or previous criminal records.[55]

A decade later, in *Oregon v Mitchell*,[56] a majority of the Court struck down a federal statute setting a minimum voting age of eighteen for all state and local elections. In reaching this result, Justice Black acknowledged that "[n]o function is more essential to the separate and independent existence of the States and their governments than the power to determine within the limits of the Constitution the qualifications of their own voters for state, county, and municipal offices and the nature of their own machinery for filling local public offices."[57] Three of his colleagues agreed that "the whole Constitution reserves to the States the power to set voter qualifications in state and local elections, except to the limited extent that the people through constitutional amendments have specifically narrowed the powers of the states."[58]

A quintessential feature of classical republican polities (discussed in Chapter One) still constitutionally reserved to the American states under their power to regulate the franchise is the power to disenfranchise convicted criminals. A majority in a state may exclude from political rights citizens it deems unfit to rule or be represented, and may determine the precise criteria (in the form of a criminal code) of that "unfitness." The consequence of this power is that 51 differently constituted (republican) electorates determine whether or not *American* citizens have the political right to choose their local, state, and national representatives. This state of affairs renders problematic the widely held view that the Fourteenth Amendment "established the primacy of a national citizenship whose common rights the states could not abridge" (Foner 1988, 256).[59] The "common rights" of the national citizenship that was established were civil, not political, and although Congress was given "enforcement power" in Section 5 of the Fourteenth Amendment, it was the judiciary that was to interpret the scope and meaning of the new, "common" citizenship rights.[60]

In the modern United States, "republican government" in the states is not *necessarily* co-extensive with an exclusionary polity, since the majoritarian state demos can decide that every adult member must be included in the *politeuma*. The state "republic" can, for instance, be equated with "liberal" or "democratic" principles, which recognize and protect the private and/or political rights of *all* citizens.[61] In Maine, for instance, citizens have decided that even prisoners should be allowed to vote, whereas in Arizona, once a person has been convicted of a felony his rights can only be restored by executive pardon. In other words, the *form* of republican government enjoyed by the states can comprehend an entire spectrum of inclusion or exclusion, depending on the will of the particular demos. Since each (majoritarian) demos inscribes its own particular "path-dependent" conception of justice and therefore of citizenship into its constitution and statutes, no specific *content* is implied by the term "republican polity." What is implied is the rule of popular sovereignty, which in a federal polity such as the United States creates distinct tensions when it collides with the "rule of law" inscribed in the Constitution. It is the combination of "republican" forms within the American polity that results in the inequality of American democratic citizenship, to be examined in Chapter Three. The following section will examine the specific content that is implied by the term "democratic" in normative political theory, which will allow me to contrast a "moral" conception of democracy with the "arithmetical," federalistic conception articulated by the U.S. Supreme Court, to be discussed in the next chapter.

4.   DEMOCRATIC CITIZENSHIP: GROWING IN "ORDERED RICHNESS"

The underlying idea of the democratic type of constitution is liberty. (This, it is commonly said, can only be enjoyed in democracy; and this, it is also said, is the aim of every democracy.) Liberty has more than one form. One of its forms [is the political, which] consists in the interchange of ruling and being ruled. The democratic conception of justice is the enjoyment of arithmetical equality, and not the enjoyment of proportionate equality on the basis of desert. On this arithmetical conception of justice the masses must necessarily be sovereign; the will of the majority must be ultimate and must be the expression of justice. The argument is that each citizen should be on an equality with the rest. *Politics,* VI. ii. 1317b.

The argument that "each citizen should be on an equality with the rest" and should therefore enjoy political rights is a normative one based on what John Dewey characterized more than two millennia after *The Politics* was composed, as "faith in the capacity of human beings for intelligent judgment and action if proper conditions are furnished" (1988, 228).[62] Stating "the democratic faith in the formal terms of a philosophic position," Dewey wrote that

> Democracy is belief in the ability of human experience to generate the aims and methods by which further experience will grow in ordered richness.

This is a moral ideal, which translated into institutional fact, means that all citizens are entitled to the "arithmetically" equal right to self-rule in the political sense. The source of this right is the equal value of the interests of each member of the polity to all members of the polity, simply in virtue of their membership, whose legal expression is their citizenship. No citizen is entitled to have his interest considered more favorably by the demos because he belongs to a particular status group, or is more virtuous, wealthy, pious or politically sophisticated than another citizen. In a democratic polity, the instrument that is the expression of his interest or consent, the vote, must therefore be equally distributed.[63] The U.S. Supreme Court has affirmed this claim in what are commonly called the "re-apportionment cases" of the 1960s, to be discussed in the following chapter.

In this section, I am distinguishing the normative, or moral, identity of democratic citizenship from the empirical or juridical identity of citizenship in a nominally democratic polity. The collective or aggregated "purpose" of the former, which is related to the polity's concept of justice in the Aristotelian framework, is to learn from one another. Democratic citizens can only learn from one another, though, as individuals in their own right (as opposed to in their collective capacity as members of demos), and according to the theory of democratic individuality, they cannot develop as such in the absence of political rights. In Dewey's words, "Democracy is the faith that the process of experience is more important than any special result attained... Since the process of experience is capable of being educative, faith in democracy is all one with faith in experience and education."

The empirical, or juridical identity of citizenship on the other hand, is a vertical relationship between the individual member of the polity and the administrative apparatus of the "democratic" nation-state.[64] From the perspective of the citizen, the purpose of this identity is to provide her with a legal identity and a set of private and public rights that shield her from intrusions of fellow citizens and the state. From the perspective of the state, the most basic purpose of the institution of citizenship is to maintain control over the inhabitants of its territory. Citizenship, as Brubaker (1992) says, "is both an instrument and an object of closure." The state needs to distinguish "insiders" from "outsiders" in order to distribute scarce resources, rights, privileges, and obligations. From a global perspective, "citizenship is an international filing system, a mechanism for allocating persons to states" (31). From the perspective of a "democratically" elected government, the identity of the enfranchised citizen corresponds to the constituent or potential constituent, whose interests must be taken into account for the government, officials, or party to survive in future elections (Manin 1997). Thus the "rationality" of the administrative apparatus consists in its power to distinguish citizens from non-citizens, whose interests need not be taken into account in political contests or decisions concerning social and economic welfare.

While both dimensions of the identity of democratic citizenship, institutionally speaking, entail equal access[65] of all (sane adult) members of the polity to the political process, the normative dimension I have selected to analyze implies an intersubjective *praxis* of consent to universal distribution of political rights whose objective is to develop individuality and maximize learning. The moral dimension of democratic citizenship is pedagogical in a practical sense.

Citizens who have the right to participate in the formal political process, to recognize one another as equals, as peers in the electoral competition, are formally positioned in the public realm, to learn from one another. I am not making the stronger claim that they do or even that they should learn from one another. Neither am I claiming in a "classical" republican vein that citizens should participate in the political process, even when they have the right to do so. High levels of voter ignorance and apathy are the despair of American political scientists, but in a "liberal"-democratic society participation cannot be coerced, only encouraged. The normative claim is that, should they choose to participate, citizens *must be* free to learn from one another as co-participants in the democratic process.

> Political rights are permanent guarantees; they underpin a process that has no endpoint, an argument that has no definitive conclusion. In democratic politics, all destinations are temporary. No citizen can ever claim to have persuaded his fellows once and for all. There are always new citizens, for one thing; and old citizens are always entitled to reopen the argument—or to join an argument from which they have

previously abstained...That is what complex equality means in the sphere of politics: it is not power that is shared, but the opportunities and occasions of power. Every citizen is a potential participant, a potential politician. (Walzer 1983, 310)

This freedom to learn—one of the "democratic liberties" implied by Aristotle in his definition of democracy—is a latent one that is an exclusive privilege of enfranchised citizens in a democracy. Their liberty may, in fact, consist in the ("negative") choice *not* to use it, to concentrate on private, rather than public affairs. Nonetheless, a moral conception of democratic citizenship seems to imply that the conditions for learning and enrichment must exist, should the citizen choose to avail herself of them. Institutionally speaking, citizens are not free to learn "in ordered richness" when members of their polity are excluded from political rights, and in this their democratic liberty is curtailed.[66] Disenfranchised citizens are not, by definition, considered political equals, and are certainly not co-participants in the civic enterprise of building a stable and flourishing polity. They are not, in the Aristotelian lexicon, "civic friends." Moreover, not only has the demos foregone the opportunity to learn from those it chooses to disenfranchise, it has deprived the disenfranchised of the opportunity to learn from *it,* by means of the formal political process.[67] Indeed, prisoners, probationers or parolees who are disenfranchised under state law are literally "removed" from the *politeuma,* such that their absence constitutes a "lack" or a negative space whose consequences for democratic learning—on both sides—demand theoretical attention.

Deprived permanently of power, whether at national or local levels, [the citizen] is deprived also of his sense of himself. Hence the reversal of Lord Acton's maxim, attributed to a variety of twentieth-century politicians and writers: "Power corrupts, but the lack of power corrupts absolutely." This is an insight available, I think, only in a democratic setting, where the sense of potential power can be recognized as a form of moral health (rather than as a threat of political subversion. Citizens without self-respect dream of tyrannical revenge." (Walzer 1983, 310)

The most immediate cause for concern is factional violence, or *stasis,* discussed in detail in Chapter One. In terms of path-dependence, majority-sanctioned private and public violence was historically used to exclude "minority" American citizens from the political process.[68] It can therefore be hypothesized that their ongoing (partial) exclusion as a result of disenfranchisement for violent and non-violent crime dynamically generates a cumulatively exclusionary polity. From the perspective of those at "the bottom" (Matsuda 1995) this polity is described by sporadic violent (urban and prison) riots, increased crime rates, ever increased budgets for "law-and-order" policies, larger prison populations, and ever-increased disenfranchisement.[69] Insofar as a polity configured by such policies renders those individuals chronically deprived of the protections of full (insider) citizenship both individually and collectively insecure in existential terms, it harbors such latent political phenomena as the "war on crime," which manufactures and exploits majoritarian "fear" for electoral purposes. Yet learning, and the creation of political "power" as Hannah Arendt (1969) argued, axiomatically precludes violence; politics and violence are mutually exclusive.[70]

Indeed, as Aristotle conceded, despite his personal distaste for "mechanics and laborers"

> There is serious risk in not letting them have *some* share in the enjoyment of power; for a state with a body of disenfranchised citizens who are numerous and poor must necessarily be a state which is full of enemies. (1281b)[71]

This is because Aristotle's overriding normative concern in the design of ideal *poleis,* and which informed his criticism of "perverted" *poleis* was stability, or *soteria,* and a state full of enemies is necessarily an unstable or "unsafe" one.[72]

From the perspective of the juridical identity of citizenship, on the other hand, *no* compelling intersubjective criteria or advance or deficit in the common good results in learning or failure to learn: the only "citizenly relation" that counts is between the citizen and the state. The relation is essentially sterile. Conceptions of the good are personal and private, or organized through partisan or "interest politics" rather than publicly conceived or debated in terms of the good of whole. The citizen may enforce her rights against the state, and the state will enforce citizens' rights to be free of interference from one another, but "liberal" citizens whose fundamental rights are protected by the state, have "negative liberty" from one another. The function of the citizenship identity as legal status is the protection of private rights against the state, and against other citizens in the state. It implies a praxis of individual consent to the state so long as it protects the private interests of the citizen, and qualifies a democratically constituted sovereign as one that aggregates individual citizens' preferences and interests by means of procedures that are "free and fair" in terms of positive law.[73] Such a praxis is clearly co-extensive with "law-and-order" politics that result in the disenfranchisement of co-citizens convicted of crimes and a diminution of democratic learning via the political process.

A normative theory of democracy whose ideal is "learning" allows citizens both the opportunity to be in the majority that "rules" (via representation) as well as in the minority that opposes government policies. It includes the right to use the political process to resist exercises of power by the sections of the demos that might be tempted to rule in their own, rather than the public interest.[74] As such an inclusive democracy that institutionalizes opposition utilizes the "power enhancing" formula identified by Arendt (1963) in order to "learn."

> [This] discovery, contained in one sentence, spells out the forgotten principle underlying the whole structure of separated powers: that only 'power arrests power', that is, we must add, without destroying it, without putting impotence in the place of power. For power can of course be destroyed by violence; this is what happens in tyrannies, where the violence of one destroys the power of the many, and which therefore, according to Montesquieu are destroyed from within: they perish because they engender impotence instead of power. (151)

Democratic legitimacy flows from the availability of institutionalized channels of dissent and protected rights of dissent just as it does from institutionalized channels of consent expressed as majority rule. Conversely, democratic "illegitimacy" flows from the stoppage of institutionalized channels of dissent via (at minimum) ex-felon disenfranchisement.

In a democratic regime characterized by the primacy of the intersubjective identity, rather than by the juridical identity of citizenship alone, citizens—whose responsibility is to govern through their representatives—are compelled to "think together" by means of organized political channels, about common issues, interests and problems. It is the responsibility of the democratic demos to make decisions about the best ways to resolve conflicts of interest between citizens and between groups of citizens in the polity, since the purpose of their citizenship—its "end"—is the good of the whole. Dewey argues that it is a contradiction to act as if the good of the whole can be served by force, by suppression of a part:

> Democracy is the belief that even when needs and ends or consequences are different for each individual, the habit of amicable cooperation—which may include, as in sport, rivalry and competition—is itself a priceless addition to life. To take as far as possible every conflict which arises—and they are bound

to arise—out of the atmosphere and medium of force, of
violence, as a means of settlement, into that of discussion and of
intelligence is to treat those who disagree—even profoundly—
with us as those from whom we may learn, and in so far, as
friends. A genuinely democratic faith in peace is faith in the
possibility of conducting disputes, controversies and conflicts as
cooperative undertakings in which both parties learn by giving
the other a chance to express itself, instead of having one party
conquer by forceful suppression of the other—a suppression
which is none the less one of violence when it takes place by
psychological means of ridicule, abuse, intimidation, instead of
by overt imprisonment or concentration camps.

In order to exercise the democratic method of self-rule and
opposition, in order to "cash in" on their political freedom and equality,
citizens must be protected by basic rights, they cannot be subject to the
whims of popular sovereignty. They need to feel secure, from the
intrusive power of the state, and from the intrusions of one another.[75]
They must also have a well-developed sense of individuality[76] and
autonomy. Failure to develop the latter qualities can result in the
inversion of democracy such that the citizens themselves are ruled in a
manner reminiscent of the "democratic despotism" Alexis de Tocqueville
worried about after his visit to the fledgling U.S. democracy. Being
deprived of the vote, which even the Supreme Court has admitted is "the
right that is protective of all other rights" in such a democracy would
appear by definition to abrogate that sense of security and autonomy that
is the basis of the identity of democratic citizenship. Indeed, as we will
see, George Kateb's theory of democratic individuality and personal
flourishing is predicated on the *right* of each individual to participate in
the political process and to be protected by due process guarantees.

5. DEMOCRATIC INDIVIDUALITY

In that it is a method of collective self-rule, democracy takes seriously
the notion of shared fate, of interconnectedness, but in order for that not
to become oppressive or despotic in the sense of a General Will, it must
also take seriously the notion of individuality, which is the source of the
individual's ability to learn, judge, discuss, convince, and act powerfully
as a citizen. The paradox of democracy is that although the people are
sovereign, so also is the person, the individual; she is sovereign only
over herself, though, which is why no power can be sovereign over her,
without her consent. This places on the collective democratic sovereign

that lays claim to legitimacy the heavy onus of non-paternalistically ensuring the conditions for the free development of individuals such that they can both discover and exercise this sovereign capacity. Democratic government, by definition, requires citizens, people who can "participate effectively in the democratic political processes that socially structure individual choices among good lives." (Gutmann 1988) It is simply not plausible to assume that citizens with the capacity to function effectively as a sovereign develop "naturally" no matter what their material circumstances—under- or over-privileged—happen to be. Since the democratic sovereign is accountable to itself for the quality of its citizens, it must do the labor, incur the costs, of securing the conditions for their development. As Sen (1999) says, this is a "two-way relationship." The analysis of development presented in his book

> treats the freedoms of individuals as the basic building blocks. Attention is thus paid particularly to the expansion of the 'capabilities' of persons to lead the kind of lives they value— and have reason to value. These capabilities can be enhanced by public policy, but also, on the other side, the direction of public policy can be influenced by the effective use of participatory capabilities by the public. (18)

Sen's analysis provides a nice complement to Kateb's more abstract analysis of democratic individuality which, while "timeless" is somewhat constrained by the "frontier" mentality of nineteenth century America, and could certainly benefit from feminist and postcolonial criticism. In this chapter I will not focus on the practical aspects of how the democratic ideal could actually be implemented, which is more Sen's focus, but on the more modest aim of sketching the normative implications of the theory.

According to Kateb, the principle of democratic citizenship is *immanent* in the method of representative liberal democracy, where "political authority is profoundly chastened by the electoral system" (38-39).

> The overall chastening that political authority receives at the hands of constitutional representative democracy (limited and nonpaternalist in its scope of action) is a chastening of all authority. At the same time the chastening is not a diminution but also an inducement to act in ways and by procedures that carry great moral significance, that teach specific moral lessons. On the one hand, the particular modes of chastening liberates citizens. On the other hand, the particular modes of chastening

may suggest an ethic of action and forbearance from action for citizens in all the relations of life. (43)

Representative democracy has these "alchemical properties," so to speak, because its electoral system is constantly being recreated by citizens whose characters are shaped by their membership in this distinctive polity that "embodies values." The central idea is that "democracy unsettles everything (though not all at once) and therefore permits the slow growth in "ordered richness" of individuality. But it unsettles everything for everyone, and thus liberates democratic individuality" (86). Insofar as its constitutional principles permit this, the democratic citizenship regime unites the criteria of equality and freedom on the same terrain. In other words, the privileged should be no freer from being "unsettled" than the underprivileged. All lives are equally works in progress and all persons can revise their opinions and make different choices.

The principle of democratic citizenship stresses the educability of citizens. Not only does the theory of democratic individuality (positively) imply the provision of equitable public education for all citizens, a punishment such as lifetime ex-felon disenfranchisement presumes and institutionalizes non-educability, and is therefore not democratic. Barber (1998) argues that what distinguishes democracy from foundationalism is that it "enjoins constant, permanent motion—a gentle kind of permanent revolution, a movable feast that affords each generation room for new appetites and new tastes, and thus allows political and spiritual migration to new territory" (23). The permanent exclusion of any "caste" of citizens from political life diminishes that feast in that its epistemology is curtailed to include only what is presumed to be "safe" and "acceptable" rather than being an epistemology that is open to different perspectives and "standpoints," particularly those of the oppressed.

> The logic of the standpoint epistemologies depends on understanding that the "master's position" in any set of dominating social relations tends to produce distorted visions of the real regularities and underlying causal tendencies in social relations. (Harding 1986, 191)[77]

Moreover, according to the theory of democratic individuality, the permanent exclusion of any individuals from political rights diminishes their chance of learning to become citizens proper through participation in the demos, and stunts their potential as human beings. It institutionalizes their chance of membership in a non-democratic shadow *polis* characterized by the political emptiness of despotism. The theory of democratic individuality is importantly different from classical "republican" theories of positive liberty, which hold that people achieve their fullest potential—their *telos*—through participation. It is the chance to participate, the status of being a voter in a community of equals, the knowledge that one has the power should one choose to use it, which is the foundation of democratic individuality. Legally bereft of that chance, citizens are members of a different citizenship regime. It is legitimate to wonder at what point different citizenship regimes can co-exist in the same polity before the polity becomes unstable and the dominant regime incoherent.

It is unusual and theoretically fruitful to think about constitutional democracy as a form of government whose institutions contain immanent rather than explicit values, since the discourse of liberal democracy presents its institutions and procedures as neutral rather than value-laden. The stated purpose of such a polity in liberal theory is to guarantee the flourishing of a plurality of conceptions of the good. Traditionally defined "republican" or communitarian citizenship regimes, not liberal democracies, are supposed to embody values. Yet for Kateb the values are not substantive in the sense of specific status honor that corresponds to the individual member of a group, such as those we analyzed in Chapter One, but relational insofar as they correspond to all members of the polity. Values are embodied first in the formal relationship established between the government and each individual citizen, and second, in the formal relationship established between all individual citizens in virtue of their collective membership of the polis. In their unsettlingness these two sets of political relationships foster an assertive individuality that allows the *citizen,* who may (or may not) use her power to change them, to develop her unique being to the fullest possible potential. In this, Kateb is, of course, very close to John Stuart Mill in both *On Liberty* and *Representative Government*. Like Mill, Kateb argues that "these relationships" (between citizens and government, and among citizens) "reach directly to many aspects of personal identity:"

> The first relationship is a crystallization of the idea that superiors (officials who make and enforce the law and policies) are inferior to those they govern, because their authority is merely temporary and revocable, and they must ask for it and win it and yet not think of themselves as deserving or meriting it. Authority is a beggar. The people's obedience is not to natural persons, inspired understandings, or naked wills, but to officeholders using their authority by means of rules and manifesting it in rules....The second relationship is a crystallization of the idea that though I am only a voter, and

only when I choose to be, I may nevertheless find in that status—as all the rest may find in it—a series of attributions to me as a citizen affirmed and acknowledged by my fellows as theirs are by me. These attributions include: I count; I count only as one; I am owed an account; I take part guiltlessly; I help to determine; I press myself forward without feeling shame; I can talk back; I have a right to be talked to; I am part of the ultimate constitution of the body politic; I take sides without wickedness; I should have access... (62)

While clearly I am sympathetic to Kateb's point of view, the claim represented in this quote raises the counterfactual question that if representative democracy indeed fosters these values, then why doesn't everyone share them? How can the same polity produce a Bull Connor and a Martin Luther King if the structures are even weakly deterministic in the way Kateb suggests? I shall try to answer this question because this claim about the immanent values of the democratic method, elaborated throughout *The Inner Ocean*, is so intuitively appealing. Probably the first thing to notice is that the "I" who claims the attributes Kateb lists is someone not accustomed to power and status, since all the "attributions" that are claimed are generally taken for granted and don't need to be articulated by citizens with "insider status." A Bull Connor wouldn't have to say "I press myself forward without shame," and would not admit that he was "inferior" to those he governs by virtue of only being in office temporarily. So the "determinism" of democratic structures comes from the bottom up, so to speak. This is why "democratization" is always the result of struggle, and appears as an expansive project, fulfilling the demands of the excluded to share power on an equal basis with people they recognize as their natural equals, but who do not recognize them as such.

Material conditions aside for the moment, the principle of democratic individuality is based on a notion of human nature that affirms the individual's inherent capacity to develop her potential when unrestrained by all but the most basic and necessary social conventions and laws. The theory of democratic individuality advanced in *The Inner Ocean* argues that democracy is the best political arrangement for such development because it allows citizens to see that social conventions are changeable rather than natural and thus compulsory or sacred. When people accept them as such, even in a democracy, they become too timid, unadventurous, and conformist (*IO,* 83). The goal of democratic individuality is to liberate human energies, to live more intensely, and since no one individual or social group can decide for another how this is to be done, all must have the power equally to decide how to live, a power they are only granted in a democracy.

In fact it is the issue of recognition, which we will come to momentarily, that is problematic for those accustomed to power as a result of their "ascriptive" status as powerholders. Buried in Kateb's argument about the democratic individual, about the "I," is a claim about the community of citizens. It is a claim for the undifferentiated *inclusion* of all members of the polity, rather than exclusion based on ascriptive characteristics or qualities of virtue that are desirable in traditional "republican" polities where political rights are distributed on the basis of status honor. The condition of my being included is that you are too, and the corollary of Kateb's beautiful tribute to representative democracy and its effects on the citizen is, of course, that when people are systematically and permanently denied the right to participate in the electoral system, those "attributions" of citizenship are not affirmed, and the individual is unable to develop all her potentials.

This claim is worded in the passive voice, but can be formulated in terms of active consent: we can say that when (enfranchised and privileged) citizens in one part of the polity consent to a regime that denies co-citizens the right to full citizenship and security, they deny those individuals the ability to develop their full potential and individuality. And conversely, when citizens actively consent to include all their co-members of the polity in the democratic process on equal terms, they are supporting the full development and flourishing of their individuality and potential without exception. The latter regime represents a democratic citizenship regime. The presence in the former of a "rejected" set of co-citizens implies a binary political relationship between a nominally "democratic" and a heretofore unidentified, but *un*democratic regime.

In other words, the theory implies that different patterns of political inclusion produce different types of individuals: the effects of democracy, which Kateb sees as independence of spirit, energy, and dignity do not manifest in excluded sectors of the polity, or are manifested in corrupt and negative forms. Based on this deduction, we can say that polities which systematically exclude certain groups or individuals from political liberty are undemocratic, or violate the principle of democracy. If we start from the premise of democratic individuality, which states that only political inclusion can potentially foster those qualities in *all* citizens, no one can be legitimately excluded because they appear to lack them, or have never been given the adequate opportunity to develop them. In fact, the argument seems to lead to the stronger claim that the demos must include all citizens in order that the formerly and currently excluded, and the fully enfranchised, might all develop the attributes of democratic individuality. The stronger claim implies, and Kateb certainly suggests it in the later chapters on Whitman and the Emersonians, who he invokes as the "geniuses" of democratic individuality, that when we exclude or despise others, we exclude and despise parts of ourselves. The interpretation is that we mutilate parts of the democratic body. This is an important claim to unpack because it implies a philosophical and political anthropology that is unusual in contemporary theoretical discourse. Kateb says,

> I see the Emersonians as trying to encourage the tendency to democratic individuality, to urge it forward so that it may express itself ever more confidently and therefore more splendidly. In their conception of democratic individuality, I find three aspects: self-expression, resistance on behalf of others, and receptivity or responsiveness (being "hospitable") to others. My judgment is that for the Emersonians the most important aspect of democratic individuality, by far, is receptivity or responsiveness. (241)

The foundation of this responsiveness is recognition of a deep ontological sameness, which is different from group "identity" or nationality based on superficial or ascriptive characteristics. The "sameness" is the life all creation (including stones, rivers, etc.) shares in its very "createdness," which can be apprehended by the individual who is not caught up in commercial society of "possessive individualism," conventional ethics, or political hierarchies. It is what Kateb calls "impersonal individualism" in that it is based in an essentially "spiritual," transcendent, vision, rather than an intellectual concept. [78]

This "impersonality" in the Emersonian vision, although inscribed in and conditioned by a foundation of liberal rights, is importantly different from the liberal perspective of the "generalized other." In that "the other" is "a rational being entitled to the same rights and duties as we would want to ascribe to ourselves," there is no need to take into account "the individuality and concrete identity of the other." Relations are governed by the norms of formal equality and reciprocity: "each is entitled to expect and to assume from us what we can expect and assume from him or her." (Benhabib 1987, 87)

Buried in this norm of generalized reciprocity is the assumption that a citizen's failure to meet its demands ("our" expectations of "citizenly" behavior) justifies rejection and punishment of the delinquent. A perspective that focuses on the particular, though, on the concrete, as feminists such as Benhabib and Harding, and critical race theorists such as Matsuda, have argued, generates a different political ethic that is closer to the Emersonian ideal of democratic individuality:

> The standpoint of the concrete other (...) requires us to view each and every rational being as an individual with a concrete history, identity and affective-emotional constitution. In assuming this standpoint, we abstract from what constitutes our commonality. We seek to comprehend the needs of the other, his or her motivations, what she or he searches for, and what she or he desires. Our relation to the other is governed by norms of *equality* and *complementary* reciprocity: each is entitled to expect and to assume from the other forms of behavior through which the other feels recognized and confirmed as a concrete, individual being with specific needs, talents, and capacities...The norms of our interactions are ... friendship, love and care...the corresponding moral feelings are those of love, care and sympathy and solidarity. (*ibid*)

In that citizens recognize one another as "concrete" rather than "generalized" others, we are recognize our particular histories, struggles, sufferings and triumphs, and are accountable to one another for those histories. The framework of democratic institutions allows citizens to translate that accountability into political involvement that supports inclusionary policies.

A significant aspect of taking the standpoint of the concrete other, which Whitman urges us to do, particularly in *Song of Myself,* and which feminist philosopher Beverly Harrison points out (1985), is that not only are we members of different groups, but our groups are related to each other within networks of hierarchy and exploitation. The values immanent in democratic institutions are activated by a certain humility of spirit and receptivity of conscience which recognizes that the apparent differences between individuals do not go as deep as the commonalities, and that the project of democracy is realized insofar as those values are translated into policy, or as the case might be, principled opposition to antidemocratic policies for which democratic citizens hold one another accountable.

> I resist anything better than my own diversity
> And breathe the air and leave plenty after me,
> And am not stuck up, and am in my place...
> (...)
> This is the breath of laws and songs and behavior,
> This is the tasteless water of souls ...this is the
> true sustenance, (*SOM,* 29)

As we can see, the transcendent nature of this existential recognition, which finds its highest institutional expression, according to Kateb and the Emersonians, in democracy, is paradoxical, what Whitman calls a "riddle," acknowledging he "contradicts himself." On the one hand, in our createdness we are all the same, we are interchangeable:

...what I assume you shall assume,
For every atom belonging to me as good belongs to you (244)
(...)
(It is you talking just as much as myself, I act as the tongue of you,
Tied in your mouth, in mine it begins to be loosen'd.) (244)
(...)
If you bestow gifts on your brother or dearest friend I demand as good
   As your brother or dearest friend,
If your lover, husband, wife is welcome by day or night,
   I must be personally as welcome,
If you become degraded, criminal, ill, then I become so for your sake. (250)

Yet on the other hand, we are all unique individuals, and representative democracy is the only form of government that affords us the opportunity to *become* those unique individuals.

Whitman's transcendent vision dissolves the apparent paradox because what is "recognized" is that the "individual" is, in fact, a composite:

Whitman's phrase is best: it is a portrait of 'a great composite *democratic individual.'* Everyone is composite, and in a democracy each one can and should see himself or herself as a 'great composite *democratic individual.'* If the (secular) soul is potentiality, an honest portrait of oneself will register one's ability to perceive, and to identify or sympathize or empathize with, all the actualized potentialities one tries to take in, and will also import the sense that no actualization is definitive of anyone. (Kateb, 249)

According to this philosophical anthropology, what citizens include, when they recognize and empathize with fellow members of their polity, is actually part of themselves—they become more self-aware. Conversely, when recognition fails, and results in exclusion; when they disenfranchise co-members of the polity, they reject a part of themselves, thereby diminishing their own awareness and power.

Whoever degrades another degrades me...and
whatever is done or said returns at last to me,
And whatever I do or say I also return.
(...)
I speak the password primeval...I give the sign of democracy;
By God! I will accept nothing which all cannot have
their counterpart of on the same terms. (SOM, 40-41)

The inverse of the recognition that Whitman hymns in his poems, and which is exercised in democratic individuality, is contemptuous resentment based on a sense of difference and superiority.[79] Resentment is aroused when citizens claim the recognition that grounds the political rights based on their natural equality and assert their "ontological sameness" with people who reject them on the basis of ascriptive characteristics such as ethnicity, skin color, gender, or sexual orientation. Nietzsche theorized that it was the masses who expressed their *ressentiment* in the face of heroic virtue, and while I won't quibble with his theory here, I would claim that it is those who believe they have more virtue than the masses who are resentful when the masses claim equal recognition on the basis of democratic values.

The democratic ideal calls forth the best in citizens who are receptive to the notion of recognition and can utilize the political liberties granted to them to pressure the legislature and other state policymaking offices to pursue more democratic policies. Claude Lefort claims that the reason this course is available to democratic citizens is that they are the beneficiaries of established democratic rights. He says that the [French Declaration] "bequeaths us the universality of the principle which reduces right to the questioning of right.(...) In other words, modern democracy invites us to replace the notion of a regime governed by laws, of a legitimate power, by the notion of a regime founded upon *the legitimacy of a debate as to what is legitimate and what is illegitimate.*" (1988, 39. Italics in original.)[80] It is the obligation of democratic individuals who want to vindicate the pedagogic potential of democracy to participate in that debate, to add their voices in whatever way suits their particular personality.

At the beginning of Section 1 I asked how the same polity could produce a Bull Connor and a Martin Luther King if the structures are even as weakly deterministic as Kateb expects them to be. Put bluntly, if those who are fully enfranchised and whose rights are protected "learn" democratic citizenship from the paradigmatic constitutional processes and protections, while those who exist (rather than flourish) in its shadows cannot, why do the former sometimes systematically and brutally deprive the latter of their political and civil rights? Where is the pedagogy of their suffrage? Why is it that the latter group, during the civil rights movement, or the "busing crises," for instance, consistently displayed the qualities of restraint, patience, forbearance and respect that were so evidently lacking in the groups of "privileged" citizens? If the source of those qualities is not their status as full citizens and electors, then to what can it be attributed? Doesn't such empirical evidence defeat the entire theory? Moreover, given the Emersonian disdain for and distrust of insti-tutionalized politics, can the ethical qualities attributed to insurgents seeking to enter the democratic process survive once the formerly politically handicapped become full citizens?

These are thorny theoretical questions that go to the heart of the foundations of political virtue, which Kateb, as we have seen, attempts to answer "institutionally" and existentially. Stephen White (2000) chal-lenges Kateb's Emersonian-based argument on the grounds that, by secularizing its essentially theistic vision, by suggesting that democratic citizens cultivate an attachment to "existence as such," Kateb creates "ontological folds" whose "weight and friction one feels continually" (30-31). By announcing that "the hidden source of democracy may always have been the death of God" (*IO,* 171) Kateb rejects the insights of "theorists as diverse as Carl Schmitt and Joseph Schumpeter [who] were probably right in pointing out that the modern creed of democracy is to be understood as a secularized version of the most elementary tenets of Christian theology." (Offe and Preuss 1992, 146)

The fact is that the impulses of the anti-slavery and civil rights movements, as well as the contemporary "sanctuary" movement sup-porting the rights of "illegals," were/are based on radical theology rather than secular institutionalism. The theology of the civil rights movement derived from, and was in large part sustained by the concept of the "Beloved Community."[81] Rev. Dr. Martin Luther King Jr.'s actions were infused with the Emersonian theism Kateb strives to deny:

> [King] insisted that civic and political life desperately needed the moral resources of black religion. He even made what to some was an outrageous argument: that the black freedom struggle could refashion American democracy. King argued that black resistance allowed America to test its ethical resolve to be a great nation and to recover the original meanings of the American republic. King shrewdly appealed to the Constitution and the Declaration of Independence, highlighting their celebration of democracy and equality. He made religious uses

of the secular documents that support civil society and embody national beliefs about citizenship. (Dyson 2000, 130)

Kateb attempts to fill the moral gap left by his denial of theism with "the wonder that stems from the Heideggerian sense of the inessentiality all things and the wonder at the uncomposed indefiniteness that contrasts with nothingness." These are "the true replacements for an untenable religiousness, glorious as it undoubtedly is, in the works of Emerson, Thoreau and Whitman." (*IO,* 171) The institutional architecture that supports this "wonder" is the constitutional framework of civil and political rights, which has both the protective and pedagogical qualities we have already reviewed. According to Kateb, it is the dialectical relationship between these subjective and objective dimensions that enables the democratic individual to do the hard labor of inner cultivation and citizenship required in order to extend the promise of democratic individuality to all members of the polity.

This, perhaps, is the beginning of an answer to the counterfactual question, why then, if the political institutions of representative democracy have this potential to foster relations of social equality, do they not simply activate democratic recognition in all citizens equally in a way that precludes struggle and violence? What inhibits the development of democratic individuality and fosters oligarchic or exclusionary tendencies in a polity that is methodologically democratic? The institutional structure of equal (political and civil) rights alone is insufficient; alone it is empty—un-infused with (theistic or atheistic) wonder and humility at our (inter-) createdness, it lacks alchemical properties. The Emersonians were advocating a democratic ideal, which they realized was difficult, morally challenging, and not universally appealing. And as I said earlier, the impulse to look, to wonder, to acknowledge others as our equals, to challenge, and to engage in transformative action rarely visits those who are comfortable with the status quo.

> In any case, democratic individuality is not an ideal that one can ever be certain to have reached. It is not meant to be so unequivocally defined as to be unambiguously reachable. It is not a permanent state of being, but an indefinite project. It allows of degrees, approximations, attenuations. Still, some persons try harder than others; some try *deliberately.* The strange result is that the egalitarian ideal is lived unequally; the cultural ideal is lived fitfully; the *telos* is often avoided. That is why the ideal must be advocated, yet the only appropriate advocacy is philosophical or poetical. (*IO,* 84)

Institutionally speaking though, insofar as enfranchised citizens who are comfortable with status quo are legally and politically insulated from the portion of the polity that is excluded from the political process, their potential to learn and look is curtailed and the development of their democratic individuality is unjustly compromised. Briefly, they may never learn.

6. FAILURES OF DEMOCRATIC RECOGNITION

Taken seriously, the emphasis on mutuality and recognition in democratic individuality reveals, for example, the travesty of "separate but equal" democratic citizenship constitutionalized in *Plessy v Ferguson*, overturned in *Brown v Board of Education*, and implicitly resurrected in law-and-order policies whose institutional consequence in high crime districts is the disproportionate disenfranchisement of minority citizens. Inner-city schools are as de facto segregated and inferior as their de jure predecessors because whites have exercised their "free market" privileges to move to the suburbs where the schools are better.[82] The inner-cities (an American euphemism for slums) themselves are no less segregated and inferior by virtue of the fact that the market, rather than the law, enforces the *im*mobility of the residents.[83]

In other words, going back to Aristotle's injunction to look at "who is a citizen?" in order to identify the type of regime, the disproportionate numbers of disenfranchised felons from minority communities are evidence of the fact that communities with high crime and conviction rates are not accorded the security, mutuality and recognition democratic political culture requires. The citizenship regime that dictates their excludable status is circular rather than open-ended and oriented toward learning. It represents vestiges of the classical republican strand of citizenship based on status honor that is not institutionally sustainable in a modern democratic polity that claims constitutional legitimacy. As we shall see in the next chapter, the presence in the polity of these vestiges of status honor renders the citizenship even of qualified American voters unequal by current jurisprudential standards. Counterfactually speaking, were American citizenship values based on the principle of democratic individuality, areas of high crime, unemployment, urban decay and their political product—felon disenfranchisement—would be considered intolerable "stains" on the democratic body as a whole. Slavery was considered just such a stain by those who sought its abolition for moral reasons: it sat like "undigested gruel on the Constitution's rights-lined stomach" (Barber 1998, 85), but the transformation of the former slaves into American citizens did not render them political equals within the federal system until a full century after the enactment of the Fourteenth Amendment.

According to the theory of democratic individuality analyzed in this chapter, the citizenship regime that produces the relationship between enfranchised and disenfranchised individuals in the national polity is not a democratic one. A polity containing citizens proper and mere citizens without political rights is one that continues to institutionalize ethical-cultural criteria of virtue and status honor in a framework of universal legal membership. The fact that it utilizes the democratic method of competition and majority rule does not mean that it has institutionalized a democratic citizenship regime. The principles of democratic citizenship described in this chapter might conceivably justify temporary political exclusion, a period of chastisement during which a convicted felon can learn to reintegrate herself into the democratic community. As such she can learn to become more worthy of it perhaps—just as it may learn to become more worthy of her when she is able to return to the demos as a full member to develop her individuality along with the rest of her co-citizens (see Hampton 1998).

To borrow an image from optical science, a normative conception of citizenship in a democracy is holographic. Every bit of a hologram contains information about the entire picture, such that any piece may be cut off or isolated, and when a laser is shone on it, the original scene appears in its entirety. The imperative of political equality in a democracy can be described holographically: if the state is "perfectly" democratically constituted, information about the political freedom and rights of just one citizen provides complete information about the political freedom and rights of each and every citizen in the state. The same holds true in that an "imperfectly" constituted democratic polity can be read off the damaged political freedom and rights of just one citizen. Equality between citizens does not obtain in such a situation, and the legitimacy of democratically produced law is compromised if just one citizen is unjustly deprived of his right to participate on equal terms with his fellow citizens.

CHAPTER THREE

Representation, Reconstruction, and American *Atimia*

INTRODUCTION

In the previous chapter I presented a normative, or moral ideal of democratic citizenship whose theory of justice prioritized the development of individuality and collective learning oriented open-endedly toward the good of the whole. The state practice of permanent ex-felon disenfranchisement appears as a "contradiction" in a polity that requires the universal distribution of political rights among free citizens in order to achieve that normative end. As such, I characterized the *aggregate* or *composite* national polity as "undemocratic" in that, while a designated set of qualified voters enjoys equal political rights, another set of "unqualified" voters is permanently excluded from the civic body. I also hypothesized the co-existence of a democratic and a shadow or "parallel" polity, comprising those citizens who possess and those who lack political rights. In this chapter I shall argue that even individual members of the (arithmetically) democratic national citizenship regime do not enjoy equal political rights, rendering the *politeuma*[1] itself incoherent.[2] This inequality is generated by the contradiction produced by combining modern representative institutions and "ancient" felon disenfranchisement practices in a single citizenship regime. The first product of that combination is the direct vote *denial* represented by disenfranchisement itself, and the second, the vote *dilution* that flows from denying votes to some citizens in some political subdivisions of the nation but not to others.

The theoretical premise of this argument is based on the institutional framework of regimes laid out in the previous chapter. Each regime has its own conception of justice as Aristotle taught, or in Montesquieu's words, its own "spirit." The laws of each regime are consistent with that spirit[3] or conception of justice such that each has its own system-wide, or structural integrity. My thesis is, therefore, that certain laws and practices such as *atimia,* or felon disenfranchisement are "just" in the context of a particular type of regime, the type based on citizenship as status honor. The non-transferable, non-generic quality of a practice such as *atimia* can be deduced from the observation that when it is transplanted into a regime that has an entirely different structure or spirit, its practice warps, or "perverts" that regime, such that the regime itself becomes "unjust" in the lexicon of ancient political theory. In other words, in lay terms, a regime is untrue to itself when it harbors elements of structurally distinct regimes. The "spirit" of the post-14th-Amendment American citizenship regime is the democratic conception of equality expressed as the right of all free citizens to be represented by winners of electoral contests between political parties in conditions of free information, etc.

Unlike the Athenian regime, which was a direct democracy comprising a minority population of citizens within a larger population of non-citizens, the United States is a *representative* republic, distinguished by "the total exclusion of the people in their collective capacity."[4] The spirit of the Athenian citizenship regime, even at the height of the democracy, was citizen equality based on shared status honor within a system-wide context of political *in*equality. As such, the retention of an institution such as *atimia* in the modern American regime "corrupts" its particular spirit and integrity, whose legal basis is *system-wide* citizen equality. Indeed, in his dissent in the 1974 Supreme Court case that affirmed the validity of the state practice of felon disenfranchisement,[5] Justice Marshall cited Judge Harrison's ruling in a much earlier state case concerning the civil rights of felons:

> The disenfranchisement of ex-felons had "its origin in the fogs and fictions of feudal jurisprudence and doubtless has been brought forward into modern statutes without fully realizing either the effect of its literal significance or the extent of its infringement upon the spirit of our system of government.[6]

I examined the ancient origins of felon disenfranchisement in Chapter One, and in this chapter I will show how it distorts the twin norms of political equality and security that are central to the national spirit of modern representative democracy based on liberal theories of social contract.

In order to show how the insertion of ancient *atimia* "perverts" the spirit of a modern representative democracy such as the United States, I construct a theoretical argument that contrasts the electoral and prosecutorial systems of the two regimes.[7] *Atimia* was the "second face" of the Athenian prosecutorial system, which like the democracy itself, was *direct,* and available only to citizens. The American prosecutorial system, on the other hand, is *indirect,* and like the democracy, administered by elected representatives who are removed "from the great body of the people." In the Athenian citizenship regime, which was predicated on direct political participation and "self-help," *atimia* had a distinct "corrective" function. In the American citizenship regime, which is predicated on a representative prosecutorial system, partisan majorities have in the past opportunistically activated state constitutional provisions and statutes that (passively) provide for felon disenfranchisement as tools of party competition in order to shrink the electorate available to the rival party.[8]

Thus an institution that was originally a system-wide corrective mechanism available to the demos as a whole has mutated in a representative democracy (configured by two-party competition) into a corrective mechanism available only to a part (the majority party). In Aristotelian terms, a regime that does not serve the good of the whole but only a part, is a corrupt regime. In modern jurisprudential terms, when citizens' votes are "diluted," the good of a (non-diluted) "part" is being served, be it the "good" of an organized political party or a particular political (or "racial") interest. A system that produces vote dilution is unconstitutional according to the Supreme Court rulings reviewed in Section 4. Moreover, *atimia* banishes a citizen from the *politeuma,* and does not provide for her rehabilitation or reintegration into a society of legal equals.

The chapter is structured as follows: Section 1 compares the direct democracy of the Athenian citizenship regime with modern American citizenship regime based on representative government and two-party competition, focusing particularly on the immediate post-bellum rivalry between the Republican and Democratic parties. Section 2 examines the administrative imperative of post-slavery African-American citizenship, the absence of a national consensus on black suffrage, and the claim of white vote dilution in the 39th Congress in the context of major party competition. Section 3 analyzes the representative nature of the American criminal justice system and compares it with the Athenian prosecutorial system, in order to make a normative argument about the "injustice" of retaining a "just" institution from an ancient citizenship regime in a modern one with an entirely different normative structure. Section 4 reviews the modern jurisprudence of individual vote dilution and the Warren Court decisions regarding political rights, which provide the discursive foundation for the modern national equality norm. In

Section 5 I conceptualize the nation as a political subdivision in its own right, and compare the voting rights of citizens in equipopulous districts across the nation, concluding that individual American citizens do not enjoy equal political rights. This section also examines the theoretical tension between the concepts of representative and electoral equality and critiques the jurisprudence of *Richardson v Ramirez*[9] in the light of all the foregoing analyses. The chapter concludes that *Richardson* perpetuates the structural contradiction that combines disparate elements of normatively distinct citizenship regimes to produce system-wide injustice.

1. ATIMIA IN THE AMERICAN CONTEXT OF REPRESENTATIVE GOVERNMENT AND PARTY COMPETITION

One of the most obvious differences between the Athenian and American democracies is that the latter is mediated by electoral representation, whereas the former, for the most part, relied on direct participation of the citizens.[10] All adult male Athenian citizens, unless disqualified by *atimia,* were entitled to vote on proposals in the Assembly, just as they were entitled to serve as magistrates to administer the laws. While there were undoubtedly what came to be known as "factions" that perpetrated *staseis,* there were no organized political parties in the Athenian polis that competed for the peoples' votes with the winner taking office and the loser temporarily excluded from a position of political power. There was no such thing, therefore, as what we know today as an electorate for general purposes, only for the selection of certain specialized magistrates and generals.[11]

The absence of representation meant that the operative principle of Athenian democracy was *isegoria,* or equality of voice enjoyed by all the citizens, their equal right to speak in the assembly.[12] In the American system, while there is theoretically equality of voice (between the competing candidates) during the electoral process—the competition for peoples' votes—once the election has taken place, only the winners have equality of voice in the assembly. Excluded from the assembly, the losers return to the electorate where they have equality of voice, which can be defined as "equal freedom of speech," only with their fellow private citizens.[13] Their civil and political rights as citizens also give them the right to organize pressure groups within civil society that can address their representatives, criticize and support policies and mobilize candidates for future elections.[14] Nonetheless, political competition for office between two organized parties in a winner take all system determines which elected officials representing which interests will have the temporary power to make the laws, and which citizens and their interests will be (directly) excluded both from lawmaking and spoils distribution.[15] It is therefore in the interest of political parties to dilute or reduce the electorate available to their rivals, if such an electorate can be clearly distinguished, in order to get their representatives elected to office. The United States, also unlike Athens, is a territorial democracy,

> Formally organized around units of territory rather than economic or ethnic groups, social classes or the like...This means that people and their interests gain formal representation in the councils of government through the location of various interests in particular places and their ability to capture political control of territorial political units." (Elazar 1972, 44).

This structural constraint means that when the local or state branch of a national party captures political control of territorial political units, its power to shape the boundaries of the franchise can take designated constituencies "out of play," thereby giving it an advantage that has national consequences. Following the Civil War, the system of representative government and two-party competition was formally re-established under the new citizenship regime of universal membership and adult (black and white) male suffrage. As we saw in the previous chapter, though, the states retained the right to regulate the franchise and distribute political rights among their members within the parameters of the Reconstruction Amendments. My point is that the former Confederate (Democratic Party) states that enjoyed the right to a "republican form of government" before their military defeat, were constitutionally entitled to that right even after the Union (Republican Party) victory. In the post-bellum American polity, free African-Americans (a clearly distinguishable constituency within the electorate) were expected to vote overwhelmingly for the Republican (and for a short period, the Populist) party,[16] so it was in the interest of regrouping (white) Democratic majorities to shrink the electoral pool available their rivals.

> From the Reconstruction to the 1890s Democratic-Republican contestation in and over the South was marked by (1) fundamental disagreement over the boundaries of the suffrage, due to a Republican commitment to contest elections in the South, and therefore by (2) intense but opposed preferences within the two parties over electoral institutions. (...) While the post-Reconstruction party system had a variety of formal democratic features, in a key respect it was unusual: one party, the Demo-

cratic party, preferred to demobilize a significant portion of the Republican Party's electoral base. (Valleley 1995, 190)

As such, it was rational for Democratic politicians to enact local restrictions on registration, one of which was the "felonization" through statutory law of behaviors attributed by those politicians to free blacks.[17] These laws, moreover, had to be enforced at the local level in order to prevent blacks and their Republican supporters from registering and voting.[18] Conversely, it was rational for Republican politicians to enact national rules so they would have a better chance of shaping electoral outcomes. As Valleley says, "In fact, the two parties did have intense and opposed preferences about electoral institutions." (191) So what was in play in the post-bellum electoral competitions was not simply the identity of the winner, or that of a particular party platform, but the electoral rules of future competitions and the very composition of the electorate. The winning majority that "shrunk" the future electorate available to its rivals did not simply change, but "broke" the rules of representative government, which require that an electorate be able to recall, or refuse to re-elect its representatives if they do not act in a way that meets their constituencies' approval.[19]

In terms of the framework of regimes and regime change discussed in the previous chapter, it is important to remember that prior to Reconstruction there was no significant Republican presence in the South. Although the Republican Party embarked on a "crash construction of a southern wing" (Valleley, 195), it was competing against the entrenched "republican" institutions of the former regime, represented by embittered Democratic party elites. As determined as they were to consolidate the military victory won by the Union in the Civil War, the Republican Party was also committed to retaining a national system of representative government and abiding by the Constitution. They did not, and could not, launch a coup d'etat, or follow Machiavelli's advice in *The Prince*.[20]

The Union neither "demolished" the republics of the South after the Civil War, nor, except for the brief period of Radical Reconstruction, imposed any type of formal punishment on the states (or individuals) that had rebelled against it, costing the country over 600,000 lives. Once chattel slavery was abolished and General Lee had surrendered at Appomattox, Lincoln's spirit of "with malice toward none," which would in time, he hoped, allow the nation to be stitched back together again, prevailed over the more usual "to the victor go the spoils" spirit of a military triumph.

Few Confederate leaders or soldiers were tried for treason or punished; those who were, or whose lands had been confiscated, were pardoned by President Johnson, and their property restored to them, often at the expense of those who had farmed it on federal "colonies" for the last few years of the war.[21] The former Confederate states, dominated by white Democratic Party elites, were eventually reintegrated into the federal system with the same "republican" powers over the franchise and criminal justice as they had before the civil war, indeed the same powers as all the states had under the original Constitution. Representative government returned to the "restored" states and to the re-unified nation, but in a climate of intense, high-stakes electoral competition between the two parties that was marked by decades of terrorist violence against African-American voters and their white supporters.

In other words, passage of the 13th, 14th, and 15th Amendments notwithstanding, both the republican institutions, and the "vitality, hatred, and desire for revenge" Machiavelli mentions, remained alive and well in the formerly rebellious states. The reasons for the brevity of the Radical Reconstruction and the inability of Congressional Republicans to fully prosecute their Civil War victory have been exhaustively analyzed in the literature.[22] The key point, though, is my claim that modern American *atimia* can be directly and rhetorically attributed to the retention of ante-bellum "republican" citizenship regimes in the states because there was no national political consensus about black suffrage when the Fourteenth Amendment was passed. The Fifteenth Amendment was passed for purely pragmatic political reasons rather than as the result of a national moral or political consensus on a new citizenship regime following the civil war.[23]

2. THE ADMINISTRATIVE IMPERATIVE OF BLACK CITIZENSHIP AND THE ISSUE OF WHITE VOTE DILUTION

The need for the entirely new definition of national citizenship articulated in Section 1 of the Fourteenth Amendment was created by the status vacuum that followed the Emancipation Proclamation and the Union victory in the Civil War. This vacuum was a problem both for the freedpeople themselves, who agitated to regularize their status, and for the government, which found itself in charge of a population that, since the *Dred Scott* ruling, had no status as citizens and "no rights any white man was bound to respect."[24] This was an untenable situation for a "republican" government, which could not "rule over" a substantial population that had been born within the boundaries of the nation, and whose "natural rights" had been recognized by the Thirteenth Amendment.[25] The government was bound by a constitutional[26] as well as an administrative imperative to regularize the status of the freedpeople within its territory by granting them citizenship.[27]

During the period between the Emancipation Proclamation in 1863 and the passage of the Fourteenth Amendment in 1867, the freedpeople were literally "stateless" in Hannah Arendt's sense of the term.[28] As "contraband,"[29] they had not lost the "right to have rights"—that right and the state of slavery were contradictions in terms. As chattel slaves, they had been property, and detailed state and national legal codes had governed their movements and behavior, as well as the behavior of whites toward them. The legal termination of their slave status did not translate into automatic legal citizenship status in the states where they had lived: they had no government or official protection save that provided by the Freedman's Bureau and the military regime. Many of the former Confederate states enacted what were called "Black Codes" to govern the freedpeople: these were essentially the old slave laws that

> Imposed upon the colored race onerous disabilities and burdens, and curtailed their rights in the pursuit of life, liberty and property to such an extent that their freedom was of little value, while they had lost the protection which they had received from their former owners from motives both of interest and humanity.[30]

As reports of the Black Codes and official mistreatment by the former Confederate states of the freedpeople arrived at the 39th Congress, Republican representatives voiced the need to encode in legislation, and subsequently in a constitutional amendment, the victory of emancipation. In citing the Black Codes in their speeches, Rep. Thomas D. Eliot and Sen. Charles Sumner of Massachusetts articulated the view that a federal "duty to protect" was inherent in formal emancipation.

> The knot which politicians could not untie during eighty years of peace, the sword of Mr. Lincoln cut at one blow. The power to liberate, which is now confessed, involved the duty to protect...Wherever we turn in our legislative path, we encounter questions of freedmen and freedmen's rights. No peace will come that will 'stay' until the Government that decreed freedom shall vindicate and enforce its rights by appropriate legislation.[31]

Only the national government could provide the freedpeople with a citizen identity—mutilated as that government was without the defeated Confederate states to complete the Union. Hundreds of thousands of the freedpeople were refugees, uprooted from their former "homes" in the South: they could not claim residency for the purpose of citizenship as could whites. It was the still the law of the land (as per the *Dred Scott* decision) that free blacks could not be citizens of *any* state under the meaning of (the Comity clause of) the Constitution.[32] Moreover, the constitutional status of the former Confederate governments was still undetermined during the 39th Congress, and few Republican Congressmen cherished the hope that once those states were readmitted to the Union, elected majorities would grant the former slaves equal citizenship status. Bitterness towards "Negroes" enfranchised under the military governments in the South, combined with the sting of the disenfranchisement of former Confederate officers would, the Radicals feared, translate into a new round of disenfranchisement once the southern states were re-admitted to Congress.[33]

The former slave states did not formally rejoin Congress until after they had ratified the Fourteenth Amendment, so did not comprise a portion of the *politeuma* whose representatives drafted the terms of the new citizenship regime. The several states individually, including the Northern states, were under no constitutional obligation to grant citizenship to the refugees since each had its own (republican, not autonomous) definition of citizenship. In other words, the whole (the national government, and national citizenship) was definitively *not* equal to the sum of its parts (state government and state citizenship) in the period of 1865-1868. Citizenship had to be redefined for all Americans, not just for the South or the "contraband," because slavery, a legally defined and minutely codified social institution that had heretofore defined national politics, had come to an end.

The "wake" of emancipation was the post-bellum administrative chaos created by the presence of "stateless" people in the South, and the influx of refugees into legally constituted states with intact rules defining their electorates. Absent legitimately constituted state power in the South, citizenship had to be redefined by the national government. And the national government was controlled by the Republican Party, which had won a decisive victory in the 1866 elections.

White Vote Dilution

The issue of political rights for African-Americans was decisively joined by the specter of a resurrected southern wing of the Democratic Party. Republican sensitivity in the 39th Congress to the prospect of *white* male (group) vote dilution in their home constituencies pushed Party leaders to advocate *black* male suffrage during the debates over the Fourteenth Amendment.

> The future of both parties was at stake, and this gave added bitterness and a frantic urgency to the debates over Recon-

struction. The constitutional deduction for Republicans was that any program which they enacted must be enshrined in amendments to the Constitution and not left at the mercy of future constitutional majorities, and thus moderates were driven towards constitutional changes that might otherwise have alarmed them. Whatever policy was agreed would also have to be enacted before the Southerners returned, because future Congresses might be unwilling or unable to pass the necessary laws. The main casualty was any program of staged development which might lead the Negroes from their depressed condition toward full citizenship." (Brock 1963, 20-23),

Knowing the federal system and the Guarantee Clause,[34] not to mention public opinion in the Northern and Western states, prevented them from directly imposing black male suffrage on the reconstructing South, the Republican-dominated Joint Reconstruction Committee proposed reducing national representation if the states did not enfranchise the freedmen.[35] Facing an increase in (Democratic) Southern representation—at least 13 new seats—once the former Confederate states were readmitted to Congress (since population-based apportionment would count freed slaves as one, rather than 3/5ths of a person), and anticipating that future Democratic Southern majorities would disenfranchise the freedmen included in the new apportionment, Republicans on the Joint Reconstruction Committee raised the cry of *white* vote dilution. According to Senator Blaine (R. ME), the key issue was

> Whether the white voter of the North shall be equal to the white voter of the South in shaping the policy and fixing the destiny of the country; whether to put it still more baldly, the white man who fought in the ranks of the Union Army shall have as weighty and influential a vote in the Government of the Republic as the white man who fought in the ranks of the rebel army."[36]

And the *Chicago Tribune* editorialized:

> Those who believe that one Northern voter should equal one Southern voter will cast their ballots for the Amendments… But those who contend that each Southerner shall count as two, by stealing the vote of a Negro, and adding it to his own, will oppose the amendment. (James 1965, 159)

In order to equalize the weights of Republican and Democratic votes in states and congressional districts throughout the country, and therefore in order to consolidate its power at the national level, the Republican Party *had to be* committed to "Negro" suffrage and to fair representation in the former slave states. Republicans' personal political ambitions and party loyalty trumped whatever reservations based on racial prejudice individual members had about whether the time had come for equal political citizenship.[37] Of course, this "rational" choice was predicated on the assumption that the freedmen—a significant and identifiable constituency—would vote the Republican ticket in local and national elections. Thus the cornerstone of the new national citizenship regime that was institutionalized after the Civil War was the nominal *political* equality of all adult male citizens, a group that had been expanded to include those who had been slaves under the previous citizenship regime. The "representation reducing" penalty of Section 2 was never enforced, though, and Southern delegations were seated even after the "disenfranchising conventions" of the late nineteenth century made it apparent that African-Americans, although included in the basis of apportionment, were to be "constitutionally" prevented from exercising their political rights.[38]

Thus despite the textual effort (Section 2) to prevent group vote dilution, state practices encoded by Democratic majorities effectuated it by means of literacy tests, poll taxes, white primaries, terrorist violence, and felon disenfranchisement. The balance of party power had shifted by the time of the infamous southern "disenfranchising conventions" and the Republican Party, which was building strength in the new Western states, no longer "needed" to win Southern seats in the House to maintain national political power.[39] Moreover as Woodward (1966) convincingly demonstrated, the national mood had turned by the "Progressive Era" and

> As America shouldered the White Man's Burden, she took up at the same time many Southern attitudes on the subject of race. (...) The doctrines of Anglo-Saxon superiority by which Professor John H. Burgess of Columbia University [et al.] justified and rationalized American imperialism in the Philippines, Hawaii, and Cuba differed in no essentials from the race theories by which Senators (...) Tillman [et al.] ...justified racism in the South. (72-74)

The price of "racial" superiority nationwide was, therefore, the weakening of the political rights of "majority" *as well as* minority citizens, or individual vote dilution in states and sections of the country that did not disenfranchise large numbers of their citizens who were counted in the bases of apportionment. The political effect of the "sectional" vote dilution the Radical Republicans had tried, and failed, to head off with Section 2 was the institutionalization of southern influence in national politics.

Long into the twentieth century, the South remained a one-party region under the control of a reactionary ruling elite who used the same violence and fraud that helped defeat Reconstruction to stifle internal dissent. An enduring consequence of Reconstruction's failure, the Solid South helped define the contours of American politics and weaken the prospects not simply of change in racial matters but of progressive legislation in many other realms. (Foner 1988, 604)[40]

The issue of vote dilution did not come to the forefront of national debate again until the early 1960s, when the Warren Court, attempting to impose a political theory of individual, rather than geographical representation, on the states came up with the "one man, one vote" rule of district apportionment.[41] Before turning to the second half of the twentieth century, though, we must look more closely at the prosecutorial systems of the Athenian and American democracies in order to see how *atimia,* opportunistically instrumentalized in a context of representative government, became an unjust institution. My claim is that it is unjust because it serves "the good" of only a part of the polity rather than the whole, as it did in Athens.

3. THE CRIMINAL JUSTICE SYSTEM AS A REPRESENTATIVE INSTITUTION

The American criminal justice system is a modern representative institution that punishes convicted citizens in conformity with standardized laws and penalties enacted by elected majorities. In order to understand how the institution of felon disenfranchisement functions in this system, and can be opportunistically "hijacked" by a political party, it must be compared with the way *atimia,* the original institution, operated in pre-representative systems. The modern criminal justice system replaced the direct, self-help, system of pre-modern societies. It gradually evolved in the United States from English Common Law practice into the statutory enactments of federal and state codes. The theory underlying state punishment in a liberal democratic society is essentially Lockean: citizens have alienated their "natural" right to punish, to defend their lives and properties, to a sovereign that will protect them more efficiently.[42]

In the Athenian self-help system that entitled all citizens to be prosecutors, the citizen who was the "victim" of a crime, or his or her

family (in the case of a murder) had to file charges against the
perpetrator on his own behalf. He represented himself. If a member of a
citizen's household (such as a woman, child or slave) was victimized, the
citizen could bring an action on their behalf against the wrongdoer. The
case was then heard by a citizen jury who would find for or against the
citizen prosecutor, much as modern juries do today.[43]

> This is an important fact. The premodern citizen around the
> globe, including the ancient Athenian, was obliged, for safety's
> sake, to understand punishment: what it was, how it worked,
> how one "did" it. Athenians of democratic Athens who thought
> that they had suffered wrong usually had to be able to deal with
> that wrong for themselves. They themselves had to be able to
> bring the apparatus of authoritative political power to bear
> against the person who had wronged them. They had to see an
> act of power through from initiation to conclusion and carry out
> the process of punishing. (Allen 2000, 4)

If the "defendant" was convicted, he suffered *atimia* as well, maybe,
as other penalties. *Atimia* and direct participation, both in the Assembly
and the criminal courts, were two sides of the same coin that was
Athenian citizenship. The former was the negative, the latter the positive
pole. Both were direct and drastically personal in their effects, and were
imposed, as we saw in Chapter One, only for serious crimes against the
demos, such as debt, certain moral transgressions, and dereliction of
civic duty.

As we also saw in Chapter One, one of the main effects of *atimia*
was to leave the, convicted citizen and the members of his household
vulnerable to assault, insult, robbery and even murder, since as an *atimos*
he lost his citizenship right to bring public and private lawsuits if
insulted or attacked. While the Athenian "criminal justice system" cannot
be assimilated to a Hobbesian "State of Nature," since it had clearly
defined laws and penalties, the world the *atimos* was cast into actually
was an (ancient) version of the State of Nature. The penalty of *atimia*
was perfectly retributive: it deprived the citizen of the protections and
honors of that status as a punishment for having transgressed the (citizen-
given) norms of the polis. An *atimos* (literally) had no honor—he was
stripped of his political, military, and religious privileges, and of the
security in his person and possessions. No "state" stepped in to ensure
him (or his family and descendents) rights of due process or protection
once the *atimia* was in force, and there was no provision for
rehabilitation or reintegration of the citizen if the *atimia* was permanent.
Although the citizen lost his right to vote, and indeed could not even
appear at the Assembly, *atimia* did not function to deprive a political

party of the disenfranchised citizen's vote, since as we said, there was no organized party competition: the citizen's individual vote was only one of six thousand or so in the Assembly. In the absence of ongoing representative coalitions such as political parties, and from the perspective of the Assembly as a whole, a single vote would not have been missed.[44]

In the United States, by contrast, which is exceptional in this regard vis-à-vis other modern democracies, locally elected or appointed District Attorneys, who represent "the People" in their law enforcing capacity, file charges against a "criminal suspect" who has violated another citizens' rights, and prosecute cases to obtain a verdict. In terms of social contract theory, when the DA prosecutes an offender and obtains a conviction, she is enforcing the law on behalf of all citizens, who have relinquished their private "right" to punish to the sovereign.[45] In the modern polity, whose central institutional feature is representation, the public prosecutor's office replaces the private (citizen) prosecutor, the institution of self-help that characterized the law enforcement function in premodern polities. In fact, though, the office of the District Attorney is a local, discretionary power, subject to no oversight and review. "To some extent [the Prosecutor] derives his authority from statute, but more largely he relies on custom. The people look to him for results in the unending war of society on crime, and if he produces results they are not likely to ask whether he has stayed within the exact limits of his powers."[46]

Compared to its continental counterparts in England and France, the American office of the public prosecutor is unique in its degree of local autonomy and discretionary power, both of which derive from the fact that it is an elective office in most states.[47] The wave of democratic zeal that expanded suffrage in the American republic during the final decades of the nineteenth century precipitated the movement to elect local officials, including judges. After it became commonplace to elect local judges, it became customary to elect the prosecuting attorney. According to Jacoby (1980) the history of the development of the office of the prosecutor has a clear theme: "local representation applying local standards to the enforcement of essentially local laws." The discretion and power of the prosecutor to charge an offender or to terminate criminal proceedings is virtually unlimited, and was the subject of several concerned commission reports and a body of legal scholarship during the 1930s. One of the articles in a series described the paradoxes embodied in the development of the local prosecutor:

> The people of the United States have traditionally feared concentration of great power in the hands of one person and it is

surprising that the power of the prosecuting attorney has been left intact as it is today. (…) Nowhere is it more apparent that our government is a government of men, not of laws.[48]

The virtually unlimited power of the local district attorney to ignore or punish an offense derives from his position as an elected representative. Not only does he (theoretically) "represent" the power of the individual citizen who has "alienated" his natural right to punish to the state, he (actually) "represents" the power of the political party, or local majority coalition that elected him, and that will vote retrospectively on his record. Unless his cònstituency rewards non-rational political behavior, he generally does not represent citizens whose political identity is tenuous, marginal, or non-existent (the already felonized and disenfranchised). He would have absolutely no reason to represent a citizen permanently disenfranchised for crime, as convicted felons now are in seven American states, since such persons can never re-integrate themselves into the *politeuma,* and rejoin their fellow citizens in a society of democratic equality. This institutional state of affairs has been described by Aristotle as a democracy where the "rule of the majority, or popular sovereignty," rather than the "rule of law," prevails. In the following passage, "decrees" can be analogized to "discretion" in administration of the criminal law.[49]

A fifth variety of democracy is like the fourth in admitting to office every person who has the status of citizen; but here the people, and not the law is the final sovereign. This is what happens when popular decrees are sovereign instead of the law; and that is a result which is brought about by leaders of the demagogic type…. The people then becomes an autocrat—a single composite autocrat made up of many members, with the many playing the sovereign, not as individuals, but collec-tively…. It grows despotic; flatterers come to be held in honor; it becomes analogous to the tyrannical temper…It is popular leaders who, by referring all issues to the decision of the people, are responsible for substituting the sovereignty of decrees for that of the laws. (*Politics* IV, iv, 192a)

The post-Reconstruction political conjuncture, which saw the rash of disenfranchising constitutional conventions throughout the South frames my comparison of the practice of *atimia* in the Athenian and American citizenship regimes. The discrepancy between the constitutional "self-help" and representative prosecutorial systems becomes particularly apparent when the Athenian regime is contrasted with the post-bellum American regime, when freed slaves were declared to be citizens under the Fourteenth Amendment. During slavery, explicit state and local legal codes evolved to regulate the movements of the slave and free black populations, and much of the discipline of slaves was left to their owners in the privacy of their plantations.[50] After Emancipation and the Northern victory, though, the situation changed dramatically, and the former Confederate states, particularly once Radical Reconstruction was over, passed legislation to closely regulate the movement and labor of the freedpeople. It is far beyond the scope of this chapter to review these provisions, but the key point is that African-Americans were now legally citizens. Under the Reconstruction Amendments and the Civil Rights Acts of 1866 and 1875, they were legally entitled to vote and to take their place in civil society along with their white counterparts.[51] They were, theoretically at least, citizens who enjoyed the protection of the law and of the prosecutor, as they went about their daily lives, participated in political campaigns, supported candidates, and voted. Again, in terms of social contract theory, they were members of the sovereign, and had no right to represent themselves, only to elect representatives.

The Civil Rights Act of 1866 was subtitled: "An Act to protect all Persons in the United States in their Civil Rights and to furnish the Means of their Vindications." It declared explicitly that

> Citizens, of every race and color, without regard to any previous condition of slavery...shall have the same right, in every State and Territory in the United States, to make and enforce contracts, to sue, be parties, and give evidence, to inherit, purchase, lease, sell, hold and convey real and personal property, and to full and equal benefit of all laws and proceedings for the security of person and property, as is enjoyed by white citizens...

The statute also had an equal protection core with declarations that all citizens: "shall be subject to like punishment, pains and penalties, and to none other, any law, statute ordinance, regulation *or custom*, to the contrary notwithstanding." (Higginbotham 1996, 76; my italics.)

Yet all citizens were not "subject to like punishment, pains and penalties" if they were members of the dominant political majority. In many cases they were granted virtual impunity for crimes against blacks, and in the most extreme cases for the terrorist violence perpetrated by the Ku Klux Klan. When district attorneys failed to prosecute people who assaulted or murdered free African-Americans, simply in virtue of the fact that they belonged to that ascribed group and were attempting to exercise their political rights, their security as citizens was compromised just as surely as that of the Athenian *atimos*. Under the system of representative government, African-Americans who were victims of white terrorist violence were not entitled to resort to the self-help system that was available to their ancient citizen counterparts.[52] They could not prosecute their assailants themselves. The representative institution of the elected prosecutor had subsumed that right, rendering them powerless to protect themselves and their families from white terrorism. Yet when plaintiffs litigated under the Enforcement and Civil Rights Acts to have their right to vote or to enjoy public accommodations enforced, the Supreme Court denied them, falling back on the pretext of states' rights as well as the need to prove intent to discriminate.[53]

So the theoretical question, what happens when representation fails, is also, of course, a practical question for those directly impacted by majoritarian sanctioned violence. What happens when the representative citizenship regime (which can, in the case of the modern American polity, be viewed as a contract between citizens and their representatives) does not represent the victims of "popular sovereignty?" When an institution that is supposed to protect and defend citizens in virtue of their membership of the polity does not represent their interests but only those of another "part" of the polity? Locke's answer to this was that citizens are in a State of War.

> For wherever violence is used, and injury done, though by hands appointed to administer Justice, it is still violence, and injury, however colored with the Name, Pretences, or Forms of Law, the end whereof being to protect and redress the innocent by an unbiassed (sic) application of it, to all who are under it; wherever that is not *bona fide* done, *War is made* upon the Sufferers, who having no appeal on Earth to right them, they are left to the only remedy in such Cases, an appeal to Heaven. (*ST*, III, §21)

Charles Mills' (1997) explanation for the failure of representation I am positing is that African-Americans were never included in the original contract and, moreover, that the original contract is actually a "racial contract:"

> In this framework (...) the golden age of contract theory (1650-1800) overlapped with the growth of a European capitalism whose development was stimulated by the voyages of exploration that increasingly gave the contract a *racial* subtext. The evolution of the modern version of the contract, characterized by an anti-patriarchalist Enlightenment liberalism, with its proclamations of the equal rights, autonomy, and freedom of all men, thus took place simultaneously with the massacre, expropriation, and subjection to hereditary slavery of men at least

apparently human. This contradiction needs to be reconciled; it is reconciled through the Racial Contract, which essentially denies their personhood and restricts the terms of the social contract to whites. (63-64)[54]

When representation is partial or incomplete as a result of outright vote denial or vote dilution, a modern citizen can suffer the material equivalent of ancient *atimia* as a result of the structure of "judicial representation" even if she has not committed a crime but has been the victim of a crime. Thus disenfranchisement can occur invisibly, informally, as well as administratively and formally after a trial and conviction. If a DA uses her statutory discretion to grant effective impunity to an offender who is known to have committed a crime, the victim or the victim's family has little or no legal recourse to punish the assailant, robber, rapist, murderer. Thus the victim or her family, or the community as the case may be, is vulnerable to violence and intimidation just as the Athenian *atimos* was because her representative, the District Attorney, has failed to represent her interests.[55] I make this point in order to show that in the American polity the decision to allow criminal behavior to go unpunished—to effectively grant impunity—is the choice of the elected representative (the DA) rather than the citizen herself. It is rather a different matter when the state, or "the People" desists from prosecuting as a result of their concept of what "the People" is, than when a victim desists from prosecuting as a matter of personal choice. As Bybee (2000, 30) says, this choice (of the elected prosecutor to act or the Court to ratify or reject a prosecutor's indictment) reaches issues of political identity:

> Political identity is central to the study of minority representation. In part, this is true because *any* debate over representation depends on political identity, with competing views turning on different notions of what people and which interests are to be represented. Understandings of political identity are also important because the Supreme Court usually justifies its own power in terms of its capacity to represent the people as a whole. When adjudicating issues of representation, the Court not only chooses between rival conceptions of "the people" at stake in public debate, but it also selects a conception of "the people" on whose behalf the Court shall speak.

The problem is, though, that by institutionalizing a criminal justice system that represents a non-inclusive conception of the People, while retaining the ancient institution of felon disenfranchisement, the American polity has combined elements of two entirely distinct regimes.

Structurally speaking, it has deprived citizens whose political identity excludes them from the People, of the self-help option available to citizens in the original regimes that integrated disenfranchisement into their structure. In those regimes, individuals whose political identity excluded them from "the people" were not citizens. They did not belong to that "status honor group" and could not represent themselves in jury trials. Each citizenship regime has its own structural integrity and coherence, and when a regime removes the positive (defensive) element from the citizen and replaces it with another system, it contradicts itself when it simultaneously retains the negative (punitive) element of the old regime. Felon disenfranchisement in premodern societies was a corrective mechanism the demos employed to restore what modern political scientist call equilibrium in areas of social, religious, and political life.

In the United States, representative government, institutional checks and balances, and party competition are modern "corrective mechanisms" that function to make both self-help and therefore *atimia* superfluous. "The People" are supposed to protect the honor and security of the citizens through their representatives. A criminal justice system in a modern representative democracy is supposed to correct and rehabilitate offenders in order that they may return to society and take their place in society alongside their fellow citizens. American *atimia* directly undermines this purpose and contradicts the spirit of representative democracy sketched in the final section of the previous chapter on democratic individuality.

The continuum of citizenship rights inscribed in the American Constitution and its Amendments reflects a movement away from violence to legal institutionalization of norms: from materially embodied struggle between the disenfranchised and the powerful, to the universalization of formal law and rights that protect all citizens. Citizenship as an institution of social and political solidarity represents freedom from the realm of violence, naked power, and what Agambin (1998) calls "bare life," the condition that allows humans who are no longer (or have never) been counted as citizens, to be killed at will by others. State-sponsored violence, in minority communities and in the prisons, are "switches" that return citizens to the material realm of "non-freedom" that is the other side of the mirror, so to speak, of citizenship. In social contract theory, the institution of citizenship "transcends" the violent material existence that was its genesis: the status embodies the freedom and rights inscribed in political discourse and legal text (statute and constitutional law.) The citizen who is evicted from that realm upon "conviction for crime" and disenfranchised, returns to the realm of material struggle where not law, but violence rules.[56] The punished "re-descend" to this pre-political level, sent on their way by those who inscribe and enjoy the rights and freedoms of citizens. The two are practically "parallel universes" of freedom and denizenship, the institution of the former being the modern polity of the hypothetical contract; of the latter the streets, the prison, the state of nature.

To sum up: in the citizenship regime where *atimia* was a just penalty, citizens had the right to represent themselves as prosecutors. Self-help, the right to prosecute, to enforce one's right to security as a citizen, was the positive pole of citizenship; *atimia,* the citizen body's right to enforce its norms, to deprive the citizen of his right to security, was the negative pole of the same citizenship regime. Both actions, both processes, defined the meaning of Athenian citizenship as a direct and personal experience of political equality. The inverse of that experience was complete social and political *in*equality, a condition shared with women and slaves. In a citizenship regime where representation, institutional checks and balances, and party competition are "just" institutions, and citizens are (theoretically at least) protected by the criminal justice system, there can be no normative justification for banishing citizens to the realm of permanent political inequality.

Since the purpose of ancient *atimia* was to render a convicted citizen forever invisible and insecure, it is both irrelevant and unjust in the modern context. For one thing, the very size of the modern American republic, which was a central reason the founders gave for the need for representation, already renders the citizen member of an electorate invisible. Theoretically, there are no non-citizen "others" in the polity to the same extent that there were in the Athenian polity into whose status group the convicted felon can be cast in order to become invisible to the rest of the citizen body. Moreover, the purpose of the modern justice system, the very purpose of the modern liberal state, is to *protect* the citizen, even when he has been convicted of a crime. The purpose of *atimia* and later outlawry, as we saw in Chapter One, was to render the convicted citizen defenseless. The reciprocal effect was to confer impunity upon the enfranchised citizenry, who could kill the outlaw (or escaped slave) at will. Comparable (albeit theoretical) modern impunity is conferred elected representatives when any group, however "politically insignificant," is subtracted from the modern "represented" electorate as a result of permanent ex-felon disenfranchisement. If universal political rights mean anything at all, it is that the potential individual contribution to the polity is incalculable, so that when the polity is deprived of the political contribution of the individual, the losses and gains are incalculable.

The stated purpose of felon disenfranchisement in the modern American polity is to remove "untrustworthy" individual voters from the electorate, either temporarily or permanently. The history of American felon disenfranchisement shows, though, that those individuals targeted for removal were so targeted because of their membership in a particular status group, which was generally thought to determine their party allegiance. Once a sufficient quantum of the negative status group, or opposition political party supporters, had been successfully removed, the dominant status group or political party secured a position of temporary impunity for policy purposes. This application represented a perversion of the purpose of the original Athenian institution though: the Assembly did not miss the votes of those who were *atimos,* because citizens did not vote in parties. In close American elections, by contrast, the political party whose potential voters have been disenfranchised may lose what could have been critical votes.[57] Furthermore, as we will see in the next section, the federalist structure of the American system of representative government means that felon disenfranchisement laws in some states dilute the votes of citizens in other states, resulting in national political inequality.

4. VOTE DILUTION, INDIVIDUAL RIGHTS AND THE WARREN COURT

Citizens' votes, the symbol of their political rights, are deemed unequal and abridged when they are diluted relative to other citizens' votes. Vote dilution typically results from the fact that electoral districts are drawn in such a way that they do not include the same number of people even though each district elects the same number of officials. As a result, those who live in larger population districts cast a vote that is diluted relative to the vote of those residing in smaller districts.[58] Individual vote dilution is subject to "strict scrutiny" since the Court has determined that under the Constitution, each person is entitled to cast a vote that carries substantially the same weight as that of other voters in the same election. The Court has derived the principle of "one person one vote" from two distinct sources. In the case of elections for the U.S. House of Representatives, the Court has read the requirement of Article I, §2, cl.1—representatives are to be chosen "by the People"—as mandating substantial equality of population among the various districts established by a state legislature for the election of members of Congress. With respect to state and local elections, the Court has extracted the same principle from the Equal Protection Clause. Under that clause "an indi-vidual's right to vote for state [officials] is unconstitutionally impaired when its weight is in a substantial fashion diluted when compared with votes of citizens living in other parts of the State." [59]

When government officials are elected on a district-by-district basis, compliance with the principle of "one person one vote" requires that state and local governments "make an honest and good faith effort to construct districts.... as nearly of equal population as is practicable."[60]

The theoretical issue underlying claims of vote dilution is interest, and the early vote dilution cases were about the "interests" of people who lived in different—rural and urban—geographical communities. They were communities of interest rather than, politically speaking, of discrete individuals, and the Chief Justice ruled that representation should not be based on interest:

> Neither history alone, nor economic or other sorts of group interests, are permissible factors in attempting to justify disparities from population-based representation. Citizens, not history or economic interests, cast votes. Considerations of area alone provide an insufficient justification for deviations from the equal population principle. Again, people, not land or trees or pastures, vote.[61]

The ruling in *Reynolds* signaled an untheorized move to majoritarian or populist democracy, and away from the more traditional Madisonian conception of republican democracy based on recognition of group interest or faction restrained by institutional checks and balances.[62]

Warren justified the Court's incursion into what had heretofore been the states' rights to plenary control over suffrage within their boundaries by claiming that "denial of constitutionally protected rights demands judicial protection." He asserted that the right to vote was federally protected[63] and tied this concept of political rights to citizenship in his famous statement:

> To the extent that a citizen's right to vote is debased, he is that much less a citizen ... A citizen, a qualified voter, is no more nor no less so because he lives in the city or on a farm.[64]

This single sentence reveals the problem of double citizenship and political rights. Warren is asserting that the right to vote is federally protected, so the citizen Warren is referring to must be an *American* citizen, yet the fact that he uses the word "qualified" to both modify "voter" and define "citizen" implies state membership, since only a state can "qualify" a voter. Thus at the same time as he is making what Harlan calls a pronouncement on the "abstract justice" of (national) citizen rights, he is also deferring to the constitutional plenary powers of the states to regulate suffrage, inadvertently exposing the disjunction of equalities that emerges when the two citizen identities/regimes are combined. When Warren said, in his *Reynolds* ruling, that "None would deny that a state law giving some citizens twice the vote of other citizens in either the primary or general election would lack that equality which the Fourteenth Amendment guarantees... The theme of the Constitution is equality among citizens in the exercise of their political rights," he was simply wrong. His error consisted in confusing the ascribed equality guaranteed by the Fourteenth Amendment with the concept of political rights, which citizens in "republican" polities may only exercise with the *consent* of their fellows.

As I discussed in the previous chapter, American citizenship has been equally distributed among the natural-born and naturalized members of the polity since the passage of the Fourteenth Amendment because it is an ascribed status, an administrative category that is neutral among persons who meet the requisite criteria. The category of *jus soli* national citizenship created in Section 1 was the only category that could comprehend the status of the freedmen after emancipation. The need to regularize the status of the minority, though, created a new universal rule of American citizenship. As Brubaker (1992, 32) says,

> Every state ascribes its citizenship to certain persons at birth. The vast majority of persons acquire their citizenship in this way.... [Ascriptive citizenship] is difficult to reconcile with a central claim—perhaps the central claim—of liberal political theory: the idea that political membership ought to be founded on individual consent. (32)

I submit that political membership in polities governed by "republican" principles is also founded on group consent, which is an active rather than tacit form of consent: the majority (status) group consents *to* include others (who then consent) into its *politeuma*. Active consent can also be negative, though, in the sense that a status group can consent to participate and legitimize an exclusionary polity. The tension between ascribed national citizenship and "consensual" state citizenship (read political rights) within the American federal system generates the political inequality inimical to citizenship in a modern liberal democratic nation such as the United States. This theoretical tension is captured in constitutional law by Sections 1 and 2 of the Fourteenth Amendment. Section 1 proclaims the rule of *jus soli* citizenship in the United States, and declares that no *state* shall abridge the "privileges and immunities"—which are not enumerated—of American citizens. Section 2 acknowledges the right of the states to control the franchise, even to the point of denying citizens the vote. It provides a penalty—reduction of national representation—should states *dis*enfranchise their citizens for anything but "participation in rebellion or other crime." Read together, Sections 1 and 2 imply that their American citizenship, bestowed automatically at birth, does not confer any right to vote on state citizens. In other words, the right to vote is not a "privilege or immunity" of American citizenship. Were it such, as (the second) Justice Harlan pointed out in his dissent in *Reynolds v Simms*, Section 2 would have been superfluous. In Justice Harlan's words,

> The second section expressly recognizes the States' power to deny "or in any way" abridge the right of their inhabitants to vote for "the members of the [State] Legislature" and its express provision of a remedy for such denial or abridgment. The comprehensive scope of the second section and its particular reference to the state legislatures preclude the suggestion that the first section was intended to have the result reached by the court today.

The "result" Harlan was referring to was, of course, Chief Justice Earl Warren's ruling that Congress had the power to regulate apportionment within the states in order to bring about fair representation in state elections. The majority ruling in *Reynolds* emphasized the equality of citizens of the nation, prioritizing the modern (liberal) democratic ideal that all individual members of the polity, rather than a select few, enjoy political rights: "Undoubtedly, the right of suffrage is a fundamental matter in a free and democratic society. Especially since the right to exercise the franchise in a free and unimpaired manner is preservative of other basic civil and political rights."[65] The fact is, though, that there was no national consensus about suffrage, particularly African-American suffrage, when the Fourteenth Amendment was framed. Insofar as such a national consensus can now be said to exist, judicial interpretations of Section 2 that adhere to original construction, concerning the states' rights to regulate suffrage in federal elections, are anachronistic and in the light of contemporary felon disenfranchisement practices, unjust.

The entirely "political" view of citizenship expressed in Justice Harlan's dissent in *Reynolds* quoted heavily from the debates of the Joint Reconstruction Committee. Harlan relied particularly on Senator Howard's assurances to his fellow Committee members that, while the purpose of the Fourteenth Amendment was to extend the Bill of Rights to the States, Section 1 did not interfere with the positive powers of the states, such as those of regulating suffrage. To make his point, Harlan quoted Howard's explanation of the meaning of the Fourteenth Amendment:

> The last two clauses of the first section of the amendment disable a State from depriving not merely a citizen of the United States, but any person, whoever he might be, of life, liberty, or property without due process of law, or from denying to him the equal protection of the laws of the State. This abolishes all class legislation in the States and does away with the injustice of subjecting one caste of persons to a code not applicable to another. It prohibits the hanging of a black man for a crime for which the white man is not to be hanged. It protects the black man in his fundamental rights as a citizen with the same shield which it throws over the white man. Is it not time, Mr. President, that we extend to the black man, I had almost called it the poor privilege of the equal protection of the law? *...But sir, the first section of the proposed amendment does not give to either of these classes the right of voting.* The right of suffrage is not, in law, one of the privileges or immunities thus secured by the Constitution. It is merely the creature of law. It has always been regarded in this country as the result of positive local law, not regarded as one of those fundamental rights lying at the basis of all society and without which a people cannot exist except as slaves, subject to a despotism."[66] (Emphasis in original)

While Section 1 of the Amendment, the "citizenship clause" declares who is a citizen of the United States, clarifies the identity of the members of the nation, and the nation's obligation to protect the "privileges and immunities" of the citizens, Section 2 explicitly recognizes the right of the states to regulate suffrage within their boundaries. Taken together, the text of the privileges and immunities and due process clauses imply that American citizens are equal insofar as they are members of the nation and beneficiaries of those rights. The privileges and immunities of American citizens do not include political rights, so they are not fundamental rights of American *or* state citizenship. The Fourteenth Amendment proclaims a politically neutered conception of citizenship that is quite distinct from the conception of classical citizenship, which always implied political rights. The reason for this was that there was no national consensus that the former slave population, or even the population of free blacks in the North, should enjoy political rights on equal terms with whites. Hence the need for a new, politically neutered, conception of national membership that regularized the administrative status and private rights of black citizens, but that excluded them from the *politeuma*.

> Modern state citizenship differs sharply in this respect from citizenship in the ancient Greek polis or in medieval towns. There it was axiomatic that some persons ought *not* to be citizens of any city. Persons lacking citizenship were not placeless; their status was not anomalous. Rather, they did not form part of the self-governing or otherwise privileged civic corporation. (Brubaker 1992, 31)

The newly minted American citizens in the post-Civil War regime were "axiomatically" citizens of the nation, but did not necessarily form part of the self-governing corporation, even when their "right to vote" proclaimed in the Fifteenth Amendment "could not be abridged on account of race or previous condition of servitude." That right although federally protected could, as the Radical Republicans on the Reconstruction Committee recognized, be abridged by elected majorities in the states for the reasons alluded to in Section 2 of the previous Amendment: "participation for rebellion or other crime." Moreover, the Thirteenth Amendment explicitly legalized slavery "as punishment for a crime whereof the party shall have been duly convicted." The power of elected majorities (political parties) in the states to control the franchise is, as we saw in the previous chapter, an essential principle of republican government, and represents the element of consent in the citizenship identity that is in deep tension with the ascribed national identity.[67] The post-Civil Rights movement national consensus is significantly different from the post-Civil War national consensus, but constitutional interpretation, by prioritizing the rights of states to republican government, has not integrated that consensus by legislating uniform national political rights.

The citizen rights of the freedmen that were explicitly protected by the federal courts under the Fourteenth Amendment were not political rights, but civil rights, what the framers of the amendment called "the fundamental rights of citizenship."

> The framers defined the rights they were attempting to secure as generic rights to life, liberty, and property, and they clarified their intent by relying on legal authorities that identified Bill of Rights guarantees with these natural rights of citizenship. Indeed, the American natural law theory of fundamental rights of citizens equated Bill of Rights guarantees with the natural rights of citizens. In light of these considerations, there is a great probability that the legislators who asserted that the fourteenth amendment and the Civil Rights Act secured Bill of

Rights guarantees expressed the general understanding of the framers. At the very least, they adopted a constitutional amendment that could be read as securing Bill of Rights guarantees, a reading that was uniformly embraced by United States Attorneys General, United States Attorneys, and legal officers and federal judges prior to 1873. (Kaczorowski 1986, 935)[68]

Such an association of citizenship with natural or fundamental rights is completely antithetical to the classical republican conception of citizenship, in which the political realm rather than the natural world defines citizenship and rights. In Hannah Arendt's view, for instance, the natural is the antithesis of the political, which is the true realm of citizenship.[69] Moreover, "Congressional framers (of the Fourteenth Amendment) acknowledged that it was the judiciary's function to determine whether a specific right was incidental to the natural rights of citizens, and thus enforceable by the federal courts." (Kaczorowski)

Thus when Chief Justice Warren stated in his opinion that "undeniably the Constitution of the United States protects the right of all qualified citizens to vote, in state as well as in federal elections," he and Justice Harlan were essentially talking past each other, since each was deploying a different conception of national citizenship. Warren's conception of citizenship was a modern one whose premise was that natural membership in a democratic nation-state automatically conferred equal political rights on qualified state citizens in virtue of their natural rights. The argument is clearly circular since Warren retained the word "qualified" in his ruling. Institutionally speaking, these rights were to be protected by the federal judiciary, which in the U.S. is a political office. Because Justice Harlan was relying on an original intent construction of the Fourteenth Amendment, which did not automatically equate natural with political rights, he viewed the Warren Court rulings in cases such as *Reynolds* and *Baker v Carr*[70] as "nothing less than an exercise of the amending power [of] the Court"[71] that created a new right [to vote] "out of whole cloth."[72] Harlan argued logically and historically, rather than abstractly, that such a usurpation by the Court of the states' authority to regulate suffrage "relegates the Fifteenth and Nineteenth Amendments to the same limbo of constitutional anachronisms to which the second section of the Fourteenth Amendment has been assigned."

By this he meant that, had Section 1 of the Fourteenth Amendment meant to include the right to vote within the "privileges and immunities of U.S. citizens, Congress would not have needed to frame either of the subsequent amendments, since "nothing is more evident than that the greater must include the less, and if all were already protected why go through with the form of amending the Constitution to protect a part?"[73]

Harlan's basic objection to the Court's interference in the states' power to regulate apportionment and voter qualifications was that it "judges constitutional questions on the basis of abstract 'justice' unleashed from the limiting principles that go with our constitutional system."[74] Such judgments spring from "impatience with the slow workings of the political process." In Harlan's view, "the vitality of our political system" is weakened by "reliance on the judiciary for political reform" with the result that in time "a complacent body politic" may develop.[75] Whether Justice Harlan was prescient or not, given contemporary voter turnout rates, is not the subject of this inquiry. His concern was that the political identity of American citizenship remain institutionally identified with the subdivisions of the states, and grounded in the political contest of interest groups. Grounded in the federal government and political contests between numerically equal population groups, political identity was meaningless, empty. Harlan's argument was that, by relocating political citizenship's center of gravity from the states to the nation, the Warren Court was "radically altering the relationship between the States and the Federal Government, more particularly the Federal Judiciary." None of the justices posited an absolute right to vote in federal elections that would be co-extensive with the status of federal citizenship and would allow state citizens, including ex-offenders disenfranchised under state law, in their capacity as American citizens, to elect federal representatives. Such a right could trump the state qualifications that stunt federal citizenship, but not abrogate states' rights to regulate suffrage vis-à-vis their own affairs. This argument has yet to be made to the Court.

5. POLITICAL INEQUALITY OF "QUALIFIED" AMERICAN CITIZENS

Although the Supreme Court has ruled that "qualified" American citizens have an equal right to vote in federal elections,[76] to be represented in the (sovereign) *politeuma,* I propose that their individual representation is actually unequal because the votes of some citizens are diluted relative to those of others. This is the product of the dynamic interaction of two apparently unrelated features of the federal system: the diverse state felon disenfranchisement laws—which result in vote denial to some citizens—and the (relatively) equal bases of apportionment of U.S. Congressional districts. Or put negatively, it is the result of the fact that the laws regarding voter qualifications for federal elections are not absolutely general, as democratic laws are supposed to be,[77] while the rules regarding apportionment are equal and absolutely general.

The Supreme Court has recognized the right of Congress to set qualifications for voters in federal (as opposed to state and local) elections, and has ruled against states that unfairly dilute citizens' votes by mal-apportioning U.S. Congressional districts.[78] There is no legal or academic scholarship that I am aware of, however, that analyzes how the equal rights of qualified U.S. citizens to vote in state and federal elections are compromised by state felon disenfranchisement laws.[79] None of the law review literature, including the briefs of lawsuits brought to challenge the practice, argues that by combining the fifty separate jurisdictions of the states into one composite national jurisdiction, the voting rights of individual U.S. citizens are compromised when compared in federal elections across the several states. Theoretically speaking, therefore, I am following the classic advice of James Madison to "extend the sphere"[80] and of E.E. Schattschneider (1960, ch.1) to "expand the scope of the conflict." The legal scholarship on felon disenfranchisement has, as I mentioned in the previous chapter, focused on the vote dilution of *minorities* affected by law-and-order policies (group vote dilution). The explicitly political national perspective[81] I am taking in this chapter will shed light on the extent to which the political rights of *all* American citizens are compromised by state laws that disenfranchise felons.[82]

6. REPRESENTATIONAL VERSUS ELECTORAL EQUALITY

The theoretical justification for extending the sphere, and conceptualizing the United States as a unitary political subdivision in its own right, for the purposes of the election of federal officers by American citizens, derives from the rhetorical references in the Constitution[83] to the People.

> What we miss is how all these references to "the People" are embodiments of the Constitution's unitary structure and the overarching spirit of popular sovereignty—of the people's right to "ordain" and "establish" and their "reserved" and "retained" rights to alter or abolish their Constitution. And when we look at the "Constitution" as an act and not a text— (...) it was the most participatory, majoritarian (within each state) and populist event that the planet Earth had ever seen. (Amar 1994, 761)

When the rhetoric concerning the People is translated into a structural framework for the analysis of electoral practices, the deficits in

political equality wrought by the diversity of state felon disenfranchisement laws become apparent. Moreover, these deficits become
apparent in terms of the Supreme Court's own voting rights
jurisprudence as applied to the states. The authoritative ruling is
Douglas's in *Gray v Sanders*[84]

> The Equal Protection Clause requires that, once a geographical
> unit for which a representative is to be chosen is designated, all
> who participate in the election must have an equal vote—
> whatever their race; whatever their sex; whatever their
> occupation; whatever their income and wherever their home
> may be in that geographical unit.

The geographical unit in question in *Gray* was the county, and at
issue was Georgia's county unit system of counting votes in the
Democratic primary elections for federal and state representatives, which
resembled the Electoral College method by which the U.S. president is
selected. The Warren Court invalidated the state's system of county
representation in candidate selection, analogizing the unequal weighting
of votes by county residence to actual disenfranchisement practices. The
majority rested this claim on the "idea that every voter is equal to every
other voter in the state."[85] *Grey* was followed by *Wesberry v Sanders*,[86] a
congressional apportionment case in which the Court relied on Article I,
Section 2 of the Constitution to invalidate Georgia's mal-apportioned
congressional districts. The majority argued that the article's requirement
that representatives be selected by the electors of the states, meant that
each individual vote was to count as equally as practicable. Referring to
the *Wesberry* ruling in *Reynolds,* Warren establishes the line of
argument:

> In that case we decided that an apportionment of Congressional
> seats which "contracts the value of some votes and expands that
> of others" is unconstitutional since "the Federal Constitution
> intends that when qualified voters elect members of Congress
> each vote be given as much weight as any other vote..." We
> concluded that the constitutional prescription for election of
> members of the House of Representatives "by the People,"
> construed in its historical context, "means that as nearly as
> practicable one man's vote in a congressional election is to be
> worth as much as another's.

My claim is that if citizens in separate Congressional districts in the
same state have the constitutional right to cast equally weighted votes for
members of the House of Representatives,[87] they must have the same
constitutional right (to cast equally weighted votes) relative to citizens in

Congressional districts in other states, since all Congressional districts are as nearly as possible "equally apportioned."[88] This logic also applies to presidential elections, since College electors are apportioned to the states by congressional delegation. In this case, though, the inequality between the rights of qualified national citizens only appears in a comparison between states with equal numbers of Electoral College votes. In other words, voters in states with equal Electoral College delegations must have a constitutional right to cast undiluted or equally weighted votes relative to one another in the same election, since their base of apportionment is relatively equal.

This argument rests on somewhat different premises than the individual vote dilution cases whose causes of action were *mal-apportioned* districts (districts with substantially different populations) since Congressional districts, as noted, have substantially equal populations. The issue is whether voters have "electoral equality" or whether residents have "representative equality," an issue the Supreme Court decisions have alluded to in stunningly confused rhetoric, but not resolved. The decisions in the mal-apportionment cases, which were based on disputes between districts with ostensibly homogeneous electorates—i.e., the parties did not raise claims of minority or group vote dilution—seemed to be based on a theory of electoral equality.

> This principle assures that, regardless of the size of the whole body of constituents, political power, as defined by the number of those eligible to vote, is equalized as between districts holding the same number of representatives.[89]

The theory of representative equality on the other hand, is based on apportionment by raw population:

> It assures that all persons living within a district—whether eligible to vote or not—have roughly equal representation in the governing body. It assures that constituents have more or less equal access to their elected officials, by assuring that no official has a disproportionately large number of constituents to satisfy.[90]

The jurisprudential problem is that Warren asserted both theories in virtually the same breath—at least on the same page of the *Reynolds* decision:

> As nearly as practicable one man's vote in a congressional election is to be worth as much as another's. (Citing *Wesberry*) [Theory of Electoral Equality]

and

Our Constitution's plain objective was that of making equal representation for equal numbers of people the fundamental goal. [Theory of Representational Equality]

Logically, the only way these two theories of equality (of voting and representation) can be reconciled, is to give all persons in the comparable districts the right to vote. As long as some persons within the boundaries of the political subdivisions are disenfranchised—or at least if the distribution of disenfranchisement between the subdivisions in the comparative set is not random—then voter equality cannot be realized. Kozinski makes a persuasive argument in his *Garza* dissent that

What lies at the core of one person, one vote is the principle of electoral equality, not that of equality of representation. To begin with, the name by which the Court has consistently identified this constitutional right—one person, one vote—is an important clue that the Court's primary concern is with equalizing the voting power of electors, making sure that each voter gets one vote—not two, five or ten, *Reynolds,* 377 U.S. at 562; or one-half.[91]

Kozinski quoted extensively from the *Reynolds* line of cases to make his central claim that "equalizing total population is not an end in itself, but a means of achieving electoral equality."

Thus the Court stated in *Reynolds:* "The overriding objective must be substantial equality of population among the various districts *so that* the vote of any citizen is approximately equal in weight to that of any other citizen in the state." This language has been quoted in numerous subsequent cases. (Emphasis in original)

As Murphy (1991) says in a "Comment" on the *Garza* case,

[Kozinski's] interpretation solves the confusion of the majority opinion. While many Supreme Court cases call for the use of population figures in apportionment, they do so only where this type of apportionment will lead to electoral equality. The Supreme Court has never required that total population figures be used when this would not advance electoral equality. Indeed, as Judge Kozinski notes, *Burns v Richardson,*[92] the only case before the Supreme Court where there was a divergence between representational equality and electoral equality, can only be explained as supporting the notion of electoral equality, for the Court approved of the departure from population figures when these figures did not provide an adequate measure of the equality of each citizen's vote.

Thus I am making my argument in terms of a deficit of electoral rather than representational equality. Although U.S. Congressional districts are equipopulous, and therefore meet *one* of the *Reynolds* standards, comparing them with one another across the national territory raises issues of electoral vote dilution for individual citizens.

The first claim, therefore, in extending the sphere to the nominally equal entire citizen body (not just qualified voters) of the United States, is that felon disenfranchisement laws in the states, and the aggregative rather than unitary nature of the electorate that selects national representatives, results in, at minimum, three subsets of relationships of political inequality:

1. Between convicted persons (Set A) in states that disenfranchise (either temporarily or permanently) and convicted persons (Set B) in states that do not;
    i. For the convicted and disenfranchised (A), the inequality with (B) is simply based on vote *denial* relative to (A) rather than vote dilution
    ii. For the convicted and *not* disenfranchised (B) the claim of inequality is based on vote *dilution* relative to voters in states that include a population of disenfranchised felons. The logic of the claim is similar to that in (3).

2. Between convicted and non-convicted persons *within* states that disenfranchise. This is also a vote *denial* claim that is constitutionally legitimate since *Richardson,* but that violates equal protection standards as in 1i, as well as the normative conception of democracy sketched in the previous chapter, and is receiving considerable scholarly attention as a violation of Equal Protection under the Voting Rights Act. The vote dilution claim legal scholars are focusing on[93] refers to the relationship between the (aggregated) minority national electorate whose vote is diluted by the disproportionate "absence" of minority felons, and the (aggregated) majority electorate.[94]

In terms of regime classification, 1 and 2 create double polities both within the state and (aggregatively in) the nation. Comparing the (non)-rights of convicted persons in all states that disenfranchise (A) with those of persons in all states that do not disenfranchise (N) does not raise a vote dilution claim in national elections. It does, however, affect popular vote totals and perhaps the legitimacy of a presidential election where the popular vote total is different from the Electoral College results.[95]

3. Between the set of non-convicted voters in states that disenfranchise (N), and the set of non-convicted voters in states that do not (D). In other words, the votes of citizens (D) who have neither committed nor been convicted of a crime, and who are therefore "qualified," are diluted relative to citizens (N) in another state, who likewise have neither committed nor been convicted of a crime. This is the claim of individual vote *dilution* that will be taken up in this section. It applies both across U.S. Congressional districts (for elections to the U.S. House of Representatives) as well as for presidential elections (for the selection of electors in the College).

Now we are in a position to see why Warren's "qualified" American citizens actually enjoy *un*equal political rights. My thesis is that state felon disenfranchisement laws that qualify citizens to vote for federal officers create inequality between citizens of the national polity, even though they could meet "equal protection" challenges in the states (since, theoretically, all felons in a state are treated alike.) So while citizens of a particular state can be said to be treated equally if *all* convicted felons in the state are disenfranchised, all citizens of the United States are not treated equally if felons are disenfranchised in some states and not in others. In other words, people in different states who have been convicted of crimes are not equally represented in national elective offices such as the Presidency or Congress if some of the convicted lose political rights (either temporarily or permanently) while others do not. Moreover, citizens who have *not* been convicted of crimes in different states—a population that includes both law-abiding citizens and (non-convicted) criminals—are *also* denied equal protection in terms of their national citizenship because of the vote dilution that results from the range of felon disenfranchisement provisions across the states.

The argument is a simple one: the basis of representation for the national offices of President and Vice-President is not, as was noted in the previous chapter, a national electorate derived from the unitary national citizenship regime described in Section 1 of the Fourteenth Amendment.[96] The populations of each state comprise the composite basis of representation for the national offices (President and Vice-President) filled through this institution. Each state is allocated a certain number of "electors" to represent it in the College, based on its congressional delegation (apportioned by population), plus two electors per state for its U.S. Senators. This distribution of presidential electors was originally thought to favor the small states, which are unequally represented relative to the large states in virtue of the two "extra" Electors each state "gets" for its Senate delegation.

Thus it is hardly news that the votes of (qualified) citizens in the large states are diluted relative to those in the small states in Presidential Elections. They are also diluted in terms of representation in the Senate, for obvious reasons.[97] The apportionment cases on vote dilution all dealt with the states and their political subdivisions, and the Supreme Court enforced the "national political rights" of citizens to equal suffrage within the states. While there have been many (unsuccessful) proposals to reform the Electoral College, there have been no legal arguments that I know of that adduce individual vote dilution within the nation taken as a single political jurisdiction. Perhaps this is because the imbalance between the small and large states has been always been compared and because the other advantages of the Electoral College are still widely believed to outweigh the disadvantages.[98]

Nonetheless, a simple thought experiment that views the nation as a single political jurisdiction shows that the qualified voters in two small states are unequal in their right to be represented as American citizens. In this case, the argument can*not* be made that it is the structure of the Electoral College that creates the vote dilution, since the two states to be compared are allocated equal numbers of electors (on the basis of population plus two for their Senators.) The vote dilution is created by the fact that one state disenfranchises felons while in prison, on parole, and once they have completed their sentence—thus all convicted felons are permanently disenfranchised, while the other does not disenfranchise at all.[99] The two states are Wyoming and Vermont, where even prisoners are allowed to vote. Both states have three votes in the Electoral College, and have roughly equal populations (479,602 and 593,740 respectively, according to Census 2000). The *fact* that crime rates may be very low in both states, and that there may be very few convicted felons relative to the population of both states, resulting in statistically insignificant vote dilution in the non-disenfranchising state, is irrelevant to a theoretical argument based on principles of abstract justice such as those adduced by the Supreme Court in the apportionment cases. The theoretical argument could be made hypothctically, based on any two states with absolutely equal populations, one of which has a population of disenfranchised felons, the other of which does not. As we saw, the problem is created by the clash of theories of representation articulated in the rulings: equal representation of voters (constituents of the nation) versus equal representation of population. Because there is no general national rule concerning electoral qualifications and citizenship rights, citizens of states whose conception of political equality is based on equal representation of voters (non-disenfranchising) are not equal to citizens of states whose conception of political equality is based on equal representation of population (disenfranchising).[100]

This particular thought experiment, which takes the nation as a single political subdivision—in other words takes seriously the claim that the American president represents all the citizens of the nation equally— is unrelated to the claim that felon disenfranchisement causes racial vote dilution.[101] That is an entirely different argument, based on empirical evidence about crime rates and "law-and-order" politics, which will be reviewed in Chapter Four. My claim is that the denial of positive political rights to the new citizens of the nation, following the Union victory in the Civil War and the consolidation of "national sovereignty," axiomatically resulted in a denial of equal political representation to all citizens.[102]

To sum up the relevant jurisprudence on political rights: The Supreme Court has developed a (contested) body of law that limits the freedom of majorities to restrict access to the franchise, but has been loath to interfere directly with registration standards and police powers that appear to operate equally on all citizens within a particular state. Although it has declared "the right to vote a fundamental political right, because preservative of all rights,"[103] it has left the distribution of that right up to the states. Almost a century after its ruling in *Yick Wo,* the Court reiterated that "No right is more precious in a free country than that of having a voice in the election of those who make the laws under which, as good citizens, we must live. Other rights, even the most basic, are illusory if the right to vote is undermined. Our Constitution leaves no room for classification of people in a way that *unnecessarily* abridges this right."[104] (Emphasis added) Relating this right to citizenship, Chief Justice Warren stated explicitly that "To the extent that a citizen's right to vote is debased, he is that much less a citizen"[105] and reiterated that "the right of suffrage is a fundamental matter in a free and democratic society. Especially since the right to exercise the franchise in a free and unimpaired manner is preservative of other basic civil and political rights, any alleged infringement of the right of citizens to vote must be carefully and meticulously scrutinized."

The problem, though, is that the "fundamental right" is actually a political one, in the sense that it is regulated by the political process: Warren admits as much when he says,

> With the birth of our national Government, and the adoption and ratification of the Federal Constitution, state legislatures retained a most important place in our Nation through the medium of elected representatives of the people, and each and

every citizen has an inalienable right to full and effective participation in the political processes of his State's legislative bodies. Most citizens can achieve this participation only as *qualified voters* through the election of legislators to represent them.[106]

We must now relate the line of the early voting rights jurisprudence to the felon disenfranchisement jurisprudence that followed it a decade later in *Richardson v Ramirez*.

Although the Supreme Court in *Richardson* ruled that the state practice of felon disenfranchisement had affirmative sanction in a federal document (Section 2 of the Fourteenth Amendment) Justice Rehnquist entered into no theoretical or jurisprudential discussion of the effect that the state practice has on national citizenship rights.[107] He simply affirmed the constitutionality of the state practice, thereby reiterating in his majority ruling the line of argument in Harlan's and Frankfurter's dissents in the apportionment cases. The plaintiffs in *Richardson* made an equal protection claim under Section 1 of the amendment, claiming that "application to them of the provisions of the California Constitution and implementing statutes which disenfranchised persons convicted of an "infamous crime" denied them the right to equal protection of the laws under the Federal Constitution." In other words, to follow my line of argument, they were asking the Court to protect their rights as American citizens. The California Supreme Court upheld their claim in *Ramirez v Brown*,[108] but an electoral official of the state of California appealed to the U.S. Supreme Court for a reversal.

The Court had no problem discerning the framers' "intent" in Section 2, which is clearly ascertainable from the documents of the 39th Congress. As we have seen, Section 2 expressly left the states with their traditional right to determine the bounds of the franchise. Knowing they could not (either constitutionally or politically) force black suffrage on any of the states, including those in the North, the framers provided a general penalty should the former Confederate states disenfranchise any adult males (including blacks) for anything but "participation in rebellion or any other crime."[109] (In other words, their intent was that states could not disenfranchise their male citizens for being black and then claim the same number of representatives for an exclusive as for an inclusive basis of apportionment.) The penalty for doing so would be reduction of their representation in Congress in proportion to such disenfranchisement.

Read positively, this statement meant that states *could* legally disenfranchise male citizens for being black, *and* could disenfranchise (any male citizen) for crime. For the first exclusion they would be penalized by a reduction of their basis of apportionment, and therefore of their national representation, but for the second there would be no penalty whatsoever. The fact that the penalty defined in Section 2 has never been invoked in a legal or political action against states that historically disenfranchised African-Americans does not mean that African-Americans were never disenfranchised simply for being black. It only meant that states found a way to associate blackness with crime, poverty, and illiteracy[110] in order to disenfranchise minority populations constitutionally.

So for the first time in its two-millennium history, the practice of felon disenfranchisement was textually associated with the institution of political representation, albeit negatively, in Section 2 of the Fourteenth Amendment. Felon disenfranchisement was singled out as the only constitutional exception to an inclusionary (adult male) basis of apportionment that would not subject the states to a political penalty. In my reading, there are two possible interpretations of the framers' insertion of this over-inclusive exception ("or other crime") without further qualification or comment (i.e. for the period of incarceration, for life, for serious crimes only). One is that they simply did not grasp the contradiction they had set up between sections 1 and 2 because it was an entirely new connection. In other words, they did not understand the connection between citizenship, which had historically (until the very enactment of Section 1 been an elite institution based on status honor, and felon disenfranchisement, a practice that represented the negation of that status honor. Before the enactment of the Fourteenth Amendment (as we saw in Chapter One) neither citizenship nor "felony *dis*-enfranchisement," (structurally speaking, a penalty with extremely narrow application) applied to the *un*-enfranchised. I can only speculate, therefore, that the framers of the Amendment could not have realized that disenfranchisement for crime would *not* continue to operate as it had before, as a minimalist practice, in an inclusionary—enfranchised—citizen body.

The other hypothesis is that if the framers never actually expected the states to *en*franchise their newly-minted black citizens, it could not have occurred to them that *dis*enfranchisement for crime would expand exponentially, since citizens cannot be *dis*-enfranchised unless they have first been *en*-franchised. The founders would certainly have expected the states to protect the new citizens' *civil* rights, as per Section 1, but having explicitly severed the civil from the political rights of citizenship by constructing two separate (but equal) sections of the amendment, the prospect that blacks would be widely *dis*-enfranchised for crime was literally incoherent. Moreover, a close textual reading of the phrase, "for participation in rebellion or other crime" conceptually associates the defeated Confederate leadership, a former political elite whose membership the Radical Republicans in the 39th Congress did explicitly expect to disenfranchise, with other criminals eligible for disenfranchisement insofar as they were already qualified to vote. These already qualified voters did not include blacks, and it is unlikely that the framers of the Fourteenth Amendment prospectively conceptualized blacks as qualified voters.

If, on the other hand, the framers expected that the emancipated slaves would be enfranchised (because states would be deterred from non-enfranchising by the representation-reducing penalty) that expectation need not have implied an awareness that disenfranchisement for crime would expand exponentially (homeostatically) with the citizen body. What the framers did with their inadvertent inclusion of the phrase "or other crime" in Section 2 was ensure that a traditionally elite penalty could now potentially include all the new citizens, any one of whom could be convicted of whatever crimes the ostensibly reconstructed demos defined as "infamous." If Rehnquist understood this watershed in the development of American citizenship, he did not acknowledge it, and stuck with a positivist interpretation of the text.

The petitioner in *Richardson,* a county clerk, claimed that the Equal Protection claim brought by the disenfranchised felons could not be sustained, since the framers of the Fourteenth Amendment "could not have intended to prohibit outright in 1 of that Amendment that which was expressly exempted from the lesser sanction of reduced representation imposed by 2 of the amendment." The Court said that it found this argument "persuasive, unless it can be shown that the language of 2 "except for participation in rebellion or other crime" was intended to have a different meaning than would appear from its face." (44) Such an intention could not be found, since felon disenfranchisement was written into the constitutions of most of the states, and appeared in an assortment of Reconstruction era legislation and documents. These included the registration oaths for citizens of the defeated states who wished to participate in elections of delegates for constitutional conventions.[111] However, if my hermaneutic interpretation of the founders' inclusion of the exception "for rebellion or other crime" is correct, no other "intention," just an unstated assumption, based on two millennia of history, about the association between citizenship and felon disenfranchisement, *can* be read into the Section. Never having inhabited a political universe in which the citizen body included former (male) slaves, the framers of Section 2 could not conceive of felon disenfranchisement operating in any way other than the "elitist" one to which they were accustomed. Disenfranchisement for rebellion or crime was a standard exclusion in the elite ante-bellum society, and it was transferred, with little or no critical analysis, into the constitutional provisions that defined the brave new post-bellum world.

The Rehnquist Court, not surprisingly therefore, found "convincing evidence of the historical understanding of the Fourteenth Amendment" and reiterated its previous decisions upholding the constitutionality of the exclusion of felons.[112] The political theory underlying what the Court called "this settled historical and judicial understanding of the Fourteenth Amendment's effect on state laws disenfranchising felons" is, as we saw in Chapter Two, the right of the states to a "republican form of government," which leaves to locally elected majorities the right to decide social policy for the community of state citizens. The felon disenfranchisement exception in Section 2, as the Chief Justice pointed out in his opinion, "was expressly exempted from the less drastic sanction of reduced representation which 2 imposed for other forms of disenfranchisement." As such, it represents the remnant of the "old regime" in the text of the Fourteenth Amendment, which created a national citizenship regime to accommodate the heretofore unprecedented status of the recently emancipated slaves.

Indeed, in his dissent Justice Marshall quoted parts of Warren's ruling in *Reynolds* and argued that "there is no basis for concluding that Congress intended by 2 to freeze the meaning of other clauses of the Fourteenth Amendment to the conception of voting rights prevalent at the time of the adoption of the Amendment." Citing the Court's evolving standards of "strict scrutiny" of state restrictions on the franchise, he argued that "constitutional concepts of equal protection are not immutably frozen like insects trapped in Devonian amber."[113] He took Warren's position that "the right to vote is of the essence of a democratic society, and any restrictions on that right strike at the heart of representative government."[114] Critics of felon disenfranchisement adopt Marshall's arguments for strict scrutiny, which would annul the practice based on the fact that states cannot demonstrate either a compelling or rational policy interest in denying former felons the right to vote. Citing the Secretary of State of California's memorandum to the Court in support of the respondents, Marshall concurred that

> The individuals involved in the present case are persons who have fully paid their debt to society. They are as much affected by the actions of government as any other citizens, and have as much of a right to participate in governmental decision-making. Furthermore, the denial of the right to vote to such persons is a hindrance to the efforts of society to rehabilitate former felons and convert them into law-abiding citizens.

Another argument Marshall adduced, following a line of 1970s Supreme Court jurisprudence, challenged the asserted purpose of disenfranchisement of "keeping former felons from voting because their likely voting pattern might be subversive of the interests of an orderly society."[115] Marshall said, "We have...explicitly held that differences of opinion cannot justify excluding [any] group from ...the franchise."[116] He also cited *Carrington v Rash*, a Texas case involving the rights of military personnel to register in the state, where the Court ruled, "[I]f they are ... residents, ... they as all other qualified residents, have a right to an equal opportunity for political representation. (...) 'Fencing out' from the franchise a sector of the population because of the way they may vote is constitutionally impermissible."[117]

Thus Marshall was reclaiming the Radical Republicans' legacy from the first Reconstruction, which attempted to impose nationwide, federally enforced electoral laws rather than the regional or local rules proposed by the Democrats.[118] His impassioned dissent, which advances a democratic conception of citizenship and political rights diametrically opposed to that of Rehnquist, is worth quoting at length:

> Although in the last century, this Court may have justified the exclusion of voters from the electoral process for fear that they would vote to change laws considered important by a temporal majority, I have little doubt that we would not countenance such a purpose today. The process of democracy is one of change. Our laws are not frozen into immutable form, they are constantly in the process of revision in response to the needs of a changing society. The public interest, as conceived by a majority of the voting public, is constantly undergoing reexamination. This Court's holding in *Davis*, supra, and Murphy, supra, that a State may disenfranchise a class of voters to "withdraw all political influence from those who are practically hostile" to the existing order, strikes at the very heart of the democratic process. A temporal majority could use such a power to preserve inviolate its view of the social order simply by disenfranchising those with different views. (...) The ballot box is the democratic system's coin of the realm. To condition its exercise on support of the established order is to debase that currency beyond recognition.

Marshall and Brennan were in the minority, though, and since *Richardson* is widely seen by legal commentators as having "closed the door" on future litigation of ex-felon voting rights, new strategies to challenge the practice under the Voting Rights Act have been formulated

(Shapiro 1993; and a law review literature that has expanded dramatically since the 2000 election). A more promising approach to the present Supreme Court bench is to demonstrate that the political rights of all Americans are compromised by the variety of state laws that deny votes to some and therefore dilute the votes of others. These political rights were affirmed by the Warren Court, albeit in the context of state political contests. Although in *Richardson* (then) Justice Rehnquist relied on the text of Section 2 of the Fourteenth Amendment to affirm states' rights to disenfranchise felons, he failed to acknowledge what has changed since that text was so cautiously yet pragmatically enacted: the fact a national consensus about African-American suffrage that did not exist at the time of Reconstruction, exists today. Although strict constructionists could interpret a Court order directing states that disenfranchise ex-felons to restore their political rights as an unconstitutional abrogation of the "Guarantee Clause," a plausible constitutional argument can be made that a democratic national polity demands uniform federal electoral rules across all the "republican" states.[119]

The following chapter considers the judicial and political justifications for American *atimia,* and the extent to which actual practices of felonization and punishment in the American criminal justice system are inconsonant with the tenets of a modern liberal-democratic citizenship regime.

Judicial Justifications of Felon Disenfranchisement and the Politics of Crime and Punishment

> *In every case the laws are made by the ruling party in its own interest; A democracy makes democratic laws, a despot autocratic ones, and so on. By making these laws they define as "just" for their subjects whatever is for their own interest, and they call anyone who breaks them a "wrongdoer" and punish him accordingly.*
>
> Thrasymachus, in Plato's *Republic*

INTRODUCTION

The very concept of felon disenfranchisement, the combination of the two words into a single phrase that denotes an institutional practice, reveals the existence of a formal link between the apparently dissimilar legal concepts of "crime" and citizenship, or a negation of citizenship, to be more precise. This chapter will explore the nature of that link by reviewing the judicial and political discourse that supports political exclusion as a result of conviction for crime. Framed in quasi-theoretical and moralistic terms, the legal and political justifications of the contemporary practice are singularly thin on the ground and unconvincing to the modern liberal democrat. Yet this practice that currently affects the lives of some four million American citizens who are permanently disenfranchised, as well to a limited extent, as the fortunes of a major political party,[1] persists, propped up only by flimsy judicial rulings that have been roundly attacked in the law review literature. There is no scholarly literature that I am aware of that argues in favor of the practice of ex-offender disenfranchisement, or responds to the growing literature that challenges the practice. This generally takes an "equal protection" tack, citing the racial disparities that characterize the American criminal justice system and result in disproportionate disenfranchisement of minorities as violations of the "results test" of the amended Voting Rights Act. Briefly, felon disenfranchisement practices unfairly dilute minority voting strength.

Why there should be no vigorous scholarly defense of the practice in response to the unanimous condemnation in the secondary literature is not particularly puzzling. First of all, I don't believe there are any compelling normative arguments available to justify ex-felon disenfranchisement in a modern democracy. Although the case can, and has been made (Hampton 1998) that prisoners who have committed violent crimes should be disenfranchised for the term of their incarceration, and possibly even for the term of their probation, ex-offender disenfranchisement is not defensible. This assumption notwithstanding, no normative arguments need to be made since, as we saw in the previous chapter, state laws that disenfranchise ex-offenders have been ruled constitutional by the presiding Chief Justice and allowed to stand. Moreover, as the official judicial justifications of felon disenfranchisement and the political rhetoric of law and order make clear, convicted felons are not entitled to collective political regard, so no rational politician (or judicial "representative") need champion their cause. Until the few scholars and political organizers who do criticize the practice make arguments that are politically, rather than only normatively and jurisprudentially compelling, those scholars who support ex-offender disenfranchisement can sit out the debate, since their position has been definitively affirmed by the Supreme Court.

The affirmative constitutional sanction, as we saw in Chapter Two, derives from the institutional framework of federalism and the guarantee of a "republican form of government." As Justice Rehnquist ruled in *Richardson*, unless popular majorities or elected representatives in the states overturn their constitutional or legislative provisions for disenfranchising ex-felons, those (often century-old) provisions will remain on the books and be enforced by the local electoral bureaucracy. Alternatively, a state or federal judge, responding to a challenge by disenfranchised felons, could rule that the practice is unconstitutional, but that ruling would then have to withstand a potential Supreme Court challenge by the Attorney General or election officials of the state.[2] Thus, in the absence of a persuasive social and political movement demanding that felons *not* be disenfranchised, the practice continues, and has a serious cumulative impact in (the relatively few) electoral districts where disproportionate numbers of minority citizens are charged with, and ultimately convicted of crimes. The "disproportionateness" of those numbers does not, however, translate into what a sufficient number of politicians would deem as decisiveness in close electoral competitions where the disenfranchised, if hypothetically enfranchised, would hold the balance of power. Rational politicians supporting ex-felon *re*-enfranchisement would have to calculate that their crusading, civil rights platform on behalf of what are considered by many citizens the dregs of society would garner them more votes from the enfranchised—the non-convicted—than their opponents campaigning on politically entrenched law-and-order platforms.

Framing this proposition negatively, it is not as though, did the practice of permanent felon disenfranchisement *not* exist in certain states as it does today, a serious political movement could successfully demand that legislatures enact the practice.[3] I doubt that it could, but given that the practice is and has been legally institutionalized (for centuries in most states), a serious political movement demanding its abolition would have to mount a convincing attack on the moralistic discourse associated with the American politics of "crime" and punishment. It is because convicted felons are, and historically have been considered morally unworthy of the political rights of citizenship that judges and politicians who support felon disenfranchisement can use a flimsy moralistic discourse to fend off challenges by ex-offenders who want their rights restored. No serious defense of the practice has to be mounted because serious attacks on the practice represent only a despised and disenfranchised minority who only, very counterfactually speaking hold a very tenuous balance of power.

This chapter focuses on the discursive justifications of felon disenfranchisement by state court judges and politicians and criticizes these justifications from the perspectives of liberal, republican, and democratic citizenship theory. My basic claim is that to the extent that concepts of "crime" and "punishment" are politicized, and conviction rates are skewed by class, race, and class-race-and-gender status,[4] moralistic claims from the bench that individual felons are "unworthy" of political rights are undermined. Yet both judicial and political justifications of felon disenfranchisement hinge on that presumption of unworthiness, conferring brands of status that constitute a caste distance, a space between felons and voters that only deepens to the extent that law-and-order policies retain political support.[5] The unstated and uninterrogated foundation of that presumption of moral and political unworthiness, moreover, is a positive presumption of worthiness whose ontological genesis is an institutional relationship (citizenship regime) of domination rather than political equality. This ontological genesis will be analyzed in Chapter Five.

By examining the substantive (as opposed to constitutional) judicial and political defenses of felon disenfranchisement, and scanning the empirical landscape of the double polity, we will see how law-and-order politics actually configure it. This does not amount to a claim that the practice of felon disenfranchisement in itself creates the landscape to be described, only that it represents the negative dimension of the political continuum of democratic citizenship within the polity. As such, it discloses aspects of the positive dimension of citizenship that might otherwise be invisible to its beneficiaries. As Jeffrey Reiman (1995) says

> A criminal justice system is a mirror in which a whole society can see the darker outlines of its face. Our ideas of justice and evil take on visible form in it, and thus see ourselves in deep relief. Step through this looking glass to view the American criminal justice system—and ultimately the whole society it reflects—from a radically different angle of vision.

The positive dimension of the continuum of democratic citizenship, which is the realm of universal political equality, reflects a commitment to a particular moral ideal, as we saw in the final sections of Chapter Two, which discussed the theory of democratic individuality. Insofar as the commitment is ideal, it is to mutual and universal, rather than partial security and protection. That protection cannot be forfeited as it was in the classical regimes when a citizen transgressed the laws of the polity, and was cast into a realm of legal and political vulnerability. Logically, it would appear that a legally institutionalized deficit of political equality such as felon disenfranchisement, the endgame of the continuum of the criminal justice system, institutionally designed to confer *in*security on offenders, and "security" on law-abiding citizens, reflects a compromise of that commitment to equality. The institutional and normative consequences of that deficit must be interrogated if citizens are to chart the course of the commitment, which is an aspect of their citizenship identity. According to Robert Dahl (1998: 64-65),

> To understand why it is reasonable to commit ourselves to political equality among citizens of a democratic state, we need to recognize that sometimes when we talk about equality we do not mean to express a factual judgment. We do not intend to describe what we believe is or will be true, as we do when we make statements about winners of marathon races or spelling bees. Instead we mean to express a moral judgment about human beings; we intend to say something about what we believe ought to be.

The practice of permanent felon disenfranchisement derives from a collective moral judgment on the part of the demos that the convicted felon, even one who has "served his time" is not, and never can be, a political equal of the non-convicted citizen.[6] Yet what this moral judgment misses is the fact that there is no legal, or even logical connection between what can be (legally or morally) named as the commission of a "criminal act," and the pronouncement of guilt following a legal process that results in conviction for the crime. By this I mean the following: if the criminal justice system is conceived of as a continuum of moments that is politically, rather than morally constituted, a cumulative process that begins with identification of a "suspect," arrest, processing, conviction and disenfranchisement, can be posited.[7] The demographics of American "punishment" and disenfranchisement indicate that African-Americans and other minorities are more likely to be subject to this continuum than members of the dominant majority, even though they have committed the same crimes.[8] In that this continuum does not necessarily exist for other persons who may have committed crimes, it cannot be said to be a morally constituted continuum. In other words, even though individual citizens may have committed the same crimes, the fact that they are less likely to be arrested, charged or convicted, means they are less likely to be involved in the continuum.[9] As such, what is presented as a moral justification for felon disenfranchisement between those "worthy" and "unworthy" of political rights as a result of crime is in fact a political justification, and has no place in a society morally committed to political equality. Disenfranchisement is a direct result of conviction for crime, not of the criminal act itself.

The fact that the socio-economic and racial biases in the criminal justice system lead to disproportionate disenfranchisement of poor and minority populations does not amount to a claim that no felons, particularly those convicted of serious crimes such as murder and rape should ever be deprived of political rights for specific periods of time such as their incarceration, which may be lifelong.[10] The most troubling exclusion is that of ex-felons, who have "paid their debt to society" and returned to the polity to live alongside their fellow (enfranchised) citizens. Moreover, the racial profiling that results in the disparate charging, conviction, incarceration, and disenfranchisement rates, particularly for drug crimes, means that since minorities are disproportionately represented in the population of ex-felons, the contemporary practice cannot be justified on normative grounds. The practice is justified, though, by state and federal judges who reject challenges on the part of ex-felons to have their rights restored. As this book goes to press, the Ninth and Eleventh Circuits have reversed lower court decisions upholding felon disenfranchisement, and have seen "the criminal justice system as a key component of the social and historical situation confronted by the minority community as it engaged in the political process. They recognized that the plaintiffs had produced significant evidence of racial discrimination within the criminal justice system."[11]

Section 1 below examines the neo-Lockean or contractarian justification of felon disenfranchisement, which deems citizens who have broken "the compact" unworthy of further membership. Section 2 looks at how judges have used the "communitarian" or "republican" discourse to justify felon disenfranchisement, positing a certain prerequisite of "moral competence" for full citizenship. Section 3 shows how contemporary political justifications of the practice mirror the contractarian and communitarian defenses. This section also evaluates how the politics of law and order constitute the continuum of the criminal justice system in order to benefit individual candidates, politicians, and political parties, thereby obviating any moral claims about the worthiness of citizens vis-à-vis felons. In order to see how the political continuum of "criminal justice" operates in the United States, Section 4 disaggregates it into the series of moments that terminate in conviction and disenfranchisement. Many of these moments are initiated by the discretionary decisions of elected or appointed officials of the criminal justice system, as we saw in Chapter Three in the discussion of the office of the prosecutor.

1. THE NEO-CONTRACTARIAN JUSTIFICATION OF FELON DISENFRANCHISEMENT

Judge Henry J. Friendly articulated a moral judgment of ex-offenders in his ruling in a New York Circuit case brought by convicted felons who challenged their disenfranchisement under the Equal Protection Clause.[12]

> A man who breaks the laws he has authorized his agent to make for his own governance could fairly have been thought to have abandoned the right to participate in further administering the compact. (…) It can scarcely be deemed unreasonable for a state to decide that perpetrators of serious crimes shall not take part in electing the legislators who make laws, the executives who enforce these, the prosecutors who must try them for further violations, or the judges who are to consider the cases.[13]

Judge Friendly's explicitly Lockean defense of felon disenfranchisement[14] has been cited approvingly by other federal judges to justify their rulings,[15] and has been upheld (by default) in the Supreme

Court of the United States, which denied *certiorari* on appeal. Friendly was using Locke ideologically, though, since Locke addressed the issue of punishment directly, from a perspective of deterrence, recommending that,

> Each Transgression may be *punished* to that *degree,* and with so much *Severity* as will suffice to make it an ill bargain to the Offender, give him cause to repent, and terrifie others from doing the like. (*ST,* §12)

Depriving ex-offenders of the vote cannot be justified from a Lockean perspective if the punishment serves no verifiable deterrent function, and if *all* felonies from the most trivial to the most serious are punished by disenfranchisement, obviating Locke's requirement that the "degree" and "severity" be matched by the punishment.

Friendly's ruling echoes and distorts Dahl's words about political equality: political equality is only for the deserving, not for those who have abandoned their right to political participation by committing "serious crimes."[16] His argument implies that those who are unworthy are cast out of political society into some unspecified non-political realm, where their status as citizens is importantly different from that of the enfranchised, and where they are forever prohibited from voting retributively against their prosecutors.[17] However, the Supreme Court had already ruled that it was unconstitutional for states to "fence out" voters from the electorate because of the way they might vote.[18] This jurisprudence affirmed a basic principle of representative democracy that voters are free to make up—or change—their minds at any time before the election: such is the purpose of debate and discussion between elections.[19]

The tension between Friendly's ruling and modern democratic theory is self-evident: if democracy means that all citizens who are subject to the laws have the right to participate in rule, it means that no citizens can be permanently ruled. Yet in Friendly's version of contract theory, as it is applied in a democracy, convicted felons are a status group that has forever lost the right to rule, and therefore may be ruled for life by the enfranchised. Consider the following hypothetical situation: a new generation of young, upper-class voters (recreational drug users who have never been charged with, or convicted of the crime) *de facto* "rules" over an older generation of ex-convicts who have lived exemplary civic lives since their release from prison.[20] In the neo-contractarian analysis, the young people are fully members of the compact, morally worthy of their status, but the ex-felons are not. This asymmetrical power relation between status groups of constitutionally equal citizens is *prima facie* incoherent in a modern constitutional democracy, and reflects the configuration of a citizenship regime based on status honor, such as those of the classical republics described in Chapter One.

This state of affairs raises a couple of epistemological issues that highlight the tension between democratic theory and ex-offender disenfranchisement. The first concern is whether or not enfranchised citizens who rule over the disenfranchised *know* that they participate in a regime that puts them in a position of rule over others, classically considered a "despotic" regime, rather a form of co-rule, traditionally defined as democratic or republican.[21] This issue goes to the heart of their identity as democratic citizens, and the description of permanent felon disenfranchisement as a betrayal of the democratic ethics that constitutes the majoritarian version of the national cultural tradition of progressive political inclusion. My analysis of the theory of democratic individuality in Chapter Two suggests that it *should* matter whether citizens with full rights know whether or not their fellow (free) citizens, anonymous or not, are political equals or not. The paradox of the interchangeability of democratic individuality rules out the possibility that one citizen should have political rights when another (free citizen) does not. The implicit notion of the shared fate of their humanness means that for democratic individuals.

> …what I assume you shall assume,
> For every atom belonging to me as good belongs to you (1)
> (…)
> I embody all presences outlawed or suffering
> And see myself in prison shaped like another man,
> And feel the dull unintermitted [*sic*] pain (74)
> (…)
> If you bestow gifts on your brother or dearest friend I demand as good
> As your brother or dearest friend,
> If your lover, husband, wife is welcome by day or night,
> I must be personally as welcome,
> If you become degraded, criminal, ill, then I become so for your sake.[22]

Kateb's (1992) interpretation of Whitman's idea of democratic individuality is that citizenship in a democracy entails both political equality *and* the knowledge of it.

> The status of equal citizenship, in which one counts equally with the rest, in which one knows that one is accepted by the rest *on the sole condition that one also accepts the rest, each*

one of them, equally—this is a status that in itself can transform the person. (160, my italics.)

Likewise, Philip Pettit suggests that

Citizenship, like any social status, naturally involves awareness: it means that the citizen, and those with whom she deals, are aware of her standing, and it means that this awareness is itself a matter of common recognition. But if citizenship or freedom involves this sort of awareness, then it also means being able to live without fear or deference; freedom connotes frankness, where 'frankness' is etymologically related to 'franchise.' (1993, 312)

Jurgen Habermas (1994) also insists on the fact that modern democratic citizenship contains this element of *mutual* recognition, that is the foundation of "self-legislating" power:

[The national] association [of the democratic state] is structured by relations of mutual recognition and, given these relations, everyone can be expected to be respected by everybody else as free and equal. Everyone should be in a position to expect that all will receive equal protection and respect in his or her violable integrity as a unique individual, as a member of an ethnic or cultural group and as a citizen, that is as a member of a polity. (24)

He goes on to claim that "The nation of citizens does not derive its identity from common ethnic and cultural properties but rather from the praxis of citizens who actively exercise their civil rights." If this is the case, then the identity of a nation where a distinctive negative status group of citizens is prohibited from actively exercising civil and political rights is more difficult to ascertain. If fully enfranchised members of the state do not *know* that they are members of a citizenship regime that constitutionally legitimizes political inequality, then their identity as democratic citizens, as effective political agents, is compromised by their ignorance. If they do know, and accept the fact that their political agency is co-extensive with the disenfranchisement of some of their fellow citizens, then they are acquiescing in, consenting to, an identity that, insofar as it implies privilege, is not a democratic identity in the ideal sense of the term. It is a democratic identity, as we will see in the following chapter, whose despotic (Aristotle) character implies a distorted form of moral knowledge (Mills 1997) that inhibits the development of progressive inclusionary social policies. (Dewey 1988)

A second agency question raised by the use of contract theory to justify disenfranchisement is whether or not the citizens who enjoyed political rights before they committed the crime that resulted in their disenfranchisement either actually or hypothetically consented to the loss of rights that accompanied their conviction. They are now part of the ongoing compact that constructs the exclusion in the sense, as Foucault (1977, 303) says that "the fiction of a juridical subject give[s] to others the power to exercise over him the right that he himself possesses over them." If the post-civil rights era formal political inclusion of African-Americans can be taken to imply their consent to abide by all the laws of the polity, including the criminal laws and disenfranchisement laws, then their hypothetical consent must have been to fair and impartial application of the laws.[23] Consent to criminal justice policies, and even to disenfranchisement policies behind any "veil of ignorance" is only rational if those policies do not profile or target the particular ascriptive group to which one happens to belong. To justify disenfranchisement, as the Friendly line of rulings does, in terms of a hypothetical contract the offender can no longer share in administering because his criminality infers anti-consent,[24] assumes that the contract itself is administered justly and according to law, rather than "popular sovereignty."

Narrowly construed, the question of consent asks whether criminals are even *aware* that conviction will result in disenfranchisement, since consent by definition entails some sort of awareness of law and the consequences of breaking it. If criminals did not know in advance that conviction would result in disenfranchisement, depriving them of political rights has no deterrent value, thereby eliminating one of the important justifications of punishment.[25] Likewise, if they did know, and were not deterred, felon disenfranchisement has no rational basis as a punishment, and must be justified on other grounds, such as retribution or rehabilitation. Since rehabilitation and permanent felon disenfranchisement are clearly contradictions in terms, the only remaining rationale is retributive (and moral). The criminal who is receiving his "just deserts" by his act of abandoning the contract, forfeits his political rights, if not temporarily, then forever, depending on the law of the state of which he is a citizen.

In that Judge Friendly's neo-contractarian analysis implies that consent can be inferred from a citizen's apparent willingness to abide by the law, [26] criminal activity that results in conviction is read as a statement of non- or anti-consent that justifies ex post facto exclusion from the compact. I am trying to distinguish the anti-consent of "crime" from the non-consent of civil disobedience, which implies prior consent and acceptance of the framework of law and the punishment that attaches to conviction when unjust laws are openly broken (Walzer 1970). In terms of the historical record, though, as Beckett (1997) and others have pointed out, dominant political elites interpreted the civil rights movement that culminated in the "Second Reconstruction," as a law-and-order issue, and civil disobedience as black criminality justifying a tough official criminal justice response. Since the discourse of compact is being promulgated in a democratic context to justify felon disenfranchisement, and one of the purposes of democratic government is to secure consent through broad distribution of the franchise to citizens, the democracy that construes civil disobedience on the part of blacks as a "crime" faces a problem of legitimacy. It must account for the presence of a significant (in some states) group of "non-consenting" individuals, and unable to distinguish between dissent and crime, fails both the political and pedagogical challenges posed by civil disobedience.[27] Worse still, since disenfranchisement removes the possibility of explicit consent (through voting) to any legislation enacted after conviction, it implies the (ongoing, indefinite) presence of a "non-consenting," multi-generational (negative) status group of (convicted) citizens within the polity.[28]

As (immanent) critics of the (neo-) Lockean justification for felon disenfranchisement have noted, it "fails to take seriously important liberal values," specifically modern liberals' belief that "prior to the social contract, individuals have fundamental rights and liberties that allow them to bargain freely but that cannot be freely bargained away."[29] According to liberal theorist John Rawls, for example, the first principle of justice is that "all citizens are to have an equal right to take part in, and to determine the outcome of, the constitutional process that establishes the laws with which they are to comply." (1971, 221)[30] Such a principle implies that "the [d]isenfranchisement of ex-offenders violates this basic tenet of modern liberalism."[31] The reason for the priority of the political liberties in Rawls' scheme is because they are "essential... to make sure that the fair political process specified by the constitution is open to everyone on a basis of rough equality" (1996, 330). Second, they are crucial "in order to establish just legislation" (*id.* at 329). As Furman (1997, 1216) observes, "this argument is based principally on pragmatic concerns: Political liberties are crucial because they provide access to the process that determines the value of all the basic liberties."[32]

Another immanent critique of the courts' use of compact to justify felon disenfranchisement claims that courts fail to take the theory to its logical extreme, selecting only the parts that are compatible with constitutional jurisprudence, a strategy that reveals the political, rather than the moral underpinnings of their position. A theoretically consistent justification of ex-offender disenfranchisement in terms of compact would render the lower courts' jurisprudence inconsistent with the Supreme Court's refusal to deprive a national of citizenship status for breaking the law. Taken to its logical conclusion, contract theory implies that if a criminal by his or her action is no longer considered a member of the state, he or she should lose all rights, not a select few.[33] The Supreme Court has refused to take this position, though, asserting that

> Citizenship is not a license that expires upon misbehavior...[C]itizenship is not lost every time a duty of citizenship is shirked. And the deprivation of citizenship is not a weapon that the Government may use to express its displeasure at a citizen's conduct, however reprehensible that conduct may be. As long as a person does not voluntarily renounce or abandon his citizenship...his fundamental right of citizenship is secure...

And

> [Denationalization constitutes a] total destruction of the individual's status in organized society. It is a form of punishment more primitive than torture, for it destroys for the individual the political existence that was centuries in the development.[34]

Thus taken together, the jurisprudence on disenfranchisement and denationalization implies that since a convicted felon retains his citizenship right and his civil rights, but not his political right, the rights of citizenship are severable, which was the explicit intent of the Reconstruction Congresses when they drafted Amendments Thirteen through Fifteen. As we saw in Chapter Three, Congress did not federalize political rights as it did civil rights because there was no national consensus about the (emancipated) African-American vote. Since the states were not ready to include free blacks in the demos, they had to retain the right to control them politically by retaining control over the franchise. They retain this control in the twenty-first century.

Severing political from civil rights is a strategy of power, or in more antiquated language, of rule. Those who do not have political rights are ruled by those who do. Those who do not have political rights cannot raise issues of justice or right, as political equals in the assembly or from the electorate, because they are labeled morally unworthy of the franchise. But political expediency—the need for social peace—has dictated in the American context that the "ruled" citizens at least have the civil rights that accrue from their nationality. It is from this constitutionally sanctioned severability of political and civil rights that the power to punish and exclude gains its cumulative strength in the

American polity. In Foucault's (1979) words, the new strategy of punishing that accompanied the consolidation of the modern state

> falls easily into the general theory of the contract. The citizen is presumed to have accepted once and for all, with the laws of society, the very law by which he may be punished. Thus the criminal appears as a juridically paradoxical being. He has broken the pact, he is therefore the enemy of society as a whole, but he participates in the punishment that is practiced upon him. The least crime attacks the whole of society; and the whole of society—including the criminal—is present in the least punishment. Penal punishment is therefore a generalized function, coextensive with the function of the social body and with each of its elements. This gives rise to the problem of the degree of punishment, the economy of the power to punish. (90)

Critics of felon disenfranchisement often cite this problem of "the degree" of punishment, and the lack of "economy" disenfranchisement represents, particularly with regard to the African-Americans and Hispanics who are convicted for non-violent, often trivial offenses, and then disenfranchised for life.[35] Nonetheless, if we take contract theory, and Foucault's commentary on it seriously, "the least offense" denotes non-consent, and therefore must be opposed by the consenting citizen body "in its entirety." If the logic and strategy of the punishment is not one of democratic justice, but a strategy of control, then it is not "uneconomical" to punish even the most trivial of crimes with disenfranchisement.[36]

Critics of the contemporary "incarceration polity" who make consequentialist, rather than deontological arguments, claim that the financial costs of incarcerating non-violent criminals, which burden federal, state and local taxpayers,[37] and cause "collateral social damage" to families and inner-city neighborhoods, miss the mark. Perhaps the incarceration polity is uneconomical from the perspective of minority interests, but in terms of an overall strategy of power and control, from the smallest unit of local government to the federal system, it is entirely economical. It brings a host of quantifiable benefits to individual politicians and their political parties, to private corporations,[38] and to the rural areas that host new prisons in the post-industrial economy.[39] Casting criminals as "outsiders" who are responsible for their situation legitimates not only the ideology of the democratic regime that incarcerates them, but the representatives of the local, state, and national polities who derive both material benefit and status from their incarceration. The policies also bring material benefits and status to the constituencies that host prisons, which reinforces their support for law-and-order policies and ultimately for the continuum that results in disenfranchisement.

Counterfactually speaking, it would be much more expensive for the state, the demos, to make itself, rather than individuals, collectively responsible for crime—to take the moral responsibility of informing itself through public debate and reputable research about the causes and effects of what is politically designated as crime. Were it to undertake such a responsibility, the nominally democratic citizenship regime would have to expend not only the symbolic resources to investigate the crime problem, but the material resources to correct the systemic problems and conditions associated with high crime areas. This would shift the focus from the individuals who commit and are convicted of crimes, to the political and historical context of criminality and impunity.[40] It would entail constructing an entirely different political discourse in election campaigns whose success would depend on building a more diverse, informed, and culturally empathetic constituency than the one motivated by (aggregated individual) fear and politicians' simplistic, "get tough" promises. Briefly, the costs of constructing such a discourse and such constituencies are far higher to politicians whose primary concern is to get elected, than are the costs of law-and-order politics.

As Beckett (1997) convincingly demonstrates, the discourse of law and order and control initiated by conservative politicians and think tanks in the latter half of the twentieth century shifted the blame for crime from social and institutional causes (institutionalized racism) to individuals.[41]

> Like conservatives before them, the Reagan and Bush administrations went to great lengths to reject the notion that street crime and other social problems have socio-economic causes. Reagan's first major address on crime, for example, consisted of a sweeping philosophical attack on "the social thinkers of the fifties and sixties who discussed crime only in the context of disadvantaged childhoods and poverty-stricken neighborhoods." This theme appeared again and again in Reagan's speeches on crime.[42] (48-49)

As the empirical data regarding the felonization rates of citizens subject to the American politics of law and order show, contemporary punishment policies appear gratuitous and demographically skewed, particularly from the perspective of minority populations. The fact that representatives of minority populations (the Black Caucus in Congress, for instance) initially supported the Presidential war on drugs, in response to their constituents' demands for tough law-and-order policies,[43] does not undercut the critique of its negative social and political consequences for those communities.[44] This critique undermines moral claims made by the demos in the person of its representatives that a (pre-offense) condition of substantial political equality obtains between all citizens, and therefore that those members who have been convicted of crimes are subsequently unworthy of political rights. The empirical analysis can be usefully linked to the concepts of compact or contract based on consent, which have different meanings for historically oppressed groups than for the founders of political society and their descendants. In Chapter Two, I described the latter's cumulative political privilege in states that enjoy a republican form of government in terms of the concepts of path dependence and increasing returns. In this section, these increasing returns can be described as "the wages of whiteness," W.E.B. DuBois' (1939) term that captures "the bottom line, the ultimate payoff for structuring the polity around a racial axis." (Mills 1998, 135)

Framing the argument in support of disenfranchisement in terms of the compact, therefore, invites critical analysis of this theoretical construct from a historical perspective informed by feminism, critical race theory and post-colonial theory.[45] This is particularly the case since, demographically speaking, disenfranchised felons in the U.S. are disproportionately drawn from groups that were explicitly excluded from the original American constitutional compact. We can see this by pairing their present status, with their pre-inclusion status. The poor (propertyless), African-Americans (slaves), Hispanics (formerly Mexican nationals), and women (largely poor and minority) fill the ranks of citizens currently disenfranchised for crime.[46] Despite the fact that, over time, these groups have won the constitutional right to vote on equal terms with the founding demos, significant numbers of their members find themselves excluded once again from the contemporary demos.

This fact lends itself to one of two (or more) possible interpretations: one is that the incarceration and disenfranchisement of minorities is profoundly bad "moral luck" distributed randomly among American citizens. The other is that there is an elective affinity between the contemporary American criminal justice system and interpretations of contract theory that grant the status honor of full citizenship only to the elect, those who have not been convicted of crimes. The fact that the power to define the criminal code as well as the electorate belongs to the states, means that political majorities in each state are responsible for determining the characteristics of the elect. The federal structure of the polity, in turn, means that the characteristics of the elect are reproduced at the national level. Rather than strengthening the inclusionary tendencies of the "democratic contract" patched together by centuries of struggle for political rights, the American criminal justice system (as a whole) reproduces the exclusionary tendencies of the original (hypothetical and actual) contract. Felon disenfranchisement is a key element in that process, since it institutionalizes the political exclusion of citizens who are convicted of, not necessarily those who have committed, crimes.

In order for the neo-Lockean justification to work, to stand as precedent in the modern socio-political context of the U.S. criminal justice system, it must smuggle in substantive elements from the republican tradition of citizenship, which emphasizes "properties" of individuals, such as virtue and love of the laws. (Viroli 1995, ch.1) These traditional elements of citizenship are explicitly articulated in the alternative, so-called communitarian defense of felon disenfranchisement.

2. THE COMMUNITARIAN OR "REPUBLICAN" JUSTIFICATION OF FELON DISENFRANCHISEMENT

The communitarian justification of felon disenfranchisement is based on the idea that the ex-convict will have a polluting effect on the purity of the electoral process. In its narrowest version, public officials worry that people with proven criminal tendencies will commit electoral fraud, or interfere in some unspecified illegal way with law-abiding citizens casting their votes. As Thurgood Marshall pointed out in his dissent in *Richardson v Ramirez,* and as various state justices who have criticized this justification have argued, this claim is redundant, so cannot serve a "compelling state interest." States have criminalized voting fraud and have systems in place to prosecute it, thereby obviating the rationale for measures (like disenfranchisement) that treat ex-offenders differently from other voters.[47] Nora Demleitner (2000) and other scholars who have analyzed felon disenfranchisement argue that

> Only a small number of all offenders are convicted of offenses connected to election fraud. While even that group is unlikely to constitute an ongoing threat to the integrity of elections, there is no empirical basis for assuming that all offenders are more likely to engage in election fraud than the rest of the population. The fear-of-election-fraud justification is also underinclusive because in some states that permanently exclude offenders from the ballot, a number of election offenses are grouped as misdemeanors and therefore do not lead to disenfranchisement. (773)

These are valid empirical and legal reasons for dismissing this legalistic communitarian justification for disenfranchisement. The broader, more normative communitarian justifications adduce the potential for social and political contamination that could follow from allowing convicted felons to vote.

The manifest purpose [of denying suffrage to ex-convicts] is to preserve the purity of the ballot box, which is the only sure foundation of republican liberty, and which needs protection against the invasion of corruption, just as much as that of ignorance, incapacity, or tyranny. The evil infection of the one is not more fatal than that of the other. The presumption is, that one rendered infamous by conviction of felony, or other base offense indicative of great moral turpitude, is unfit to exercise the privilege of suffrage, or to hold office, upon terms of equality with freemen who are clothed by the State with the toga of political citizenship. *Washington v State*, 75 Ala. 582 (1884)

In more modern language, judges have upheld the constitutional standard of a "compelling state interest" to deny equal protection claims challenging felon disenfranchisement. These claims are usually based on the argument that a state has an interest in "preserving the integrity of [its] electoral process by removing from the process those persons with proven anti-social behavior whose behavior can be said to be destructive of society's aims."[48] What is most striking about this latter justification of felon disenfranchisement is not so much its arguable assumption of an ascertainable set of "society's aims," but its implicit claim about the weakness of the democratic process. "Criminality, like disease, the court seems to say, must be contained so as to prevent contagion." (Furman 1997) The alternative perspective, which conceives of the democratic process as robust and fundamentally healthy, would obviate worries about the political participation of those "with proven anti-social behavior."

The author of a 1989 Harvard Law Review "Note" on felon disenfranchisement calls the moral competence argument "a prop in [the] act of communal self-delusion." The self-delusion involved lies in the casting, by the enfranchised, of criminals as "hopelessly different moral defectives," a perspective that "blinds us to the social and political components of crime." (1316)

As George Herbert Mead pointed out, crusades against despised outsiders can generate strong feelings of communal cohesion: "The attitude of hostility toward the lawbreaker has the unique advantage of uniting all members of the community in the emotional solidarity of aggression."[49] The process resembles that which occurs in wartime. The enemy in war is typically a foreign nation, but in a very real sense, criminals in our society are permanent outsiders, and the effort to oppose them is understood as a "war on crime."[50]

From the perspective of the theory of democratic individuality outlined in Chapter Two, such a "solidarity of aggression" by definition blocks the learning potential inherent in democracy, and prevents citizens from being able to apprehend, let alone begin to correct, "the social and political components of crime." (*ibid.*) While it may be gratifying in the short term from a communitarian point of view, it is ultimately self-defeating, which is why it cannot meet the criteria of a utilitarian justification of punishment, the object of which is the greatest good of society as a whole. Casting criminals as permanent outsiders resonates with the Schmittian theory of the political,[51] but flies in the face of both normative theories of democracy and the classical theory of republican citizenship, which gives normative value to individual political participation. The Deweyian and Emersonian approaches resonate with this normative value in that they are based on the claim that democracy's strength lies in its limitless potential to expand, to include, and to learn from all its members, who in turn become better citizens as they participate on an equal basis with their peers.

The dualistic or exclusionary approaches to the political that justify disenfranchisement are based on the assumption that inclusion of those cast as felons, even ex-felons, would weaken American democracy. Yet the fear and revulsion generated by the identification of an enemy that supposedly consolidates the moral identity of the community creates a weak rather than resilient community that requires the juridical justifications of felon disenfranchisement cited above. What has been whipped up from the popular culture fear of crime is "a community founded upon victimization (by predatory criminals, by 'Them') and victimization constitutes the necessary entry subscription."

> The community that results is, of course, a simulacrum of community; a phantasm that speaks of a nostalgic desire for oneness and unity, while at the same time structuring itself around its dependence upon fear, alienation, and separateness for its elements to make some sense. Thus modernist criminal justice offers an impoverished pale version of community. Recognition is not based on shared friendship, but on shared risk and danger. (...)

> Languages of crime, words like punishment, murder, and arrest stir deep emotions and powerful feelings in all of us. These feelings are a desire to sacrifice (...) Those that are outlawed by government, by popular culture, by criminology, are being

sacrificed in order to maintain a fragile community. (Young, 1996, 10)

Critics of the communitarian justification who approach it from a deep republican, rather than communitarian perspective recognize that

> The renovation of political communities, by inclusion of those who have been excluded, enhances everyone's political freedom. (...) Because direct participation, as an equal, in the determination of common affairs...is for individuals an interest both positive and primary, republican communities may not be built by fencing out those at the margins.[52]

Moreover, given that one of the traditional aims of punishment is rehabilitation, such that punishment is a process of restoring the individual who has committed an offense to the community, facilitating his participation in public life should be a priority. The republican tradition emphasizes the salutary effects of political participation on the individual, its deepest, most Aristotelian strains identifying participation as essential to individual wholeness and development. Therefore denying convicted felons the right to participation, even when they have paid their debt to society implies that the criminal is an essentially different type of human being than the enfranchised, non-convicted citizen in that he is *not* capable of developing toward wholeness. Such logic contradicts the theory of democratic individuality presented in Chapter Two, which is premised on the assumption that we are all essentially the same, and that it is our commonality that makes possible not only language and speech, but empathy, solidarity, and participation in the political itself.[53] Permanent disenfranchisement represents a political judgment that denies the offender's ability and opportunity to change and reintegrate herself, and in effect denies a basic premise of republican political theory, that political participation can have a transformative effect on an individual. Therefore disenfranchisement can be said to have a negative effect on the offender's resocialization, especially when combined with other exclusionary measures, such as employment and housing restrictions and private discrimination.[54] Ex-offender disenfranchisement is an institutional contradiction of classical republican ideals of friendship and citizenship.

3. THE POLITICAL JUSTIFICATION OF FELON DISENFRANCHISEMENT AND THE POLITICS OF LAW AND ORDER

One cited political (as opposed to judicial) defense of felon disenfranchisement implies that the non-political realm into which criminals are cast after their conviction is defined by Section 1 of the Fourteenth Amendment. This Section distributes American and state citizenship to all persons born in the U.S., and protects their equal civil, not political rights.[55] Florida House Speaker Tom Feeney, a Republican, articulated   the   standard   political   justification   of   felon disenfranchisement, which mirrors Judge Friendly's neo-Lockean justification:

> At some point, you have to ask yourself whether or not—with an electorate that is increasingly less likely to be literate—expanding the franchise to just everyone who has two arms and two legs is the best way to govern a democracy for the future. It's less important to me that I have the right to vote than that the people who do are upholding the integrity and legitimacy of the society and culture. The fact that an individual, because he has permanently lost the right to vote, for example, is not going to be able to vote every two years—as long as the voters who do vote, vote responsibly—it shouldn't affect his ability to enjoy the blessings of the First Amendment and the Twentieth Amendment and all his constitutional rights. (cited in *Rolling Stone* 8/30/01)

Feeny's political justification of felon disenfranchisement also contains echoes of the (non-contractarian) communitarian justification of felon disenfranchisement used by state court judges who cite a compelling state interest in maintaining "the purity of the ballot box." He is distinguishing between "types" of human beings, some of whom are competent (he selects literacy as a marker) and others who are not, and should therefore not be allowed to vote.

The 2000 Presidential election, which drew both scholarly and journalistic attention to felon disenfranchisement laws, has forced states to debate legislative measures to ease the process of restoring ex-offender voting rights. The report of the bipartisan National Commission on Federal Election Reform (2001), recognizing that "in states that enact a permanent loss of the right to vote, this feature, combined with the demographics of the criminal justice system, produces a significant and disproportionate effect on black citizens, to the extent that as many as one-sixth[56] of the black population is permanently disenfranchised in some states." Accordingly, the Report, while recognizing that "the question of whether felons should lose the right to vote is one that requires a moral judgment by the citizens of each state," recommends that

> Each state should allow for restoration of voting rights to otherwise eligible citizens who have been convicted of a felony once they have fully served their sentence, including any term of probation or parole.

In general, Democratic Party legislators favor facilitating restoration of rights, and Republicans oppose such a process, although no clear consensus either in the national or state Democratic parties recommends sweeping changes in the law.[57] Opposition to changing restrictive laws is clearly self-serving on the part of Republican legislators, based on the demographics of disenfranchisement. The majority of disenfranchised felons are African-American and Hispanic, groups that normally vote for the Democratic Party (Uggen and Manza, 2001), although see *The New York Times* 7/10/04 on Hispanic voters in Florida and records of felony convictions.

In Virginia, a state that had denied the vote to ex-felons (more than 250,000), the legislature passed a bill to facilitate the clemency process.[58] Opponents, such as Roger Clegg, vice-president of the Center for Equal Opportunity, defended Virginia's process (of restoring ex-felon's rights through a cumbersome clemency process) as "a good approach that properly screens each individual on a case-by-case basis."[59]

> We don't let everyone vote. We require that people meet a minimum level of trustworthiness and loyalty to our system of government. Consequently, we don't let children, noncitizens, or people who are certifiably insane vote. Just as these groups don't meet the basic requirements, those people who commit serious crimes don't either.[60]

"The fact that somebody has served out his prison sentence does not mean that society is obliged to ignore the history of that individual... There should be a presumption [to deny restoring the right to vote] until they have shown that they can be trusted with that right again,"[61] said Clegg, a former top official with the Civil Rights Division of the U.S. Department of Justice. Clegg echoed Judge Friendly's neo-contractarian interpretation when he said, "I think people who have committed serious crimes have shown a lack of trustworthiness and loyalty. Someone who has shown they won't follow the laws should not have a role in making the laws themselves."[62] Clegg's rhetorical position, using words such a "serious crimes," "trustworthiness" and "loyalty" belie the actual situation, though, which is that the majority of felons are convicted for petty crimes, largely non-violent drug offenses. The assumption that there is an empirical connection between possession of marijuana and loyalty, which justifies stripping a citizen of voting rights is tenuous at best. Many citizens might agree with Clegg that serious crimes such as murder, rape, treason, bribery and electoral fraud warrant a period of disenfranchisement, possibly even permanent disenfranchisement if the offender is incarcerated for life, but these crimes constitute a tiny minority of those for which citizens are currently disenfranchised.[63]

In that felon disenfranchisement works as a tool of group (blacks, drug addicts, youth, "the dangerous classes" in general)[64] exclusion that by default, rather than intent, enhances the status, honor, and power of partisan political elites and their constituents, it is a perversion of the original institution of *atimia*. As we saw in Chapter One, *atimia* was an integral institution of the Athenian democracy and its particular conception of justice and democratic citizenship. *Atimia* was used as a defensive tool by the classical demos to exclude individuals who were derelict in their clearly defined duties toward the state; this dereliction sullied the collective status honor of citizenship. In a constitutional democracy such as the U.S., which has formally overcome the legal and political systems that defined American citizenship in terms of status honor, disproportionate punishment and felon disenfranchisement of minority groups indicates that the site where status honor is enforced is in the *in*formal realm. The informal realm is constituted by the multiple discretionary moments available to elected and appointed officials who represent "the public"—the enfranchised political majority—within the criminal justice continuum described in the final section of this chapter.

Although there are bills pending in several states to either restore the vote to ex-felons, or to facilitate a former prisoner's application for political rights once his sentence is completed, supporters of such legislation, even incumbent Democrats, usually find themselves in a minority. Such support would create the fatal perception, which would be jumped on by electoral opponents, that incumbents or candidates will appear "soft" on crime and/or drugs if they endorse voting rights for ex-felons in the current climate. Political campaigns since the late 1960s have made toughness on crime and a moral stance on drugs, a key credential for candidates from both parties.[65] Appearing to be tough on crime as both a candidate and an elected official is a rhetorical requisite for American politicians, "who have made crime-related problems central campaign issues and struggled to identify themselves as tougher than their competitors on crime, delinquency and drug use." (Beckett 1997, 3). This discursive use of the concept of "crime" is a factional tool in the *staseis* between the two major political parties in their struggle for the elusive political "center." According to Beckett, the politicization of "crime," which constitutionally speaking is the province of state and local governments, rather than the federal administration, followed the enactment of the Voting Rights Act in 1965 and the subsequent breakup of the Democratic Party's New Deal Coalition.

It was thus the civil rights movement that finally cut the South from the Democrats and enabled the GOP to make a bid for that region... By drawing significant public attention to the plight of blacks in the South, civil rights activists forced the national Democratic party to choose between its southern white and northern black constituencies. The high degree of support among nonsouthern whites for the civil rights cause prior to 1965 and the increasing numbers of northern black voters eventually led the Democratic party to cast its lot with blacks and their sympathizers... This decision, however, alienated many of those traditionally loyal to the Democratic party, particularly southerners. "Millions of voters, pried loose from their habitual loyalty to the Democratic party, were now a volatile force, surging through the electoral system without the channeling restraints of party attachment."[66]

These voters were available for courting, and courted they were. (Beckett 1997, 41)

Beckett argues that the Republicans courted the solid south, urban blue-collar workers, Catholics, and the farm vote to form a "New Majority" coalition "that could dominate electoral politics." The rhetorical vehicle for the coded anti-black message used to attract these voters was law and order. "As the traditional working-class coalition that buttressed the Democratic party was ruptured along racial lines, race eclipsed class as the organizing principle of American politics. By 1972, attitudes on racial issues rather than socio-economic status were the primary determinants of voters' political self-identification."[67] Law-and-order campaign promises and positions taken by elected officials and translated into policy have resulted in the large numbers of both prisoners and disenfranchised populations in some states, populations that can be seen as the collateral damage of the war on crime.

4. THE CRIMINAL JUSTICE SYSTEM AS A CONTINUUM OF MOMENTS

Just as American citizenship can be represented dynamically in terms of a continuum of political rights (ranging from total enfranchisement to partial disenfranchisement to lifetime disenfranchisement), rather than as a static , vertical administrative institution, so too can the criminal justice system be represented as a continuum of events or moments. From the perspective of the "system," this continuum begins with the competition for election by local and national candidates, who as representatives enact and enforce laws defining prohibited behaviors and penalties. During the competition for office, they present policies and platforms they hope will capture the electorate's attention and votes, making ideological use of conceptually distinct notions of law and order. The politics and economics of crime and drugs have captured the American electorate's attention since the late 1960s, as we saw in the previous section. Those politics constitute the starting point of the continuum. Furthermore, from the "system" standpoint, the endpoint of the continuum is the enforcement of felon disenfranchisement provisions at the local level, which results in the elimination of potential voters from the next (local, state, or national) electoral competition.

From the perspective of individual lifeworlds (both the offender's and the arresting officer's), the criminal justice continuum can be said to begin (clearly it could actually begin much earlier with the victimization of both or either) with arrest of the offender by an officer of the law,[68] and terminates with her disenfranchisement following release from prison.[69] Because disenfranchisement for crime in the states that practice it is attendant on a felony conviction, which generally involves incarceration, it is analytically implicated in the politics of law and order, which are deployed at the local, state and national levels. Most obviously, it is implicated in the very concepts of crime and felony, which have no objective existence, but are contingently defined by the "collective consciousness,"[70] expressed institutionally by elected majorities. Moreover, individual police officers, prosecutors, and judges are representatives and enforcers of the collective consciousness when they select (profile), charge, and convict offenders, or decline to profile, charge and convict.[71]

The politics of law and order are directly implicated in the high rates of felon disenfranchisement evident in the contemporary American polity in that these rates are an apparently unintended consequence of the escalated conviction and incarceration rates that have defined the domestic war on drugs since the 1980s.[72] One of those consequences has been the historically unprecedented loss of political rights by so many citizens, a disproportionate number of them African-American.[73] Felon disenfranchisement has therefore been the target of journalistic and scholarly critique in recent years, particularly in the wake of Election 2000, when inaccurate lists of disenfranchised felons were deployed in the close Florida race for electoral votes.[74]

Notwithstanding the fact that many of the state laws mandating disenfranchisement of felons date from the colonial period, constitutional and statutory provisions prohibiting convicted felons from registering to vote are not archaic legal relics states do not enforce like, say, laws punishing adultery or sodomy. They *are* enforced, and they do have political significance.[75] Although in practice subject to bureaucratic error and mismanagement, in theory an officer of the court delivers lists of names of convicted felons to the county or district clerk responsible for maintaining the electoral rolls. When a convicted person tries to register or vote, she is turned away until (again in theory) a pardon, or court order releasing her from probation or parole, directs the clerk to restore her name to the list of eligible voters.

Just as the decision to arrest and prosecute an offender is local, corresponding to the smallest political subdivision in the state, the administrative function associated with striking or restoring an offender's rights is also local, although controlled by state law.[76] Thus the local, discretionary, often personal decision of a police officer to "profile" and arrest a suspect, and the decision of a prosecutor to charge and or plea bargain, must be analytically distinguished from the state or federal law (the "system" perspective) that classifies crimes according to felonies or misdemeanors.[77] The discretionary moments that constitute the front end of the continuum of the criminal justice process must also be distinguished from the later moment, which is the sentencing that follows conviction, a moment that is no longer discretionary.[78] Nonetheless, discretion and personal choices of state officials do permeate later moments along the continuum in the form of the behavior and attitudes of correctional officers towards inmates in jails and prisons, as well as in the decisions of parole boards and probation officers. When disenfranchisement is co-extensive with the term of incarceration, probation, and parole, as it is in some states, a felon might remain in the system for as long as a prison guard, probation officer, or parole board can find reason to punish him. This is why I believe that although some seven states have removed ex-felon disenfranchisement statutes from the books since I began my research, the cumulative impact of all the moments along the discretionary continuum can keep fellow citizens effectively disenfranchised for life. In other words, *plus ça change, plus c'est la meme chose.*" In states that require an executive pardon for the restoration of political rights following conviction, the discretionary role of the governor is a key moment.[79]

What becomes apparent, when sentencing and conviction rates in the polity as a whole are viewed in terms of this continuum of discretionary moments, is that the political rights of all American citizens are hostage to the individual decisions of thousands of elected and non-elected public officials in local political subdivisions throughout the United States. The interior of the apparently secure and seamless exterior edifice of American citizenship defined in constitutional text and affirmed in Supreme Court rulings is actually shot through with holes that represent discretionary decisions of criminal justice system officials at each moment of the continuum that extends between profiling, arrest, and disenfranchisement.

I identify the discretionary moments that occur along the continuum of the punishment process and distinguish them from the positive content—the "substance" of the criminal law—in order to highlight the difficulty of generalizing about a philosophy, or justification of punishment, associated with a particular system in any given state. State punishment policies are usually discursively legitimated in terms of whether they are retributive, rehabilitative, deterrent, or a combination of any of the three. These legitimations are based on a formal conceptual connection between the concepts of crime and punishment. The discourse surrounding policy debates on criminal justice, and the association of particular sentences with particular crimes, may indicate the preference of policy makers for one justification over another, but the way the system actually operates on the ground is the key to the mechanics of felon disenfranchisement. The application of punishment is independent, in other words, of any formal philosophical links. It is the key to how the politics of the practice configure the double polity. Two of the major American justifications, retribution and rehabilitation, are discussed in Chapter Five.

The methodological problem of analyzing criminal justice regimes in the several states, whose laws as we have seen, control felon disenfranchisement, is that few generalizations can be made about policy, since each state constitutes its own distinct political universe. There is no single punishment regime in the contemporary U.S. that can be analyzed and criticized as such, just as there is no single citizenship regime, as we saw in Chapter Two. For analytical purposes, scholars rely on elite discourse that justifies or criticizes national penal policy in the context of legislative appropriations and/or political legitimation.

Critical analyses of the wars on crime and drugs, and racial disparities in the criminal justice system typically present aggregated (state) data in order to discuss an "American" problem, referring to particularly shocking and illustrative state cases to drive home a point. There are single- and multiple-state studies on crime and incarceration rates, and data on state incarceration rates broken down by demographic categories are available from the Department of Justice, but even the DOJ emphasizes aggregated data for both state and federal prisons in its reports. In other words, the scholarly and journalist critiques of the contemporary criminal justice system, including felon disenfranchisement (as we saw in the previous chapters) implicitly reproduce concepts of American nationhood and citizenship that are unitary (and therefore incoherent) rather than carefully dissected.[80] The arguments and statistics they present bespeak patterns of discrimination that are common to the profiled states and raise questions about the legitimacy of a polity that tolerates injustice in all the various criminal justice systems that comprise the (mythic) nation as a whole.[81]

African-American males, who represent less than seven percent of the U.S. population, comprise almost half of the prison and jail population in the country. This statistic represents the cumulative consequence of hundreds of thousands of discrete, local decisions. Insofar as these discrete local decisions bear no formal relation to constitutional principles, they cannot be construed as the result of a legally organized conspiracy, or of a concerted national policy. Justice is blind, and the law, including the laws providing for disenfranchisement of felons, knows no formal color. That, for the sake of argument being the case, it becomes imperative for a democracy that aspires to legitimacy to address local patterns of discretionary enforcement through concerted national policy, directed by political conversations in which all citizens, not just those designated as morally worthy, are allowed to participate.

As we saw in Chapter Two, though, the political conundrum is that the national electorate is a fragmented federal one, rather than a unitary democratic one, full of the holes or negative spaces represented by disenfranchised felons in the states. That political conundrum can only be addressed by the Supreme Court (if a suitable case reaches it), and by Congress (if the relevant bills can get out of committee). Both these institutions have the constitutional right to disaggregate national from local and state elections and restore voting rights to ex-felons in their capacity as members of the American electorate.[82] It is doubtful that either institution will exercise that right in the absence of a challenging national conversation about race, criminal justice policy, and the institutional legacies of slavery, a conversation the U.S. formally opted out of at the World Conference on Xenophobia and Racism in Durban, South Africa in 2001. It is up to American citizens, many of whom are doing so, to initiate such a conversation on home ground if the unresolved issues that precipitate such national denial are ever to be addressed. The strong presence of American NGOs in Durban suggests that this unfinished business of historical and institutional racism will not be shelved despite, and maybe because of, the context of the present "national emergency."

Such a national conversation, begun in local constituencies, would reveal the tension between the institutions of "law" and "order;" "justice" and "the police," a tension epitomized in current racial profiling policies carried out under the apparently neutral guise of law. Theorists of legitimacy cite the necessary generality of law, and the fact that when law singles out groups or individuals it by definition loses its generality and becomes illegitimate. The contemporary American statistics from the war on drugs exemplify how racial profiling illegitimately dilutes the law of its generality.

The following, final chapter identifies the double polity configured by criminal justice and disenfranchisement policies as a neo-colonial citizenship regime. It argues that the genesis of the contemporary polity was the original colonial regime based on the domestic political binary citizen/slave, which was not only uninterrupted by the Founding, but was consolidated in the Constitution. It further argues that the legal abolition of slavery following the Civil War did not constitute an accounting for the national crime of slavery and therefore, from the perspective of a theory of retributive justice, allowed that crime to stand. The chapter presents one philosopher's analysis of how racist interpretations of social contract theory have historically justified structural relations of domination between whites and non-whites to ground a moral epistemology and ethics antithetical to democratic equality, learning, and social justice. It is my view that the modern American practice of felon disenfranchisement provides structural support to the original and ongoing racial contract, notwithstanding the fact that its institutional origins in the Athenian polis were innocent of the concept of race. The irony is that Athenian *atimia* was a practice that preserved and supported classical democracy and its particular concept of political equality, while modern American felon disenfranchisement subverts and undermines the American ideals of democracy and political equality. Briefly, Athenian *atimia* was internally consistent with the democratic idea of justice in the ancient polis, whereas American *atimia* represents an internal contradiction of the democratic idea of justice in the modern polis.[83]

CHAPTER FIVE

The Double Polity Identified

"Laying claim to and denying the human condition at the same time: the contradiction is explosive."

Sartre[1]

INTRODUCTION

The previous chapter analyzed the contemporary American neo-contractarian and communitarian judicial defenses of felon disenfranchisement, both of which claim in different ways that the convicted felon is morally unworthy of full citizenship rights and should therefore be legally exiled from the polity. I argued that the claim of moral unworthiness cannot stand in a universal democratic citizenship regime, given racially disparate arrest, incarceration, and conviction rates which result from the combined discretionary and political structure of the continuum of the criminal justice system. I also suggested that the negative designation of unworthiness used to justify exclusion implies a reciprocal, positive conception of worthiness, whose ontological basis will be examined in this chapter. I argued that the institutional consequence of the cumulative rates of disenfranchisement in the American context of four decades of law-and-order politics has been the creation of a negative status group of non-ruling or ruled citizens in a polity of formally equal citizens. This status group is (indirectly) ruled by those non-convicted citizens who enjoy political rights and comprise the visible, positive democratic citizenship regime of enfranchised equals. This chapter seeks to identify the type of regime that is constituted by these two politically related groups of citizens.

I claimed that the non-convicted, enfranchised citizens actually possess a double political identity, whether they are aware of it or not, an identity that exists behind their backs, so to speak,[2] in that they are simultaneously political equals (with their enfranchised peers) and rulers (albeit distant, over their disenfranchised co-citizens). The disenfranchised, on the other hand, only possess one, negative political identity, which those who seek to register to vote, even after their release from prison, are painfully aware of. Institutionally speaking, the fact that citizens can both co-rule and rule over fellow citizens in a single territorial unit denotes a double citizenship regime, or a double polity, simultaneously comprising a democratic regime and a despotic regime. Judicial defenses of felon disenfranchisement, particularly the neo-contractarian defense, legitimize the existence of the double polity and the double citizenship identity of the enfranchised.

One aim of this final chapter is to use the disciplinary lens of empirical political theory to identify the double polity and double citizenship identity in terms of a modern, rather than ancient, taxonomy of regimes.[3] I intend to argue that the United States has the highest rate of incarceration in the free world (699 per 100,000 population)[4] and that Americans "of color" are disproportionately incarcerated for drug crimes, and therefore disproportionately disenfranchised, because the United States is, in fact, a neo-colonial regime. Its old colonial roots lie in the slave society instituted during the English regime, which were constitutionalized in the new republic.[5] Although these roots were formally excised after the Civil War, the ethos and mores that structured the American slave society remained vital throughout the nation well past Reconstruction, finding institutional expression in both legalized segregation and in the continuum of the criminal justice system described in the previous chapter. The multiple opportunities for discretion and coercion available to representatives of that system at the informal level have consistently combined with the formal practice of felon disenfranchisement to configure a subordinate polity whose members are disproportionately drawn from poor and minority groups of citizens. Legitimized by the formal guarantees of the Fourteenth Amendment, and explicitly by Section 2's affirmative sanction of felon disenfranchisement, the institutional relationship between the dominant and subordinate groups comprising these two polities can be described as neo-colonial.

This argument cuts across the positivist claim that all inmates are in prison and all felons are disenfranchised simply because they were arrested for breaking the law, tried, and duly convicted. Yet as we have seen, even the claim that *all* lawbreakers are punished equally is ethically troubling given the sheer recent numbers and trends of incarceration, in both the American and international context. It is also ethically and logically troubling, given the racial and social discrepancies between drug use across the population as a whole and arrest, conviction, and sentencing patterns that have appeared in the war on drugs. As we saw in the previous chapter, these patterns cut across the basic liberal tenet of state punishment that "like crimes be treated alike." The tension between the publicly legitimated regime—a constitutional liberal democracy—and penal policies that violate its "colorblind" equal protection norms raises political as well as theoretical and institutional questions about such a regime's claim to legitimacy and challenges the self-identification of the regime.

The previous chapter presented historical-political explanations about why so many citizens are now being "punished," and by extension disenfranchised—why the numbers started escalating dramatically when President Reagan expanded the wars first on crime and then on drugs initiated by Richard Nixon. It did not, however, probe the rationality (beyond the material and symbolic gain to politicians, parties, and corporations), of policies that deprive the most vulnerable members of our highly modern society—the poor, the illiterate, and the addicted—of their freedom and their vote in a country where freedom and the vote are quintessential political values. Beyond pointing to the civil rights movement and Democratic party dealignment as "efficient causes," the chapter did not attempt to analyze why men and women of color—the descendants of slaves and immigrants—are punished in numbers vastly disproportionate to their national population and offending rates. Nor did the chapter attempt to probe why the majority continues to tolerate such policies enacted in its name. The purpose of this chapter is to analyze the theoretical genealogy of the punishment polity and associated citizenship identities from the perspective of two related critical discourses: post-colonial theory and an immanent critique of social contract theory, called "The Racial Contract." I turn to these discourses because I find the received, or mainstream, discourses inadequate explanations of the current state of our polity.

The most common explanation/critique from the left of the contemporary punishment polity is that incarceration trends track the liberal demand for social peace, and are a necessary condition of elite property accumulation in the unstable, globalizing world.[6] Incarceration is simply, albeit tragically, a politically attractive method of social control that enables elites to manage rising (economic) inequality and populations rendered surplus by capitalist development (Parenti 1999.) Inner city dwellers, the chronically poor, have always been stuck to the bottom of the great American melting pot and are now a surplus population, a dangerous class to be segregated and incapacitated (Gordon 1994.) The problem with this explanation is not its quasi-Marxist theoretical assumptions, which are, arguably, vindicated by empirical developments on the ground. It is that the explanation does not challenge the liberal-democratic or the republican self-understandings of the United States on their own ideological terrain. I am more interested in immanent critique (hybridized by a postcolonial perspective) than a critique of ideology performed from distinct theoretical premises. I want to see how the internal rationality of modern liberal democracy can account for such an apparent contradiction as contemporary incarceration rates, which chart the fact that poor and minority citizens are disproportionately represented as felons, and are disenfranchised for crime.

The problem with using any of the received political theory discourses alone—liberalism, republicanism, discourse theory, democratic theory, systems theory, multiculturalism, or Marxism—to track down the genealogy of contemporary disenfranchisement rates, is that none of them can, or will, account for institutional racism. Mainstream political theory ignores the fact of slavery; it does not acknowledge its legacy, which confers the political and socio-economic privileges of whiteness whose reciprocal condition is the institutional subordination of Americans of color, a fact that challenges the normative legal narrative of individual equality. All of these received ostensibly colorblind discourses (with the exception of Marxism, which has trouble dealing with race) share the "homogeneous empty time" perspective of the nation state (Benjamin 1973, cited in Anderson 1983). This means that the mainstream discourses start where "we" are, which in the American case means a constitutional state of formal legal equality. Historically speaking, the myth of the Revolution vindicates and sanitizes the violence of the first founding, obscuring the contemporaneous institutional violence of slavery, which the second founding, the Civil War, was supposed to have overcome.[7] Yet the narrative of that second founding, inscribed in the Reconstruction Amendments, obscured the contemporaneous institutional violence of the convict labor system, just as the triumphalist legal narrative of the second Reconstruction, the civil rights movement, obscures the moralistically sanitized violence of the class- and race-coded law-and-order polity. Mainstream political theory shrouds this cumulative violence behind a thick veil of what can only ironically be called ignorance, an ignorance that is willful because the history and narratives that could obviate it are widely available.

The postcolonial critique of liberalism is useful because it brings in race, punctures the linear, nation-centered narrative of modern political theory and development, and reconfigures the coordinates of contemporary problematics along more disruptive and theoretically fruitful axes of space and time. According to Stuart Hall (1996, 249),

> In the re-staged narrative of the postcolonial, colonization assumes the place and significance of a major, extended and ruptural world-historical event. By 'colonization' the 'post-colonial' references something more than direct rule over certain areas of the world by imperial powers. I think it is signifying the whole process of expansion, exploration, conquest, colonization and imperial hegemonization which constituted the 'outer face' the constitutive outside, of European and then Western capitalist modernity after 1492.

The genesis of the present American metropolis/colony relation is the original imperial relation with England, a relation whose structural binary of citizenship/slavery was reproduced with the Founding in the newly independent polity. Insofar as that structural dynamic was never emphatically rejected through a retributive or compensatory process, it continues to be expressed through ostensibly neutral structures such as the criminal justice system.

The United States was institutionalized as a ready-made (with regard to the Native and slave populations) colonial regime of republican liberty that has evolved discursively through extension of universal suffrage into a modern constitutional liberal democracy. In the contemporary polity, the enfranchised, free citizens are members of what can be described both symbolically and materially as a metropolis. Through their elected representatives, they administer what can be described (both symbolically and materially) as a periphery, prisons and the high crime areas that supply those prisons with their occupants, who are disenfranchised after being convicted of crimes.[8] In states where convicted felons are disenfranchised for life, even after serving their time, the enfranchised and the disenfranchised citizens live and work side by side, unbeknownst to one another. Both are free, but only one set of citizens has the right to vote on Election Day.

As Hall says, this post-colonial type of configuration does not amount to direct rule by the metropolis over certain areas of the United States, or over certain clearly designated colonized peoples, as in the saltwater empires.[9] The indirect nature of representative democracy and the fact that the enfranchised and the convicted share the status of American citizenship preclude such a broad claim. My theoretical arguments merely gesture to the fact contemporary high rates of felon disenfranchisement reveal that polity and nation state are not co-extensive in the United States. The corollary claim with regard to citizenship is that only members of the metropolis enjoy the full benefits of national citizenship, which entail privileges and protections denied to those who populate the (legal and symbolic) periphery and are thus more vulnerable to state coercion.

The U.S. can be described as a post-colonial polity because its legal experience as a British colony terminated in 1776. Yet I would argue that the anti-colonial revolution that resulted in its birth as a white republican nation and the myths of civic identity (Smith 1997) produced to legitimize its birth and development have governed its jurisprudence ever since. My argument rests on an intuition that what could be posited as the colonial continuum has never been effectively disrupted such that the national ideological "switches" set during the original colonial period—which saw the institutionalization of slavery—could be re-set to configure a fully inclusive polity.

Although the legal abolition of slavery followed the Union's military victory in the Civil War and the Republican political victories of Reconstruction, abolition in the absence of any type of restorative justice process did not amount to an accounting for the national, not just the Southern crime of slavery.[10] This rather glaring deficit in the national narrative implies that the United States lacks an account of justice that can provide a sufficient normative framework for its self-evaluation. Bearing in mind the caveat emphasized in the previous chapter about the difficulty of generalizing about a single regime or philosophy of punishment, criminal justice in the United States has, until very recently, been predicated on the reformative or rehabilitative principle of punishment, which is oriented toward the individual offender. The purpose of reform is, whenever possible, to create good citizens who do not commit crimes—the criteria of which are decided by the collective consciousness as we will see in Section 3. This principle of criminal justice—reform of the individual—was never applied to white slave-masters, federal officials, or Confederate officers, who formed part of that collective consciousness, albeit a treasonous part. The reformative, individualist principle simply lacked the normative foundation to address such an enormous task of determining collective accountability, and as we saw in Chapter Two, no significant punishment of the Confederate leadership ever took place.[11] That leadership was granted virtual impunity (the concept of which is to be discussed in Section 3 of this chapter) for both the rebellion and for slavery.

Until its recent demise, the rehabilitative account of punishment was premised on a collective—or at least majoritarian—consensus about the lineaments of good citizenship and how state punishment could secure them. The traditional rehabilitative account suffered from the mid-twentieth-century rejection by the anti-war and civil rights movements of all majoritarian/consensual versions of good citizenship. In that the success of the civil rights movement changed the political equation of American politics, conservative Republicans, who interpreted the civil disobedience of the civil rights movement as crime, were challenged to either come up with a new justification of punishment or change their interpretation of American citizenship. A sincere national commitment to reform and rehabilitation of criminals incarcerated in the wake of the civil rights movement would have implied the commitment to accepting those reformed criminals as fully fledged members of the polity upon release from prison.

Rather than accepting such a commitment, the new American Conservatives (Wallace, Goldwater, Nixon, Reagan, Bush) trumped the radical democratic interpretation of the civil rights movement by changing the rules of the game of punishment from reform to retribution. Instead of rehabilitation based on a conception of universal consent to the revised contract formulated by the success of the civil rights movement, punishment was justified by the Conservative conception of Right, or what the neo-retributivists called "just deserts." The account of Right they produced, though, was exceptional, American, not universal—it was opportunistic, partial—raised to support the good of a part of the polity, based on a political agenda whose goal was to restore its pre-civil rights movement hegemony, which was not the good of the whole. Because African-Americans were demanding equal citizenship rights, the bar of citizenship had to be raised. In other words, prisons could no longer serve as schools of citizenship, and the definition of citizenship as an inclusive collective enterprise had to be changed. If the mission of prisons was to educate and reform criminals (both black and white) so they could be worthy of citizenship, then unless blacks who demanded civil rights and committed civil disobedience were eventually to be received as equals, that mission had to change.

Should the rehabilitative account be revived in a different political climate than that prevailing today, its legitimacy will depend on its parameters being defined in the context of inclusive democratic deliberation about the criteria of good citizenship. An honest accounting of good citizenship that catalogs and presents the harms of slavery for democratic judgment calls for insertion in the broader philosophical framework of retributive justice, to be reviewed below. Briefly, the American tradition of reformative or rehabilitative punishment has always been context-dependent: its theories evolved in the context of a slave society whose concept of justice legally comprehended negative and positive status groups. Citizens were reformed within that context whereas slaves were simply punished. Philosophically speaking, the universal perspective of retributive punishment transcends the (ethical) context of status groups and re-establishes natural Right where Right has been infringed by harm.

This framework demands acknowledgment, accountability and redress for wrongdoing, or harm on the part of all participants in crime, which may well be collectively (and officially) endorsed and perpetrated, not just individually executed. It implies that when the wrongdoer is (or wrongdoers are) punished, and/or reparation made to the victim(s), the polity is restored to the state of equilibrium that was disrupted by the crime. Although in the case of slavery, there was no prior (pre-slavery) equilibrium that could be restored by punishment or reparations, the abolition of slavery alone could not "cancel the cancellation" of right[12] represented by the crime of slavery. Insofar as no such process or accounting has ever taken place in the United States to interrupt or cancel the harms caused by slavery to both the victims and the beneficiaries of slavery, the harm continues to all parties.[13] This can be attributed to the fact that the United States, since the Founding, has never formulated a national code of justice, and this in turn can be attributed to the fact that the United States was founded as a federal, race-based slave society.

If this argument is correct, slavery is the unfinished business of the post-colonial United States, and its legacy, much like buried but still "hot" radioactive waste, continues to harm the polity.[14] The ideological well-spring of the extremely effective construction and manipulation of racialized law-and-order discourse by the Wallace, Goldwater, Nixon, and later Reagan and Bush presidential campaigns is the legacy of original American herrenvolk colonial republicanism.[15] The institutional counterpoint of the thick conception of virtuous citizenship associated with that political tradition was, of course, slavery, just as the contemporary legal/symbolic counterpart of the ideal drug-free modern American citizen is the incarcerated (disenfranchised) felon.[16] The invocation of retributive punishment theory to justify contemporary racialized (war on drugs) incarceration policies, and the subsequent stigma of unworthiness that attaches to the criminalized and disenfranchised, is cynical and opportunistic, since retributive theory has never been invoked to account for the historical crimes of slavery. In the words of Dr. Ronald Walters:

> We are in a period where we are told that morality and ethics are the key to civil (*sic*) virtue. Well one of those most immoral acts of the development of the United States has been the enslavement of the Africans. This immorality has been compounded by the modern failure to acknowledge that the grandeur of this country was based in substantial part on the monumental resources made possible by African labor.

This failure to acknowledge that fact is an act bereft of virtue, which is the basis of modern racial subordination, and which fosters such cynicism and alienation that it prevents the acceptance full faith of the institutionalized version of the American dream. It is the basis of the differential acceptance of the O.J. Simpson verdict by blacks and whites, the Los Angeles rebellions after the Rodney King verdict, and other racially charged incidents, and gives evidence of the sleeping, seething, consciousness of the history of slavery, and its links to the modern dehumanization of black people.[17]

Before turning to a more detailed exposition of postcolonial theory, Section 1 reviews the retributive account of punishment, in order to reveal the gap between normative justifications of state punishment and its politicized application. Section 2 provides an overview of the rehabilitative or reformative justification of punishment, which has been the dominant account in the U.S. since the founding, and has only recently been replaced by a neo-liberal version of retributivism. Section 3 is divided into two parts, the first of which, "The Concept of Crime" looks briefly at how crime is defined in political philosophy and social theory. The second part, "Crime, Consent, and Impunity," interrogates the institutional consequences of *not* punishing what is defined as "crime," by a community of consenting citizens. Section 4 looks at one philosopher's critique of the use of social contract theory to justify racial domination in the liberal state. Section 5, finally, presents an overview of postcolonial theory and challenges the U.S. self-identification as a liberal-democratic citizenship regime.

Identifying the contemporary citizenship regime as neo-colonial demystifies, de-moralizes the criminal justice policies that result in the incarceration and disenfranchisement of large numbers of poor and minority citizens. Revealing those policies and practices as the cumulative institutional expression of a multi-century pattern of racialized group domination (colonial) rather than the aggregated statistical expression of individual or personal moral failure (liberal) opens the way for political conversation and action to alter those practices. I hope to convince the reader that operation of what Charles Mills (1997) calls "The Racial Contract" and the effective institutionalization of a neo-colonial citizenship regime in the American polity damages the polity as a whole, and enfranchised citizens individually, not just those individuals and groups that constitute the periphery.[18] From the perspective of the theory of democratic individuality outlined in Chapter Two of this book, exclusion of any individual, or members of any ascriptive group, compromises the potential for collective learning immanent to the citizen body of a truly representative democracy. The theory of the Racial Contract clarifies how such a pattern of political exclusion creates moral and epistemological deficits in the dominant group, the enfranchised citizens that comprise what I argue is the metropolis of the double polity. To name the damage and the deficits is to take the first step in the praxis of overcoming them in order to realize the full potential of the democratic form available to American citizens.

1. OVERVIEW OF RETRIBUTIVE THEORY

The retributive account of state punishment is based on the idea that the crime "is an intentional assault on the sovereignty of an individual that temporarily places one person (the criminal) in a position of illegitimate sovereignty over another (the victim)" (Reiman 1990, 193). The moral and legal equality of citizens that is disrupted by the criminal act can only be restored by retribution, which [gives] "the victim authority over the criminal comparable to the authority over the victim that the criminal arrogated to himself." The victim, in the modern state is, of course, legally represented by the state, the People, in the American criminal justice system. Politically speaking, as we saw in Chapter 3, the victim is represented by the *enfranchised* People in the person of the elected prosecutor, and more specifically by the majority party he belongs to. In systems where retribution for harms is not governed by law, but by personal or popular power, punishment is synonymous with revenge, which Hegel insists is a judgment of "subjective interest" and a "contingency of power, rather than "punitive justice."[19]

Kant and Hegel's philosophical justifications of punishment derive from their conceptions of the person as an autonomous, rational individual who has the right to be punished for his act by a state that is legitimately constituted by contract (Kant) or by Right (Hegel). In modern European political theory (versus Old Testament theology), retributive accounts of punishment are legitimated by the concepts of social contract and right (both in the case of Kant, and only Right in the case of Hegel, who did not believe the state was a contract).[20] The basic idea is that retributive punishment restores the alleged symmetry and reciprocity present in the original, rights conferring social contract in which all participants are equal. It satisfies the apparently innate ontological requirement of balance or reciprocity implied by the justice of contract or by the justice of Right. When punishment acts as "cancellation" (*Aufheben*) of a crime, it constitutes "retribution" insofar as punishment, "by its concept, is an infringement of an infringement." Retribution has its ontological grounding, as it were, in natural equality:

> [R]ight is a certain equal relationship of sovereign authority between the wills of individuals. Crime disrupts that relationship by placing one will above others, and punishment restores the relationship by annulling the illegitimate ascendance. (Reiman 1990, 193)

Hegel's account of retributive justice requires both an "injury" and natural equality—shared by a perpetrator and a victim—to make sense, which is why the contemporary (neo-liberal) application of retributive theory to the war on drugs, which justifies the incarceration of non-violent drug felons, is philosophically incoherent. According to retributive theory, punishment restores the original natural equality between victim and perpetrator, natural equality that reaches its highest form of realization in the state.[21] Felony crimes such as drug trafficking and possession lack the retributive prerequisites of victim and injury unless the victim is construed as society itself, and the injury as one done to society as a whole. For the sake of argument, if that were the case, then all drug crimes would have to be punished, since each and every infringement of the drug laws would represent a harm to society. As we saw in the previous chapter, the racially discriminatory law enforcement policies that constitute the war on drugs cannot support this dual requirement of injury and (universal) punishment: selective law enforcement, in the retributive view, compounds the injury, it cannot possibly fix it. Hegel insists that if a crime, which is an infringement of Right is not punished, the (criminal) deed will stand as valid. In other words, impunity will ensure the continued operation of the negativity created by the infringement of the victims' rights, particularly if the victim is the People.[22]

Moreover, the substantial element in Right and crime is universal, although both assume different specific "shapes" in different cultures and over time. This universal element in both means that punishment is a matter of justice because it cancels crime, which is an infringement of Right, not simply a contextual expression of the collective consciousness. Reiman (1990) suggests that the source of the justice in Hegel's theory is "the lasting quality of moral relations," which refers to "the relations among people as relations among their degrees of actual freedom:

> If one person subjugates another temporarily, then, even after that subjugation is ended, it remains true that (everything else equal) the first has obtained an increment of freedom to pursue his sovereign interest over the course of his whole lifetime that

is at the expense of the freedom that the other has for pursuing her sovereign interest over the course of her whole lifetime. (192)

The argument is that since moral relations are co-extensive, reciprocal, and ongoing, the state's failure to punish an injury by asserting a like authority over the criminal as he asserted over his victim "lets the indignity stand though the injury itself is healed" (194). The result is that injustice is allowed to stand, legitimized, and the ongoing universal moral relations of equality between members of the polity are disrupted.

Retributive theory can help us to understand why the American practices of slavery and legalized segregation cannot simply be relegated to history, and why the question of reparations is both normatively and politically compelling. The citizens and institutions that perpetrated and profited from the harms and "injuries" of two and a half centuries of slavery were never held accountable for their actions, and the victims never compensated for their loss. Most obviously this was because slavery was not considered a crime, and the injuries that constituted it, which today would be classified as serious felonies (kidnapping, rape, assault, murder, incest, robbery, etc.), were not considered crimes.[23] Since the very legal and institutional framework of slavery legitimized those injuries, it would have been a grammatical contradiction to talk about kidnapping or rape as crimes perpetrated by owners or slave traders. Insofar, however, as slavery is now recognized as a crime, the crimes it sanctioned must also be named as such.[24]

As I said above, a condition of retributive theory is the equality of all members of the polity, all (potential) victims and all (potential) perpetrators, and slaves were never, by definition, considered the equals of white citizens. Thus in the context of positive law, retribution or punishment of the crimes of slavery was incoherent. The ideal universe of Right, though, is not limited by positive law—"it is something *utterly sacred,* for the simple reason that it is the existence [*Dasein*] of the absolute concept, of self-conscious freedom" (*PR,* §30). Returning to the American situation: the freed slaves' (natural) right to (civil) equality was recognized by the Reconstruction Amendments that abolished slavery and bestowed equal (state and national) citizenship upon all Americans, including the former bondsmen. This new enactment of formal equality, however, could only function prospectively: it comprehended no retroactive recognition or provision that because the former slaves were actually equal—or equal enough to be constitutionally inscribed as American citizens—they should be compensated for the harms they suffered as slaves. Presumably formal citizenship was compensation enough, and since American law prohibits retroactive punishment, no formal mechanism could be activated to hold the "offenders" of the slave system responsible. From the Hegelian perspective, though, this (deficit in positive law) robs those wrongdoers, who were co-equal members of the pre-Reconstruction polity, of their right—which is not circumscribed by positive law—to be punished. A key element of retributive justice, which is retrospective, demands that the wrongdoer be held accountable because it is his right as a rational being, and it is this element that has always been missing from the multigenerational American drama of slavery.[25]

The retributive justification of punishment has never enjoyed much currency in the U.S., though, and has only recently been overhauled by penologists to justify twentieth-century incarceration policies.[26] American punishment policy, whose Enlightenment origins reflect the influence of Beccaria, has traditionally been justified by the classical ideal of rehabilitation.[27] The purpose of the quintessentially American institution of the penitentiary was to produce good citizens, as we will see in the following section. Those citizens, as I argued in Chapter One, were predominantly white, since the U.S. had a dual system of criminal law until Reconstruction, which punished slaves and citizens differently. The reformative justification remained the dominant American account until the 1970s, when its perceived failure in the wars on crime and drugs precipitated professional and political interest in "retribution."

As we saw in the previous chapter, the rise in incarceration and, consequently, disenfranchisement rates accompanied what David Garland (1990) calls "a more punitive anti-modernism." Moreover, the judicial defenses of permanent felon disenfranchisement we reviewed imply that the convicted felon cannot be rehabilitated or reformed to rejoin the polity as a fully equal participant. Nevertheless, since the vast majority of currently incarcerated prisoners are released to the larger society, the official rejection of the aim of "reform" has serious social consequences for the polity.[28] The demise of the rehabilitative justification, and the rise of retribution can be interpreted as a measure of return, albeit in a modern context, to a dual system of law, and what I have posited as a dual polity in which different citizens are punished differently and relegated to different political statuses.

Federal or state abolition of permanent felon disenfranchisement laws would entail reviving and overhauling the rehabilitative tradition in order to convincingly reintegrate convicted felons into society. A significant part of this effort would imply a democratic conversation, rather than just a dialogue between criminologists, about the broader goals of criminal justice policy, which would take into account the conditions that precipitated the "liberal reaction to the excesses of the therapeutic state." Such a democratic conversation would put the problem of the exclusion of ex-felons from the polity at center stage, since to be maximally effective in terms of its pedagogical and therefore policy potential, that conversation would have to include ex-felons who wished to participate. As we saw in Chapter Two, the *telos* of the moral conception of democracy developed by John Dewey, idealized by the Emersonians, and developed as democratic individuality by George Kateb is to maximize the potential of both individual citizens and society as a whole to learn. The ongoing experience of (personal and political) learning is expressed as good public policy enacted by elected representatives. Insofar as citizens are criminalized, incarcerated, and disenfranchised, and accounts of state punishment de-emphasize rehabilitation and reintegration in favor of retribution or incapacitation,[29] democratic learning would appear to be compromised.

We will now review how the reformative account of punishment was justified and operationalized in the early American polity.

2. THE MORAL, OR REFORMING JUSTIFICATION OF PUNISHMENT

> *"A strange thing our punishment! It does not cleanse the criminal, it is no atonement; on the contrary, it pollutes worse than the crime does."*
>
> *Nietzsche[30]*

Who does it pollute? Although clearly Nietzsche disagreed with both of them, thinkers as far apart in historical and political time as Plato and Dr. Benjamin Rush[31] believed that punishment could reform the soul of the individual criminal, make him or her a better person. The genesis of this reformative lineage is each thinker's vision of an ideal society, one whose values were divinely inscribed, and were perceived by and had to be imposed by an enlightened elite or legislator for that ideal to become reality. Both Plato and Rush believed that virtue, a requisite of the ideal individual, as well as a collective ideal, could be instilled in the deviant citizen by means of pedagogical punishment.[32] "I should wish the citizens to be as readily persuaded to virtue as possible; this will surely be the aim of the legislator in all his laws" says the Athenian in Book IV of the *Laws*.[33] Rush believed that through medical practice "it is possible to produce such a change in [man's] moral character, as shall raise him to a resemblance of angels; nay more to the likeness of GOD himself."[34] Plato recommended both corporal punishment (whippings and branding) and prison, to promote improvement, and Rush believed that the penitentiary, a site where social alchemists such as could transform devils into angels, was the ultimate (supposedly non-violent) medical, psychological, and social institution.[35]

Thomas Dumm (1987) interprets the reform/penitentiary movement as an institutionalized effort to produce the conformist liberal subject.[36] The central argument of *Democracy and Punishment: Disciplinary Origins of the United States*, which is a genealogical study of the Pennsylvania system, is that the liberal democratic state must be repressive in order to constitute the self-controlled (as opposed to other-controlled in a feudal or hierarchical order) liberal democratic individual.

> Inside the walls of the penitentiary, the absence of freedom had the ironic effect of establishing the conditions necessary for the reconciliation of liberal and democratic assumptions about the behavior of men. The penitentiary was already liberal and was to become democratic. It was liberal because the entire force of its operations was designed to reconstruct the psychology of individual persons. It was to be democratic because the same operations applied to each individual. All were to be made into republican machines through the use of the same technique. And that technique was derived from Rush's work...which concerned the mechanics of moral health." (95)

Dumm's argument echoes Alexis de Tocqueville's premonition about the dark side of democracy, and the dialectical connection between the penitentiary and the democratic despotism alluded to in both *The Penitentiary System in the United States* and Book II of *Democracy in America*.[37]

> It must be acknowledged that the penitentiary system in America is severe. While society in the United States gives the example of the most extended liberty, the prisons of the same country offer the spectacle of the most complete despotism. (Beaumont and Tocqueville 1883)

My argument that the United States is a double polity, comprised of American fully enfranchised citizens with two identities, one "despotic" in that they rule over the disenfranchised, and the other democratic, in that they co-rule the polity, restates Tocqueville's contrast of American democratic freedom and the despotism of the penitentiary in theoretical terms.

The reformative justification of punishment, which critics deemed paternalistic and racist, remained the dominant institutional account in the United States until the early 1970s, when neo-liberal retributive accounts based on just deserts, the philosophical analog of law-and-order politics, supplanted it. Pressure from both the right and the left forced the retreat of the reformative justification, with the left (ironically the Quakers, who had presided at the birth of the penitentiary) challenging the justice of the American tradition of mixing treatment with coercion.[38] Reformers from the left suggested short, determinate sentences that were not subject to discretion during any part of the process. The right, on the other hand, whose position was articulated by criminologists such as James Q. Wilson and Robert Martinson, claimed that the function of the corrections system should be to isolate and punish.[39] Because "nothing works," criminals should receive long determinate sentences so at least law-abiding citizens were protected from their predations. Conservative discourse won decisively with the Reagan Administration, and in terms of penal policy, has been hegemonic ever since, hence the synthetic justification of incapacitation and retribution we have today, which results in the highest incarceration rate in the "free world."[40] The replacement of an official commitment to reform with retributive and incapacitation justifications has serious social consequences, as Lin (2000) argues, since the vast majority of (unrehabilitated) convicted felons are released into the community, subsequently exhibiting high rates of recidivism. Absent a serious effort on the part of the entire criminal justice continuum to provide prisoners with the wherewithal of citizenship while in prison, the claim that nothing works becomes a self-fulfilling prophecy and the lineaments of the double polity only become further entrenched.

The following section is divided into two parts. The first reviews the several different theorists' definitions of the concept of crime, which according to Rusche and Kirschheimer (1939), must be disarticulated from punishment.

> The bond, transparent or not, that is supposed to exist between crime and punishment prevents any insight into the independent significance of the history of penal systems. *It must be broken.* Punishment is neither a simple consequence of crime, nor the reverse side of crime, nor a mere means which is determined by the end to be achieved. Punishment must be understood as a social phenomenon freed from both its juristic concept and its social ends. We do not deny that punishment has specific ends, but we do deny that it can be understood from its ends alone. (p. 5; Italics added)[41]

I hope in this first section to show how this disarticulation facilitates the use of crime as an ideological tool that can be used to punish individuals more harshly for crimes by virtue of their membership of a negative status group. The second section glances briefly at the under-theorized concept of impunity, defined in the OED as "exemption from punishment or penalty,"[42] an exemption touched on in the discussion of Reconstruction Era violence in Chapter Two. Impunity is relevant to this study of felon disenfranchisement because, as we saw in the previous chapter, although white citizens break the drug laws at equal or higher rates than black citizens, their objective rate of criminalization indicates that many are exempt from punishment or penalty. This impunity, as I claimed, obviates the moral justification adduced by judges for felon disenfranchisement, which in a polity where the law was enforced impartially, would have a more compelling claim to legitimacy.

3. THE CONCEPT OF "CRIME"

From a positivist perspective "crime" is defined by the state, which circumscribes its definitions in penal laws that classify crimes as felonies and misdemeanors. Wilson and Herrnstein (1985, 22) define a crime as "any act committed in violation of a law that prohibits it and authorizes punishment for its commission."

Emile Durkheim's (1893; 1984, 39) approach to the question of crime is more functionalist and sociological: "an act is criminal when it offends the strong, well-defined states of the collective consciousness." Durkheim defines the collective consciousness as "the totality of beliefs and sentiments common to the average members of a society." These form "a determinate system with a life of its own." The collective consciousness is "the entire social consciousness, that is co-terminous with the psychological life of society, whereas, particularly in the higher societies, it constitutes only a very limited part of it." Judicial, governmental, scientific or industrial functions appertain to the psychological order, but "they clearly lie outside the common consciousness." "What characterizes a crime is that it determines the punishment. Thus if our own definition of crime is exact it must account for all the characteristics of punishment" (44). Punishment is a function of consciousness, not of the objective criminality of an act. Crime is "conduct which, if duly shown to have taken place, will incur a formal and solemn pronouncement of the moral condemnation of the community" (Tunick 1992, 90).

As we have seen, Hegel defined crime as an infringement of Right, which is grounded in natural equality.[43] Jeffrey Reiman (1990, 193) explains how Hegel's notion of "crime" depends upon a pre-existing political relationship: "[R]ight is a certain equal relationship of sovereign authority between the wills of individuals. Crime disrupts that relationship by placing one will above others..." Hegel explicitly denied that the state was a contract, though, and allowed that an act or a practice, including slavery, could be criminal—in that it was an infringement of Right—even if it was not negatively sanctioned by positive law, or in fact officially sanctioned.

However, according to theorists in the social contract tradition (Hobbes,[44] Locke,[45] Kant, and Beccaria), a crime is an intentional breach of the social contract by a member of the contract who thereby harms society (Beccaria 1764, 1995, 24).[46] The key institutional point is that the criminal must be a member of society, a well-informed signatory of the contract in order to be punished as an equal. There is no discussion that I am aware of in classic social contract theory of extra-contractual violations that are defined as crime. By this I mean that there is no civil equivalence between contractual insiders and outsiders (those who are not political equals) as there is between contractual insiders *tout cort.* The concept of crime committed by contractual insiders on outsiders is incoherent. This is why contract theory cannot, strictly speaking account for the crimes of slavery discussed in the previous section as theoretically although not positivistically amenable to retributive justice.

From the perspective of contract theory, crime is a category that applies only to insiders—it is a political act, which is why Kant (1991, 154) defines it as "an infringement of public law that renders the guilty person incapable of citizenship." So a crime is not simply an individual moral mistake within the context of a lifetime that may perhaps be adjudged as good, but an act that is helplessly perpetrated in the context of a (collective) political relationship. The people who are in relationship are citizens: equally autonomous "Members of the Society" who have given up their "joynt power" to "that Person or Assembly" (…) "Their Power in the utmost Bounds of it, is *limited to the publick good* of the Society. It is a Power, that hath no other end but preservation, and therefore can never have a right to destroy, enslave, or designedly to impoverish the Subjects."[47] Thus although under the terms of the contract equal citizens cannot impoverish or enslave one another, there is no prohibition on enslaving those outside the contract, and their enslavement or impoverishment does not count as crime.[48]

Each definition of crime given above implies a continuum of political moments: first is the moment of the constitution of the state between naturally equal individuals who are then designated citizens. Second is the moment when those citizens designate a representative or representatives who formulate the laws, including a penal code that defines society's expectations, and third is the moment when the law is transgressed by one or more citizens. This is followed by the moment of punishment. In the context of that continuum, the transgression that is called crime generates the legitimate right of the modern state to punish its citizens. An immanent critique of the practice of punishment from the political theory perspective can enter the continuum of the definition of crime at any of those moments. In other words, it can interrogate the constitution of the state and/or the designation of citizen and/or the subsequent representativeness of the sovereign who creates and administers the penal law.

All the above definitions of crime assume the horizon of a community or consensual collective consciousness against which transgressions clearly appear as crime. This assumption can be problematized theoretically, by disaggregating the continuum of moments implied by the production of the category of crime, as well as empirically, by demonstrating how definitions of crime vary according to the exigencies of particular historical conjunctures.[49] The interrogation of the function of representation in determining the political use of the category of crime may disaggregate the fairness of the procedures whereby representatives are chosen, and/or the procedures whereby, once chosen, representatives formulate and enforce penal laws. The latter interrogation reaches all the way down into the debates about deliberative democracy, the education of citizens, the availability of information, and the vitality of "civil society." This is well-trod ground that will not be explored in this book.[50]

The definitions of crime formulated by the elected representatives of state polities, and the way in which the criminal law is enforced through punishment reinforces the political identity (collective consciousness) of the original citizen body whose genesis was the original exclusionary constitution (and subsequent post-bellum refounding) of the American state. Were that not the case, counterfactually speaking, there would be no patterns of racial disparity in arrest, incarceration and disenfranchisement rates. Justice Harlan's claim in his *Plessy* dissent that "In view of the constitution, in the eye of the law, there is in this country no superior, dominant, ruling class of citizens,"[51] would be vindicated. The empty set, so to speak, of my argument is that the criminals who are excluded and disenfranchised today are a different species of citizen who are more inclined to criminality than those who are not excluded.[52] Should it be the case that criminals are a different species of citizens unfit for political rights, democratic theorists would need to direct their attention to a different anthropology of citizenship than that assumed today. Were like crimes actually punished alike, such that the criminal justice system was effectively color blind, one could hypothesize that the cycle of reinforcement of political identity produced by crime had been interrupted, and perhaps even refounded.

4. CRIME, JUSTICE, AND IMPUNITY

The review of two of the classical moral justifications of criminal punishment in Section 2 suggests that the patterns of penal sanctions that describe the contemporary American criminal justice system and constitute the front end of the continuum that terminates in disenfranchisement, fail the normative test of just "punishment," since they are neither consistently retributive nor consistently reformative. Rehabilitation has been explicitly discarded as a penological justification; most observers agree that the other traditional justification of punishment—deterrence—has no value in the drug war, and question the utility of pursuing an expensive and failing policy. (Bertram et al. 1996) Since, strictly speaking, the retributive account of punishment requires that all harms be punished so that the social and moral equilibrium disturbed by the offenses be restored, the requirements of the classical retributive account are not met. Deontologically speaking, therefore, policies that punish the same crime differently cannot be considered just, and justice is not done, even when an actual crime is properly punished, if the same or other crimes are left unpunished, elsewhere in the polity.

In fact, the failure to punish universally according to the retributive mandate is a structural feature of the double polity, a requirement of the Racial Contract, to be discussed in the following section. If, in the perfect retributive universe, the victims of slavery were given authority over the criminals (the slave traders, holders, and profiteers of slavery) comparable to the authority over the victim that the criminal arrogated to himself, justice would indeed be served. But it was not until 2001 that American slavery was formally defined in a United Nations document as a crime,[53] at an international meeting boycotted by the United States in part because its leadership did not want to endorse a call for reparations. To be seen to endorse such a call would add fuel to the nascent reparations movement in this country, which is political anathema to dominant political elites because reparations are seen as antithetical to white interests.[54] I would dare to say that a fully inclusive debate on reparations, along the lines suggested by proponents of deliberative democracy, would reveal that reparations—in whatever form might be ultimately decided upon—would not be as antithetical to white interests as might appear at first glance. This intuition is based on the observations of colonial and postcolonial theorists that colonialism (and slavery) and the intergenerational effects that flow from both institutions damage not only the victim, but the perpetrator as well, albeit in dramatically different ways.[55]

Postcolonial theory refers to the longevity of the original colonial relation because its unrepaired legacy continues to negatively impact the descendants of both the denizens of the periphery and the citizens of the metropolis. When both sets of persons are simultaneously integrated into one polity as citizens, then the polity as a whole suffers from the unexcavated or unacknowledged legacies set in motion by the original relation of domination. Hence repairing, or *re-pairing*, the colonial legacy is in the interests of all citizens, not just the descendants of the formerly colonized. From a Hegelian perspective, it honors the descendants of the former colonizers. In contemporary jargon, reparations are not a zero-sum game when approached from a normative perspective.

My reading of the theory of retributive justice suggests that the source of the contemporary distortions in the American justice system, produced by disparate enforcement policies and revealed in demographically skewed arrest and incarceration policies, is the national failure to account for the crime of slavery. Although this claim is a positivist oxymoron, it is not a normative one. The root of the systemic distortion is the collective American impunity for slavery, and I say "collective" because democracy implies collective accountability. The democratically sanctioned criminal justice system, as well as the mass media, continue to blame the victim of the racial contract, rather than to rewrite the contract in terms of its original normative ideals. Such a revision of the contract would generate different political, moral, and epistemological norms based on the meta-norms of equality and universal consent, rather than on group domination and impunity.[56]

This normative claim does not obviate the fact that in most cases minority citizens who are processed through the criminal justice system have broken the law and should therefore be subject to formal sanctions. The point, though, as we saw in Chapter Four, is that the majority of their white counterparts who have broken the same law are not processed through the criminal justice system. It is their impunity that allows the system of criminalization and disenfranchisement to reproduce itself. Their relative impunity suggests that the law was not written, or the prisons not built, for them.[57] George Jackson, writing from prison, makes this point:

> I thought most blacks, especially those of our economic level, understood vaguely at least, that these places were built with us in mind, just as were the project houses, unemployment offices, and bible schools.[58]

Until the contemporary democratic citizens of the United States take responsibility for the criminal past perpetrated by the antecedent citizens of their nation, they are granting themselves, and the nation itself, impunity for crimes committed against "persons," whether "slaves" or not.[59] Impunity is the inverse of absolute civic accountability for transgressions of the contract, which according to the neo-contractarian justification of felon disenfranchisement warrants forfeiture of property and political rights. Ongoing citizen consent to the terms of the racial contract signifies that the historical system of white supremacy that legitimized and profited from human slavery with impunity can continue to function with impunity. Uninterrupted by the discourse of justice, impunity has a cancerous effect on institutions, which, as we saw in the review of the concept of path dependence in Chapter Two, continue to function inefficiently or dysfunctionally so long as they produce increasing returns for their beneficiaries. In terms of the bottom line of the racial contract, these are the "wages of whiteness."[60]

5. THE RACIAL CONTRACT

Philosopher Charles Mills, building on Rousseau's class critique of the social contract in *Discourse on the Origins of Inequality* and on Carole Pateman's feminist critique in *The Sexual Contract,* developed a theory of the racial contract. The purpose of this descriptive and normative tool is to decode the historical and contemporary operation of white supremacy in the modern polity. Mills distinguishes his approach from Rawls, and uses the concept of contract "not merely normatively, to generate judgments about social justice and injustice, but descriptively, to explain the actual genesis of society and the state, the way society is structured, the way government functions, and people's moral psychology" (1997, 5). A central explanatory "fact" Mills highlights is what he calls "the reality of group domination," in contrast to the focus on individual consent, which operates normatively in the classic contract.[61] The argument is that although the classic contract is normative and based on the ideal of universal consent, whites as a group formulated and consented to an actual racial contract, leaving the dominated (non-white) group outside the contract. The purpose of this bifurcation of the (legitimating) ideal contract into a legalized inside and outside was to prevent white exploitation of black labor (slavery/colonialism) from being construed as an offense (as it would be under the terms of the ideal contract). The system of white supremacy the racial contract creates is made normative by the fiction of universal consent of those inside to the domination of those outside.

Mills' theory draws explicitly on the work of Herbert Blumer, who argued that racism should be understood not as "a set of feelings" but as a "sense of group position" in which the dominant race is convinced of its superiority, sees the subordinate race as "intrinsically different and alien." The dominant group has proprietary feelings about its "privilege and advantage," and fears encroachment on these prerogatives.[62] From this perspective, Mills claims that "race and white supremacy are therefore seen primarily as a system of advantage and disadvantage but only secondarily as a set of ideas and values. The individualist ontology is displaced or at least supplemented by a social ontology in which races are significant socio-political actors."[63] This social ontology creates a "racial self" whose identity is constituted by relations of group domination and privilege. For my purposes, in the context of a discussion of state punishment and felon disenfranchisement, that identity is a dimension of the status of citizenship, which both passively reflects and actively determines the allocation of rights and privileges in the polity.

The theoretical counterpoint of the racial contract is the inclusionary imperative of democratic individuality outlined in Chapter Two, which, because it is based on recognition of universal equality, serves the purpose of individual and collective learning and moral development. By contrast, the racial contract, which is based on a politics of domination of groups outside the contract by those inside and an ethics of superiority based on group position, mutilates the polity and results in individual and collective ignorance.[64] I have argued in previous chapters that the practice of permanent ex-felon disenfranchisement institutionalizes that segmentation of the polity into honored and dishonored status groups, and therefore precludes the collective learning essential to the formulation of good public policy.

Herrenvolk ethics are inscribed geographically, in the spaces that are normed by the racial contract. The original spaces are the "wild," "savage" untamed areas inhabited by those subpersons who are in the "state of nature," who must be supervised and governed by the civilized, those who have exited from the state of nature and granted themselves civil and political rights.

> Part of the purpose of the color bar/color line/apartheid/jim crow is to maintain these spaces in their place, to have the checkerboard of vice and virtue, light and dark space, ours and theirs clearly demarcated so that the human geography prescribed by the racial contract can be preserved. For here the moral topography is different and the civilizing mission as yet incomplete. (*ibid.* 47-48)

In the contemporary American polity, which has constitutionally abolished the color line and jim crow, the cartography of vice and virtue is symbolized by (although clearly not perfectly coextensive with) the inner cities and the suburbs,[65] and the (predominantly) black prisons and the white rural counties that host them. In terms of symbolic space, that cartography is represented by the metropolis (of enfranchised citizens) and the periphery (of disenfranchised felons.) The cartography of vice and virtue is encoded in the statistics tracking "minority" and white drug use, arrest and incarceration rates, and numbers of felons who are disenfranchised because they are considered morally unworthy of full citizenship.

Mills' analysis of the racial contract's norming of space and identity corroborates my argument that contemporary American felon disenfranchisement practices create a double polity of enfranchised and disenfranchised citizens. In that the enfranchised enjoy all the rights of citizenship, they are members of a democratic nation-state that bases its legitimacy on the rights of its citizens to elect their representatives. In that the disenfranchised are deprived of political rights, they are members of a (symbolic, rather than territorial) polity that is ruled, governed, by the representatives of the enfranchised. The racial contract can be used to explain the double citizenship identity of the rulers, and their awareness or lack thereof of that identity, and whether or not it matters to them that a number of their fellow citizens are not their political equals, but their subjects.

Furthermore, since the specific context of the criminal justice system and felon disenfranchisement explicitly frames crime and punishment as individual and moral issues, or issues of public safety, the disciplinary (and racist) dimensions of the system are all but invisible to those who are not subject to it.[66] However, when the racial demographics of arrest, incarceration, and felon disenfranchisement are mapped against the racial demographics of drug use and specific drug crimes, the spatialized coordinates generate a picture of inter-group political conflict that obviates judicial and political claims of individual immorality and unworthiness. The epistemological dimension of the racial contract blocks individual citizens' awareness of what I call their double identity. The cognitive handicap that "usually comes with social privilege" obscures the fact that they are simultaneously democratic citizens— insofar as their relationship with their fellow non-convicted citizens is concerned—and despots—insofar as their relationship with their fellow convicted citizens is concerned. They do not necessarily see their double identity because, as Mills says

> The requirements of "objective" cognition, factual and moral, in a racial polity are in a sense more demanding in that officially sanctioned reality is divergent from actual reality. So here, it could be said, one has an agreement to *mis*interpret the world.

One has to learn to see the world wrongly, but with the assurance that this set of mistaken perceptions will be validated by white epistemic authority, whether religious or secular. (1997, 18)

Under the racial contract, the identity of democratic citizen is subjectively available to (non-convicted) Americans who (actively or tacitly) support policies of law and order that currently incarcerate over two million of their fellow citizens, and the (cumulative) disenfranchisement of over four million on any one national Election Day.

In the context of this book, whose subject is contemporary felon disenfranchisement, the notion that can be rethought in terms of the racial contract is punishment, the apparently innocent practice that accounts for the incarceration policies under investigation. By definition, state punishment in a liberal-democratic polity is neutral and legitimate,[67] yet the demographics of the inmate populations in the U.S. disrupt the formal requirements of universality and justice built into the modern concept of punishment, rendering the policies that produce those inmate populations illegitimate. Those demographics also challenge the self-understanding of the polity as liberal-democratic, and challenge theorists to identify the regime they configure.

6. A POSTCOLONIAL PERSPECTIVE ON THE AMERICAN PUNISHMENT POLITY

Mills' interpretation of the classic social contract can be described as a form of what is called postcolonial critique.[68] As useful as the concept of the racial contract is for my argument, Mills' works are self-consciously written as political philosophy, and my concern in this book is to do nuts-and-bolts empirical political theory. I want to use the contemporary American practice of felon disenfranchisement to classify and name the citizenship regime represented by the U.S. While Mills' work takes me very far in my criticism of contemporary liberal and communitarian justifications of the regime, it does not help me name the double polity I have mapped.[69] Postcolonial critique, by taking the original colonial polity as its starting point, explicitly acknowledges that history— as told by those at the margins, as well as those at the center— is the DNA of the (damaged) citizen identity of the modern nation-state. The history of the colonial polity, a double helix of freedom and oppression, engenders the contemporary political identities of citizenship, including the negative identity of the disenfranchised felon.

According to postcolonial critique, the facts of racial profiling, mandatory minimum sentencing that results in the over-incarceration of minorities, and the permanent disenfranchisement of more than one-third of the adult black male population in some states,[70] are not contemporary anomalies or epiphenomena. They represent parts of the shadow self the nation has been dragging for centuries; its legally inscribed yet unexcavated identity whose narrative has been repressed and segregated by the celebratory narrative of the (ethnocentric) center:

> The 'epistemological limits' of those ethnocentric ideas, are also the enunciative boundaries of a range of other dissonant, even dissident histories and voices—women, the colonized, minority groups, the bearers of policed sexualities. For the demography of the new internationalism is the history of postcolonial migration, the narratives of cultural and political diaspora, the major social displacements of peasant and aboriginal communities, the poetics of exile, the grim prose of political and economic refugees. (Bhahba 1994, 5)

The postcolonial interpretation traces the roots of the contemporary problem under consideration (racialized incarceration and disenfranchisement) to (at least) three co-constitutive ideas and practices that emerged in the seventeenth century: the nation-state (Anderson 1983, Poole 1999), imperialism (including the slave trade),[71] and liberal thought. To take a postcolonial perspective is to locate the contemporary American incarceration and disenfranchisement crisis as yet another coordinate in the plane of the shadow history that tracks the national narrative from the negative quadrant of political space. The received national narrative that tracks it from the positive quadrant celebrates the progressive democratization of the polity. It hails the gradual extension of rights to the excluded, through the American Revolution, Jacksonian democracy, the Civil War, and the Civil Rights Movement; it is textualized in the Declaration of Independence, the Constitution and its Amendments, and contemporary colorblind Supreme Court jurisprudence.

The (postcolonial) shadow history begins (arguably—this is a relatively arbitrary starting point) with the European colonization of the Americas, and meticulously documents the genocide and colonization of Native Americans.[72] It comprehends the transcontinental trade in African people, the constitutional codification of plantation slavery in the antebellum South, and the Fugitive Slave Laws in the North. It connects the violence and failure of the First Reconstruction,[73] the jim crow era and lynching,[74] the massive Black diaspora to what became the Northern ghettoes, the violence and eventual failure of the Second Reconstruction, and the international drug trade, which has wreaked social havoc on the American inner cities.[75] When a situation such as the incarceration crisis "forces us to rethink the profound limitations of a consensual and collusive 'liberal' sense of cultural community," (Bhabha 1994, 175) the postcolonial perspective offers the tools of the "bricoleur" (Spivak 1988). These allow us to formulate a more useful and comprehensible response than that articulated by the moral and disciplinary opacity of the individually oriented practice of punishment.

Post-colonial is a hybrid word that denotes an altered structure of the contemporary world state system, not necessarily altered national values on the part of the former colonial powers.

> [Post-colonial] refers to a general process of decolonization which, like colonization itself, has marked the colonizing societies as powerfully as it has the colonized (of course in different ways). Hence the subverting of the old colonizing/ colonized binary in the new conjuncture. Indeed one of the principle values of the term post-colonial has been to direct our attention to the many ways in which colonization was never simply external to the societies of the imperial metropolis. It was always inscribed deeply within them—as it became indelibly inscribed in the cultures of the colonized. (Hall 1996, 246)

Racism is the key colonial "value," as Albert Memni (1991) noted in his celebrated analysis of colonialism:

> Racism appears... not as an incidental detail, but as a consubstantial part of colonialism. It is the highest expression of the colonial system and one of the most significant features of the colonialist. Not only does it establish a fundamental dis-crimination between colonizer and colonized, a *sine qua non* of colonial life, but it also lays the foundation for the immutability of this life. (74)

The post-colonial state system forces the former colonial powers to structurally internalize the racism they were previously able to externalize in their empires. Moreover, because liberal and democratic values determine the citizenship regimes in the U.S., as in most European countries, the structural internalization finds its ultimate institutional expression in the apparently *a*political, rights-protecting criminal justice system, in the prison, which I interpret as an anchoring institution of the periphery. The United States, originally a slave society whose plantations can be represented as miniature internal colonies, attempted to solve its race problem via external colonization of former slaves and freedmen during several epochs of its history but, being unsuccessful,[76] was forced to institutionalize legal forms of (ostensibly apolitical) domestic repression. The fact that former slaves and their descendants were the primary victims of convict labor systems, and several generations beyond slavery are still over-represented in American prisons and jails, suggests that the racist impulse to colonize, albeit internally, persists. Likewise, contemporary European (as well as British, Canadian, Australian and New Zealand) incarceration rates reflect a "chickens coming home to roost" syndrome of former colonial, or indigenous, subjects settling in the motherland and being over-represented, population-wise, in prisons and jails.

> The race relations that are put into place during colonialism survive long after many of the economic structures underlying them have changed. The devaluation of African slaves still haunts their descendants in metropolitan societies, the inequities of colonial rule still structure wages and opportunities for migrants from once colonized countries or communities, the racial stereotypes...still circulate, and contemporary global imbalances are built upon those inequities that were consolidated during the colonial era. A complex amalgam of economic and racial factors operates in anchoring the present to the colonial past." (Loomba 1998, p.129)

Because the present public policy of incarcerating non-violent drug felons is legitimized by a self-identified liberal democratic regime, the moral opprobrium that is built into the classical notion of punishment can be successfully conferred by the criminal justice system onto a specified caste of people, an "underclass." Their forced removal from the larger polity of free and equal citizens, and their return to the polity as lower-status disenfranchised citizens, is thereby legitimized as punishment, for individual transgressions of the law. By identifying the U.S. as a postcolonial regime, however, the criminal justice policies implemented under the auspices of the war on drugs appear not as punishment, but as repression. Furthermore, one analytical requirement of the concept of colonialism is that the periphery produce a raw material that benefits the metropolis. In the neo-colonial American polity this requirement is met by the production of symbolic, rather than material goods (Bourdieu 1988). By selecting and removing all convicted felons into the periphery, what the criminal justice system produces for U.S. citizens who comprise the metropolis, is their freedom, one of the essential attributes of the identity of citizenship.

7. THE COLONIAL IDENTITY AND RACIALIZED SPACE

Political agency, as we saw in the discussion of the racial contract, is related to spatial position, and we can identify sites of freedom and sites of domination—where the dominators act as free members of the polity, and the dominated as outcasts in the neocolonial polity. This spatial analysis reduces in fact to the coordinates polis/prison; suburb/gated community/ghetto, and in a colonial analysis, to the terms metropolis and periphery. Analyzing the spatial configuration reveals the "ever-shifting social geometry of power and signification in which the material and ideological are co-constitutive. This is by no means a settled notion of space, but rather a troubled social/spatial dynamic" (Jacobs 1996). In the context of a "modernity [that] is inherently globalizing," (Giddens 1990) the contemporary consolidation in the United States of the eminently *local* (eighteenth century) institution of the penitentiary, along with other (medieval) punishments such as civil death and forfeiture, appears paradoxical. Giddens follows his declaration by acknowledging the dialectical nature of the process in that "[l]ocal transformation is as much a part of globalization as the lateral extension of social connections across time and space." Herein lies a clue to the apparent paradox. While globalization theorists intone the demise of the sovereign nation state, the legislative organs of that very same entity (federal and sub-federal) are strengthening and committing ever more resources to local institutions whose function is to concentrate and punish citizens.

Also, Michael Watts (1991:10) proposes that globalization "does not signal the erasure of difference, but rather the reconstitution and revalidation of 'place, locality, and difference.' (…) Imperialism in whatever form, is a global process—it occurs across regions and nations—but even in its most marauding forms it necessarily takes hold in and through the local. The embeddedness of imperialist ideologies and practices is not simply an issue of society or culture, but also, fundamentally of place… It is precisely in the local that it is possible to see how the past, including imperial and pre-imperial pasts, inheres in place. This is not an archaic residue, but an active and influential occupation."[77] As I argued in the previous chapters, the offices of local criminal justice officials are key coordinates in the continuum of moments that results in the disenfranchisement of so many minority American citizens for drug crimes, and drug trafficking itself represents a quintessential instance of globalization.[78]

Giddens suggests that "The undue reliance which sociologists have placed upon the idea of society where this means a bounded system, should be replaced by a starting point that concentrates upon analyzing how social life is ordered across time and space—the problem of time-space distanciation." I shall use this as a preliminary analytic framework because I expect it to be theoretically more fruitful than the simple claim that contemporary U.S. criminal justice policy is a product of an overtly racist nation-building process that reproduces categories of domination/subordination that have obtained since the Founding. Instead, I shall analyze the policy as a product of "colonial time" rather than linear, historical time. The central claim is that the colonialism that constituted the genesis of what is now the United States is perennial and endemic, given certain conditions or the lack thereof, in even the formally modern post-colonial constitutional democracy. The historical period of colonialism, which can be clearly marked off in chronological time (ending for the U.S. as a colony in 1776), set the stage for the period of post-coloniality, in which the U.S. can be identified as a neo-colonial power.[79] "In postcoloniality, every metropolitan definition is dislodged. The general mode for the postcolonial is citation, reinscription, rerouting the historical" (Spivak 1993, 217).

Furthermore, I interrogate the place pole in Giddens' framework of time-space distanciation, redefining the historical and contemporary American metropolis in terms of the spaces occupied by captured Africans on the lower decks of slave ships making the Middle Passage, spaces mirrored by the almost identically sized cells in modern penitentiaries. Another space to be interrogated is that bounded by the lines of tension, the songlines[80] that stretch between the inner cities, the rural prisons, and the international arena that is the setting for the global financial system and the drug trade. As Radhika Mohanram (1999: 200-201) says, "Place is of tremendous importance within postcolonial discourse... Colonialism was about the seizing of place, draining it of its resources, its history, and the meaning attributed to it by its primary occupants. The centrality of place is made visible in postcolonial discourse by its interrogation of the meaning of locations, the excess or lack of resources in these locations, the equitable sharing and withholding of resources."

The contemporary criminal justice system gives the inner cities and the prisons pride of place in the periphery that institutionalizes the disenfranchised identity. If, as I hope, I have established that the primary function of the contemporary racialized prison is not to punish, in the classical sense, then a postcolonial critique may provide a key to its true function. Foucault's answer that the prison's function is "to discipline" begs the question, because liberal citizens do not discipline (in the Foucauldian sense of the term) their co-citizens who are free and equal members of the same polity.[81] Therefore, if the function of contemporary prisons is indeed to discipline, then the objects of that discipline must not be free and equal co-citizens. In the Foucauldian interpretation, discipline engenders a subordinate polity of unfree and unequal subjects whose function as denizens of the periphery is the traditional function of all colonized subjects, to augment the power of the metropolis and to generate commodities. The American prisons, which control and incapacitate (Zimring and Hawkins 1995) people who are considered social surplus, produce goods in the symbolic economy (Bourdieu 1998), namely the freedom and honor enjoyed by citizens who can live their own individual private lives unencumbered by substantial concern for the so-called underclass.

The challenge is to account for the reproduction, the longevity, of the colonial relation I am asserting, when a nation-state such as the U.S. is formally post-colonial and considered a legally unitary[82] nation-state from the perspective of international relations.[83] A plausible account can be derived from the ongoing nature of the moral relations between the members of the metropolis and the periphery. Colonial domination, as Edward Said (1978) pointed out in *Orientalism*, relies on the construction of an inferior Other "against which flattering and legitimating images of the metropolitan Self were defined." Although no formal legal category of "Other" (except perhaps *il*legal "aliens") can be posited in the contemporary American polity, the informally structured Othering of African-Americans by whites has been established by historical, anecdotal, and empirical study.[84] The problem, though, is that because this Manichean binary, as it is called in postcolonial theory, is a fiction, it is inherently unstable, always challenged by the Other, always potentially overturned. Hence the institutional requirement of actual violence and coercion on the part of the colonizer that reflects the symbolic binary:

> The colonial world is cut in two. The dividing line, the frontiers are shown by barracks and police stations. In the colonies it is the policeman and the soldier who are the official, instituted go-betweens, the spokesmen of the settler and his rule of oppression...In the colonial countries, the policeman and soldier, by their immediate presence and their frequent and direct action maintain contact with the native and advise him by means of rifle butts and napalm not to budge. It is obvious here that the agents of government speak the language of pure force.[85]

Jacobs attributes the "vitality of such binary concepts" to "their being anxiously reinscribed in the face of their contested or uncontainable certainty."

> It is, in part, this anxious vitality that gives racialized categorizations elaborated under colonialism such a long life and

allows them to remain cogent features even of those contemporary societies that are formally 'beyond' colonialism. (3)

The epistemological foreshortening or damage created by the racial contract described by Mills accounts for the anxiety Jacobs notes in the metropolitan Self, anxiety that is not assuaged by an ever more draconian criminal justice system whose inmates themselves are perennially existentially insecure.[86] Moreover, since one dimension of the inter-citizen (ongoing moral) relation between the "races" in the contemporary U.S. is constituted by the unretributed crimes of slavery and segregation perpetrated by a historically prior group of citizens, I have claimed that the criminal justice system is itself normatively unstable. The culturally constructed category of the Other has been applied to African-Americans (as well as other minorities, of course) throughout the national narrative. Just because the naming of insuperable difference is a dialectical and contextual activity, though, does not mean that the protean nature of the hegemonic relation is in any way obviated.

This is another way of articulating Rogers Smith's (1997) thesis about the longevity of ascriptive identities in an apparently liberal-republican ideological (multiple traditions) framework.

Defenders of ascriptive inegalitarian arrangements will not lack for arguments recognized as intellectually respectable and principled; they will have opportunities to design new systems of ascriptive inequality recapturing some desired features of older ones, such as overall white supremacy. Indeed, the very success of liberalizing and democratizing reforms is likely to unsettle many, creating constituencies for rebuilding ascriptive inequalities in new forms. (9)

Smith's argument is predicated on what he implies is citizens' "natural" desire for "peoplehood," which produces political discourses and institutions to stabilize those unsettled identities. Citizenship laws are formal responses crafted by political elites to meet two basic political imperatives: first, aspirants to power require a population to lead that imagines itself to be a "people," so this population must be formally defined.[87] Second, they need a people that imagines itself in ways that make leadership by those aspirants appropriate. These needs drive political leaders to offer civic ideologies, or myths of civic identity, that foster the requisite sense of peoplehood, and to support citizenship laws that express those ideologies symbolically while legally incorporating and empowering the leaders' likely constituents... Most liberal democratic positions are, however, less effective than ascriptive views of civic identity in fostering beliefs that a certain group is a distinctive and especially worthy "people."

Although Smith doesn't use the language of psychoanalysis like the postcolonial theorists such as Bhahba (1994), he still is speaking about needs, drive, and identity. It is not clear if these are ontological, core, human desires, and Smith does not provide the theoretical framework defining them: he elides that issue by calling such desires political. He cites the protection that citizenship brings, and the fact that citizenship laws constitute a collective civic identity. "They proclaim the existence of a political "people" and designate who those persons are as a people, in ways that often become integral to individuals' sense of personal identity as well" (31). If force is not to be used to directly constitute a people, political leaders need compelling stories to convince their constituents. In other words, ascriptive identity is a silent partner of competitive democracy in a racialized state.

As Said (1993, 332) emphasizes, processes of social construction of identity are not simply mental exercises but also "urgent social contests involving...concrete political issues such as territory, violence, law and policy. Social constructs and the meanings and practices they generate are at the very heart of the uneven material and political terrains of imperial worlds." To describe the contemporary American citizenship regime configured by law-and-order politics as neo-colonial, comprising a democratic metropolis that rules over a periphery of the politically disenfranchised, is to reframe the moral discourse of crime, punishment and disenfranchisement in political terms. Because a constitutional democracy that enshrines equal civil and political rights for all citizens cannot legally exclude those people certain political elites and their followers consider less desirable fellow citizens, those elites must operationalize a constitutional, apparently apolitical, socially clinical as it were, mechanism of exclusion without compromising democratic legitimacy. In the contemporary U.S., the legislative enactment and executive and judicial prosecution of criminal justice policies fulfills this task through the continuum of moments reviewed in the previous chapter. This process enables American constitutional democracy to juridically legitimate large-scale exclusion, rather than inclusion. Juridical legitimation does not, however, a national democracy make. It is not just that American representative democracy lacks the institutional resources to withstand the strong communitarian winds that result in a punishment polity,[88] the punishment polity is actually theoretically immanent to Anglo-American liberal democracy in a post-colonial world.

CONCLUSION AND SUMMARY

The legal end of segregation, brought about by patient organizing during the first half of the twentieth century, allowed the United States to officially identify itself as a "color-blind" liberal democracy. Constitutionally speaking, all American citizens were entitled to equal protection under the law and equal access to the political process via universal suffrage. Yet this second Reconstruction (Marable 1991) was widely acknowledged to have failed by the mid-1970s. Dr. Martin Luther King Jr. had recognized by 1966 that the "legislative and political victories did very little to improve" Northern ghettoes, nor did they do much to "penetrate the lower depths of Negro deprivation." In 1966 King acknowledged that the progress that had been made had been "limited mainly to the Negro middle class" (Dyson 2000, 87).

In terms of the argument of this chapter, the "Negro middle class" and black elites King and Marable (1991) distinguish, form part of the metropolitan core, the enfranchised, non-incarcerated, non-inner city dwelling minority who have become citizens proper in Aristotle's terminology.[89] The neo-colonial argument is not entirely racial—not framed exclusively in terms of black and white. The relevant sociological axis is framed as elite/underclass,[90] which for the most part breaks down to white over black, a material binary configured by structural discrimination in areas such as housing, employment, tax, or labor law. (Thomas 1999, 334) The corresponding political axis is citizen/disenfranchised felon, and the regime analog is metropolis/core.

As Beckett (1997) convincingly argues, the backlash against the political success of the civil rights movement, and the subsequent enfranchisement of Blacks who identified with the Democratic Party, engendered the Republican-led, now bipartisan, "wars" on crime and drugs. The "collateral damage" of these wars has been the substantial loss of civil and political rights won during that era.[91] The civil rights movement effectively challenged the political economy of property in white citizenship, such that its value for conservative Southern elites (and white supremacists throughout the country) as a scarce and exclusive resource was diminished. In the quest to restore that value, and the honor that is a core component of citizenship as status, white supremacist political elites (beginning with George Wallace) have engaged in *stasis*, which currently takes the form of "the war on drugs."

The point is that the contemporary relation between fully enfranchised citizens and disenfranchised felons, between metropolitan and core, between free and incarcerated, is a neo-colonial relation based on status honor within the territory of the nation-state. The contemporary

American relation originated between English and European settlers on the American shores and Africans who were brought to the colonies as slaves. Slaves who were emancipated after the Civil War (or for that matter any slaves who were ever freed) were not compensated for their labor. No serious effort has been made since the passage of the Thirteenth Amendment to provide the material wherewithal necessary for those who were collectively and systematically denied the protections and advantages of citizenship for so many generations to catch up with their white counterparts. The United States has a history of extending constitutional rights to excluded minorities on the one hand, and withholding the material wherewithal for their fulfillment on the other.[92] The institutional expression of this pattern is the double polity—the bifurcated citizenry of rulers and ruled, enfranchised and disenfranchised, whose original genealogy was the positive colonial relation that was symbolically and materially supported by slavery. The result, for modern enfranchised American citizens, is a post-colonial political identity:

> With us, to be a man is to be an accomplice of colonialism, since all of us without exception have profited by colonial exploitation. This fat, pale continent ends by falling into what Fanon rightly calls narcissism...with us there is nothing more consistent than a racist humanism since the European has only been able to become a man through creating slaves and monsters. While there was a native population somewhere this imposture was not shown up; in the notion of the human race we found an abstract assumption of universality which served as a cover for more realistic practices...the elite shows itself in its true colors...it is nothing more than a gang. Our precious sets of values begin to molt; on closer scrutiny you won't see one that isn't stained with blood.[93]

The periphery comprising an over-incarcerated population of criminals and free citizens permanently disenfranchised for crime performs several functions for the dominant metropolis. Prisons isolate and confine those the metropolis rejects as full citizens, those who, natally disadvantaged by their membership of what dominant groups designate the underclass, do not rise to either liberal or republican standards of national citizenship.[94] Prisons hide these unfortunates from view; they draw a veil over the dominant society's distaste and failure regarding the fellow citizens it has chosen to discard. Because the United States is supposed to be a colorblind democracy, prisons disguise the "selection" enacted through the criminal justice process as natural, and displace the shame of the original crime (the kidnapping, forced labor, rape, and murder of Africans brought to the United States as slave laborers) onto its victims so the descendants of the perpetrators will not have to be accountable. Albert Camus (1956) suggests why this may be the case:

> People hasten to judge in order not to be judged themselves. What do you expect? The idea that comes most naturally to man, as if from his very nature, is the idea of his innocence... Each of us insists on being innocent at all costs, even if he has to accuse the whole human race and heaven itself.

And James Baldwin (1963) relates Camus' general observation about human nature to the American desire for innocence:

> In our image of the Negro breathes the past we deny, not dead but living yet and powerful, the beast in our jungle of statistics. It is this which defeats us, which lends to interracial cocktail parties their rattling, genteel, nervously smiling air: in any drawing room at such a gathering the beast may spring, filling the air with flying things and an unenlightened wailing... Wherever the Negro face appears a tension is created, the tension of silence filled with things unutterable.

The justice system is able to perform its labor of occlusion because criminal law treats present time as absolute. It suppresses and invalidates history and memory, ignoring in its focus on the individual the reproduction and mutation of the bloodlines generated by the original categories of citizen and slave birthed at the (post-colonial) founding.

The prisons that hold the over-incarcerated populations and discharge them as our disenfranchised co-citizens are key (pre-modern) institutions in the (modern) political economy of citizenship: they "shelter" and "educate" (in the Foucauldian sense) those who are considered a charge on the polity of free citizens. The citizens of the metropolis are both legally and politically free because they do not have to perform the labor of democratic citizenship required to draw every last natural born citizen, however unfortunate, into the fold of the polity. Only such labor can make what was originally a slave-based *herrenvolk* republic a fully mutual and just modern nation-state where prisons would hold only the most dangerous and evil of our number, rather than the illiterate, the mentally ill, the addicted, and the poor. This labor involves the recognition, built into the theory of democratic individuality, that the hierarchy of legal and political status created by felon disenfranchisement denies the fact that all citizens in the polity are equals in imperfection, by virtue of their humanness. The abolition of such hierarchies, and the institutionalization of truly democratic politics predicated on universal political inclusion, is essential for maximizing the potential for learning inherent to the democratic form. At the very least, universal political inclusion institutionalizes the conditions favorable for the development and implementation of policies that, in these very critical times, serves what Aristotle pragmatically called the "good of the whole" rather than that of just a part.

Endnotes

Introduction:

1. My research began in 1997. As this book goes to press, organizational efforts since the 2000 elections have resulted in a total of almost 500,000 people regaining the vote. See Uggen and Manza for The Sentencing Project, *Impact of Recent Legal Changes in Felon Voting Rights in Five States.*

2. For an excellent study the relationship of felon disenfranchisement and modern citizenship theory, see Jason Schall, Harvard Law School unpublished paper "The consistency of felon disenfranchisement with citizenship theory."

3. For an ongoing compendium of these efforts, see The Sentencing Project website.

4. This does not belie the fact that it was not necessarily theoretically significant, just that it did not attract any particular attention until incarceration rates began to rise dramatically, and therefore with them, disenfranchisement rates.

5. The European Community is facing similar questions regarding voting rights of citizens and non-citizens in member states. According to Brubaker 1992, 197n.25, "In Sweden, the Netherlands, and elsewhere, non-citizens are now allowed to vote in local elections. But the campaign for local voting rights for resident non-citizens has emphasized the categorical difference between local and national elections, local and national politics...The argument for extending local voting rights to non-citizens concedes to citizens the legitimate monopoly on electoral participation in the politics of the national state."

6. An oxymoron, since "free" and "franchise" share the same etymological root.

Chapter 1:

1. The Greek term signifying the Athenian penalty depriving a citizen of political rights for transgression of specific written and customary law. Literally, "dishonor."

2. The Latin term signifying loss of civic honor, but not necessarily political rights, following transgression of Roman written and customary law.
3. The English Common Law penalty of "tainting" of blood following conviction for high crimes such as treason.
4. Patterson 1982, Wyatt-Brown 1982.
5. This is consistently verified in the Athenian, Roman, and American (until 1964 –*Loving v Virginia*) laws on intermarriage or "miscegenation."
6. *SOL*; VIII, 3.
7. According to Finley, one reason the Athenians were able to indulge in fratricidal activity, or *staseis* "was the presence of others who possessed no rights. On this subject the Greek view was virtually unanimous: there was no contradiction, in their minds, between freedom for some and (partial or total) unfreedom for others, no notion that all men are created free, let alone equal." (81) *Democracy Ancient and Modern* "Freedom of the Citizen."
8. See Weber 1978, 1311 "Stages and consequences of democratization in Greece" for original development of the concept of democratic citizenship.
9. Cited in Nussbaum 1980, 417.
10. Clearly white women from privileged ethnic status groups received different protections than slave or free women of color or Native American women.
11. Even though the New York general assembly "still unable to act on emancipation, passed a comprehensive slave code that sought to minimize some of the most unpleasant aspects of slavery…the dual justice system was still very much in evidence. It was still a crime for a slave to strike a white person, regardless of the circumstances; the punishment was imprisonment. And the right of a slave to testify was limited to capital cases." (Higginbotham 1978, 141-142) On the colonial and postcolonial legal systems, see Berlin 1974; Fredrickson, 1981, 1987, 1988, 1996; Morris, 1996.
12. McKeon translates Homer's phrase more poetically as "like a dishonored stranger."
13. "Membership of the governing body depends on a property qualification – a kind which it seems appropriate to call 'timocratic' (…) Timocracy is the worst [type of regime]." The footnote to this passage reads: "The Greek word for 'property qualification' is *timema*, based on *timē* or honor." *Ethics*, Aristotle (Trans. Barker) 1160a31. See also Plato, *The Republic* Book VIII, 548-550.
14. See also Wyatt-Brown 1982 on Southern honor and its relation to the criminal justice system. "As reflected in law, the ethic of honor required the unfeigned willingness of slaves to bestow honor on all whites. For instance, in slaves merely pretended to offer respect, the essence of honor would be dissolved; only the appearance, shabby and suspect would remain. Hence it was important that blacks show obedience with apparently heartfelt sincerity. Grudging submission to physical coercion would not suffice. In part the slave codes were designed to meet this end. They heavily penalized the slave for infractions to deference." (363)

15. This conception of citizen dignity as collective honor was articulated in the American context by President Lincoln in his 12/1/1862 Message to Congress: "Fellow citizens, we cannot escape history. We ...will be remembered in spite of ourselves. No personal significance or insignificance can spare one or another of us. *The fiery trial through which we pass will light us down in honor or dishonor to the latest generation*...We ...hold the power and bear the responsibility." (Italics added.) Cited in Higginbotham 1978, ix.

16. As Wyatt-Brown notes, "If there had been a rankless democracy in the Old South, honor would soon have become irrelevant, its ubiquity cheapening its value." (365)

17. "The democratic conception of equality maintains that all are entitled to an equal share, and the poor, when deprived of such a share envy the wealthy and resent their privileges. The oligarchic version of equality, on the other hand, maintains that those who are better (e.g. wealthier) deserve a greater share of power and influence. When denied that greater share under a democratic constitution, such individuals feel insulted by being placed on an equal footing with their inferiors. These competing notions of equality thus produce different answers to the most basic political question of who should rule. Accordingly whenever either side does not share in the constitution according to the fundamental assumption in each case, they resort to stasis." (*Politics* 1301a37)

18. See Finley, "The Freedom of the Citizen in the Greek World," for the responsibility of the rich for funding the military. The difference between permanent and temporary *atimia* applied to state debtors. Both were subject to total *atimia*, but state debtors could be restored to their civil rights when they paid the debt. If they failed to pay state debts or other fines the *atimia* became permanent and hereditary.

19. See Weber 1978, 386-7: "Patriarchal discretion was progressively curtailed with the monopolistic closure (...) of political, status or other groups and with the monopolization of marriage opportunities; these tendencies restricted the *connubium* to the offspring from a permanent sexual union within the given political, religious, economic and status group. (...) The conventional *connubium* is far less impeded by anthropological differences than by status differences."

20. "A Greek had his freedom severely restricted by law in any activity that entailed the introduction of new members into the closed circle of the citizen-body. That meant, in particular, tight restriction in the field of marriage and family law. The state determined the legitimacy of a marriage, not only by laying down the required formalities but also by specifying the categories of men and women who could, or could not, marry each other, and in so doing they went well beyond the incest taboos. Pericles' law of 451 or 450 BC, prohibiting marriage between a citizen and non-citizen is only the most famous example. Violators may not have been punished personally, but their children paid the heavy penalty of being declared

bastards, *nothoi,* and therefore being excluded from the citizenship roster."
Finley, "Freedom of the Citizen in the Greek World."

21. According to Demosthenes, an Athenian citizen who did not appear when
called up for military service was liable to automatic *atimia.* Also, if the
prytaneis and *proedroi* did not place the appointment of *nomothetai* on the
agenda of the fourth Assembly in the first *prytany,* each *prytanis* was to pay
a fine of 1000 dr. to Athena and each *proedros* one of 40 dr. These fines
were enforced by no court decision, but if the offenders did not voluntarily
either pay or, as state-debtors and *atimoi* resign their offices, any citizen
could summarily have them denounced by an *endeixis* and sentenced to
death.

22. "Within the *polis* equality in status under the laws specifies the type of
participation to which every citizen is entitled. Office and its rewards are to
be assigned to those who deserve them by reason of ability and
achievement. Every citizen is free not only to participate in the life of the
city but also to pursue his own ends, and each will be able to do so all the
more successfully by reason of that participation... To be wronged,
therefore, as a citizen would involve willful and unnecessary interference
with one's activities by another person. The laws on a Periclean view are to
be regarded with fearful respect because they protect against such wrongs."
MacIntyre 1988, 51.

23. See, for instance Plato's *Gorgias,* 486b,c and 508c,d: Kallikles compares the
danger of being unable to express oneself to *atimia,* saying that a man
without any skill in rhetoric is legally just as unprotected as an *atimos.* He
has "no power to save either himself or others, when he is in the greatest
danger and is going to be despoiled by his enemies of all his goods, and has
to live, simply deprived of his rights of citizenship. He being a man who, if I
may use the expression, may be boxed on the ears with impunity." See also
Manville 1990, 147-48.

24. Kleisthenes' reforms regularized Athenian citizenship through the system of
the neighborhood demes, which enrolled and authorized their members as
citizens and selected members for the new Council (*boule*). Membership
could be challenged or confirmed at the central administration, rather than
being determined by tribal descent as it had been during the *diapsephsimos.*
Manville says that "demes became the bridge of representative government
that linked the individual formally to the polis – and thus translated
practically the vision that the "state" was the sum of its citizens."(193) As
such, *atimia* was a punishment determined by law rather than the whim of
whichever tribe had won the most recent round of *stasis.*

25. This also fits with Weber's definition of a status group based on honor,
which he says "may come into being: a) In the first instance by virtue of
their own style of life, particularly the type of vocation (...) c) through
monopolistic appropriation of political or hierocratic powers: political or
hierocratic status groups." (306)

26. After the American Civil War, the former Confederate leaders of the rebellion were disenfranchised for a maximum period of ten years. See Foner 1988 on the Confederate disenfranchisement.

27. I would venture to suggest that this is because in Rome, manumitted slaves automatically became Roman citizens, so different types of punishments preserved the distinction between former slaves and "true" Roman citizens. Upper class citizens could be executed in more or less humane ways, if they did not choose exile instead, but there are cases of *honestiores* being thrown to the beasts, burned alive, or crucified, depending on the Empire or the period under consideration.

28. "*Existimatio* is, in fact, defined for us as *dignitatis illaesae status*. It was so far a conception similar to that which the old Roman law knew as *caput*, and which the later jurists generally described as *status*." (Greenridge 1894, 5)

29. "The history of the Roman Infamia is a history of special disqualifications, based on moral grounds, from certain public or quasi-public functions: by the latter are meant those functions, such as postulation in the praetor's court, which, though based primarily on the rights of the individual in private law, yet necessarily bring him into contact with an official of the state." (ibid, 8)

30. Greenridge, who published the only book-length study of *infamia* calls it "the most unsettled in the whole province of Roman Law." (3)

31. About the self-chosen penalty of exile, which resulted in disenfranchisement, Cicero said: Exile is not a capital punishment; it is an escape from punishment. In *lex* of ours is exile a punishment for a crime. Those would avoid imprisonment, death, or disgrace (*ignomia*) seek refuge in exile as if at a sanctuary. If they remained at Rome, they would only lose their citizenship when they lost their lives. But when they go into exile, they do not lose their citizenship by law, they are stripped of it by their own act of abandonment. The fugitive loses it as soon as he becomes an exile, that is, when he acquires the citizenship of another state. (quoted in Bauman 1996, 14)

32. These were considered "obligatory relations" of the citizen and their neglect, followed by public condemnation according to Cicero, involved a "serious breach of *existimatio*," the "reason being the peculiar moral turpitude involved in such breaches of faith." (See Greenridge, 26, text and footnotes.)

33. "The drawing up of the census gave the censors very considerable powers to oversee Roman morality, since they could mark a man with *infamia*, remove him from his *tribus*, remove him from the Senate or ranks of *equites*, or increase the tax he had to pay. This they could do arbitrarily, though they had to give reasons for affixing the *nota censorial*, both censors had to be in agreement, and the man who was to be punished was usually given the opportunity to defend himself. The censors were able to use their powers fairly systematically to deal with wrongful conduct which was otherwise not punished; for instance, an *ingenuus* marrying a *liberta*, an over-hasty divorce, or too severe a punishment by a *pater familias*." (Watson 1974, 87)

34. Interesting in the light of the Abu Ghraib scandal as well as treatment of prisoners in U.S. prisons.

35. (In 2002) Alabama, California, Idaho, Indiana, Iowa, Maryland, Minnesota, New Mexico, New York, Ohio, Rhode Island, Tennessee Washington, Wisconsin and Wyoming. Many laws are changing as this book goes to press, though. See The Sentencing Project website for updates.

36. Itzkowitz and Oldak cite C. Calisse, *A History of Italian Law* (1928, 300-424).

37. I take issue with von Bar's use of the term "citizen" here, since technically there were no "citizens" in the received sense of the term, during the feudal period.

38. von Bar 1916, 111, on Medieval Germanic Law.

39. Condemnation to hard labor in the mines. This under the Empire "was regarded as the heaviest punishment after that of death, and as in the case of the latter, was preceded by scourging. It carried with it the loss of liberty and necessarily of property and other rights." (ibid. note 22, p. 272)

40. "When the sentence of death, the most terrible and highest judgment in the laws of England, is pronounced, the immediate inseparable consequence by the common law is attainder. For when it is now clear beyond all dispute that the criminal is no longer fit to live upon the earth, but is to be exterminated as a monster and a bane to human society, the law sets a note of infamy upon him, puts him out of its protection, and takes no further care of him than barely to see him executed. He is then called stained or blackened. He is no longer of any credit or reputation; he cannot be a witness in any court...he is already dead in law. (...) The consequences of attainder are forfeiture and corruption of blood." Blackstone, *Public Wrongs, Book IV, Commentaries on the Laws of England.* "Judgment and Its Consequences," p.952.

41. Burdick (1929) attributes the prevalence of English Common Law in the U.S. to the dominance of Blackstone. "Published in England in 1766, and followed by an American edition in 1771, it became a sort of gospel upon the law for all American judges, lawyers and law students." (35) The states of the Louisiana purchase, the Southwest, and Florida, were all influenced by French and Spanish law derived from Civil Code. New York was once under civil law from Dutch. Civil law has influenced much of Common Law. "English feudal law has been changed by such doctrines in every one of our states." (54) There is debate over how much English law, and hence U.S. law, was influenced by the Civil Code. Blackstone saw them as two distinct traditions. Others, former chief justice Holt, said "it must be owned that the principles of our law are borrowed from the Civil Law." Sir William Jones "Thought few English lawyers dare make the acknowledgement, the Civil Law is the source of nearly all our English laws that are not of feudal origin."

42. According to Itzkowitz and Oldak, "the use of this criminal sanction (outlawry) is evident from the fact that the outlawry statutes of New York and North Carolina were struck down in the 18th century." New York

retained the punishment of attainder until the turn of the 18th century, though, despite the constitutional provisions against it. See Walsh 1948.

43. U.S. Constitution, Article I, §9. The most notorious cases successfully challenging state and federal statutes that required loyalty oaths, as unconstitutional "bills of attainder" were the post-bellum cases *Ex-parte Garland*, and *Cummings v State of Missouri*. Both the rulings and (powerful) dissents contain interesting exegeses of the laws of attainder and the practices of felon disenfranchisement.

44. U.S. Constitution, Article III, §3.

45. In order of enactment: Va. (1776), Ky. (1799), Ohio (1802), La.(1812), Ind.(1818), Miss. (1817), Conn.(1818), Ill.(1818), Ala. (1819), Mo.(1820), NY (1821). Itzkowitz and Oldak, 725, n.37

46. *Ex parte Wilson*, 114 US 417, 422; State v Clark, 60 Kan. 450; *Com. V Shaver*, 3 Watts & S. (Pa.) 338.

47. *Davis v Carey*, 141 Pa.314.

48. A 1705 statute reiterates the provision that it is not a felony for a master to kill his slave. Person shall be acquitted as "if such accident never happened." People of color couldn't raise their hands against "Christians" though.

49. "Even in cases extreme enough to be brought to court, the masters were acquitted." Higginbotham cites a 1735 case of master beating his slave to death. "The coroner's jury held that the slave's death could be attributed to "a work of God;" judgment was rendered in favor of the defendant." This and the other cases Higginbotham cites are all evidence of dual system of law, the legally "segregated judicial system in New York." "Slaves charged with minor offenses received no court hearings; flogging was the mandatory form of punishment."

50. Moreover, white American *citizens* who transgressed the strict interracial codes of both ante- and post-bellum society made themselves vulnerable to both legal (state) and extra-legal sanctions and violence.

51. See Burton, Cullen, and Travis 1987 for detailed discussion of state statutes regulating the collateral consequences of felony convictions, some of which still include the penalty of "civil death."

52. See Parenti 1999 in particular on contemporary police and prison violence. See generally Miller 1996 and Conover 2001, Franklin 1998, and Christianson 1998 on prison violence.

53. This claim comes from a statement of Aristotle's regarding who is "justly a citizen" in *The Politics*, which is discussed in detail in the following chapters.

54. *Plessey v Ferguson*, 163 U.S. 537 (1896). See Brook 1997; See Woodward 1966 on the history of jim crow laws.

55. See also Tourgée 1989 for discussion of this period, as well as DuBois 1939.

56. Carter 1995, 1996; Glazer 1996, Beckett 1997 and the Democratic Party de-alignment and the Southern development of the Republican Party.

57. Alabama, Arkansas, Georgia, Kentucky, Missouri, Ohio, South Carolina, North Carolina, Oklahoma, Texas.

58. For the post-civil war criminal justice regimes in the "reconstructed" states, see in particular duBois 1939, Higginbotham 1996, Oshinsky, Shapiro 1993, Davis 1991, Waldrep 1998, and Myers 998.

59. Miscegenation and intermarriage between racial groups was a felony offense in many American states until *Loving v Virginia* declared the statutes unconstitutional. Judge Leon Bazile articulated the seriousness of a felony conviction in the lower court ruling: "Parties [to an interracial marriage] are guilty of a most serious crime...Almighty God created the races, white, black, yellow, malay, and red, and he placed them on separate continents... The fact that he separated the races shows that he did not intend for the races to mix. The awfulness of the offense [of interracial marriage] is shown by the fact...[that] the code makes the contracting of a marriage between a white person and any colored person a felony. Conviction of felony is a serious matter. You lose your political rights, and only the government has the power to restore them. And as long as you live you will be known as a felon. "The moving finger writes and moves on and having writ/Not all your piety nor all your wit/ Can change one line of it." Transcript of Record at 8, reproduced in *Loving v Virginia*, 388 U.S. 1 app. At 42 (1967).

60. The Supreme Court overturned the "moral turpitude" clause in the Alabama Constitution in *Hunter v Underwood*, 471 U.S. 222 (1985) one of the few cases where felon disenfranchisement has been successfully challenged. The court recognized that the clause was a violation of Equal Protection because the law had a disproportionate impact on blacks and was adopted with racially discriminatory intent. The president of the 1901 Alabama constitutional convention that adopted the disputed section had declared to his fellow delegates "And what is it that we want to do? Why it is within the limits imposed by the Federal Constitution, to establish white supremacy in this state." Cited in Shapiro 1993, 570. Shapiro argues that plaintiffs no longer have to prove discriminatory intent, but only discriminatory results under the Amended Voting Rights Act (1982).

The fact is that the "moral turpitude" clause operated unchallenged in Alabama for over eight decades, resulting in the legal disenfranchisement of (literally) untold numbers of citizens. Although it is possible to estimate how many ex-felons are disenfranchised today, it is impossible to estimate how many have been disenfranchised over time, since the passage of the relevant statutes in the states. Thus there is no way of quantifying the extent of the loss to the polity from what is now legally recognized as "illegal" disenfranchisement under the "moral turpitude" clause. If, as many of the scholars who criticize the contemporary American practice argue, ex-felon disenfranchisement insofar as it disproportionately affects minority communities, is unconstitutional, it is just a matter of time before a future Supreme Court recognizes it as such. The "illegal" cumulative damage that

will have been done to many state polities – the loss of so many citizens' votes – will be incalculable.
61. Subject to residency, citizenship, and property ownership restrictions. See Keyssar 2000, Table A.9
62. See Miller 1996 on drug laws and forfeiture.
63. July 6, 1775, Franklin, Rutledge, Johnson, Livingston, John Jay, Jefferson and Dickinson. *Declaration of the Causes and Necessities of Taking Up Arms*.
64. See, in particular Patterson 1982 for the relationship between honor and slavery. See also Davis 1975 and Patterson 1991 for analysis of the dialectical relationship between slavery and freedom.
65. Van den Berge 1978. To be discussed in detail in Chapter Five, below.
66. *Richardson v Ramirez* 418 U.S. 24 (1974).

Chapter 2:

1. For a recent bibliography of new research and analysis, see Pamela S. Karlan 2004, "Convictions and Doubts, Retribution, Representation and the Debate over Felon Disenfranchisement" Stanford Public Law and Legal Theory Working Paper Series, footnote 8, p.2.
2. Hampton's article was written in the context of the debate over whether the provision disenfranchising prisoners should remain in the revised Canadian constitution. No such debate has taken place in the U.S., although it is long overdue.
3. Two articles, respectively, the Harvard Note (1989, 1301) and Demleitner (2000, 795) recognize that felon disenfranchisement must be "rejected by the legislatures of those states in which it occurs" and "[C]ourts are unlikely to invalidate the denial of voting rights to felons. Therefore legislative action offers a more promising approach for reform, since disenfranchisement presents normative questions that fall squarely in the legislative realm." The majority of critics of the practice, however, argue that it is unconstitutional and calls for judicial action: "[…] the continued imposition of this disability, which effectively operates as an additional punishment for the commission of felonious crimes, is cruelly excessive and is thus prohibited by the eighth amendment of the [U.S] Constitution." Tims (1975) "The disenfranchisement of ex-felons is unconstitutional. (…)Upon the grounds usually advanced – prevention of antisocial voting and election fraud --- [it] constitutes a violation of equal protection." Reback (1973, 845) "My argument is that when properly understood as a continuation of *infamia*, disenfranchisement for the commission of "infamous" crimes or felonies should be regarded as unacceptable in the American constitutional system." Fletcher (1999, 1902) "The most viable way to break the silence imposed on millions of disenfranchised offenders and ex-offenders is through vigorous litigation under the Voting Rights Act." Shapiro (1993, 564-5) "The cycle of exclusion has come nearly full circle, and it will not end until the Supreme Court returns to the true meaning of equal protection, protecting minority citizens "with the same shield which it throws over the

white man ... [both] being alike citizens of the United States...." Hench (1998, 789) "Where legislatures fail to repeal old laws that infringe upon such fundamental rights as voting, and that since their adoption may have become unlawful under statutory developments, courts should take "a 'second look' [through] the eyes of the people" ... directly and indirectly affected by such laws, and take steps to correct their harmful effects." Harvey (1994, 1189)

4.   "The United States shall guarantee to every State in this Union a Republican Form of Government..." U.S. Constitution, IV, iv.

5.   See Fletcher 2001, 146-147 on the "negative strategy" of the Reconstruction Amendments.

6.   Police power is "the acknowledged power of a State to regulate its police, its domestic trade, and to govern its own citizens." Marshall, C.J. in *Gibbons v Ogden*, 22 U.S. (9 Wheat.) 1, 208 (1824), cited in Tribe 2000, 1046, n.1.

7.   "The House of Representatives shall be composed of Members chosen every second Year by the People of the Several States, and the Electors in each State shall have the Qualifications requisite for Electors of the most numerous Branch of the State Legislature." Article I, ii.

8.   418 U.S. 24 (1974).

9.   "Representatives shall be apportioned among the several States according to their respective numbers, counting the whole number of persons in each State, excluding Indians not taxed. But when the right to vote at any election for the choice of electors for President and Vice-President of the United States, Representatives in Congress, the Executive and Judicial Officers of a state or the members of the Legislatures thereof, is denied to any of the male inhabitants of such State, being twenty-one years of age and citizens of the United States, or in any way abridged *except for participation in rebellion or other crime*, the basis of representation therein shall be reduced in proportion which the number of such male citizens shall bear to the whole number of male citizens twenty-one years of age in such State." (Italics added.)

10. The California Supreme Court ruled that disenfranchisement of ex-felons violated the Equal Protection Clause of the Fourteenth Amendment and directed the county clerk to register the ex-felons. Petitioner Viola Richardson, Mendocino County Clerk, appealed the ruling to the Supreme Court, which reversed the California Supreme Court.

11. Interestingly enough, California law was subsequently amended following the *Richardson* decision to permit ex-offenders to vote, while continuing to disenfranchise those in prison or on parole. See *Flood v Riggs*, 80 Cal. App. 3rd 138 (1978). Also, New York law was amended to abolish ex-offender disenfranchisement after a court decision upholding the practice (*Green v Board of Elections*, 380 F.2d 445, 1967) to be discussed in Chapter Four. Moreover, Massachusetts, which until 2000 was one of the few states allowing prisoners to vote, just passed a referendum disenfranchising felons for the term of their incarceration. See The Sentencing Project web site

http://www.sentencingproject.org for the most recent changes in state disenfranchisement provisions.

12. Harlan's dissent in *Carrington v Rash* 380 U.S. 89; 85 S.Ct. 775 (1965).

13. *Reynolds v Simms*, 377 U.S. 533 at 625.

14. The European Community is facing similar questions regarding voting rights of citizens and non-citizens in member states. According to Brubaker, 1992, 197n.25 "In Sweden, the Netherlands, and elsewhere, non-citizens are now allowed to vote in local elections. But the campaign for local voting rights for resident non-citizens has emphasized the categorical difference between local and national elections, local and national politics...The argument for extending local voting rights to non-citizens concedes to citizens the legitimate monopoly on electoral participation in the politics of the national state."

15. For two prominent authors who discuss the ideology of American identity, membership of a "single nation," and the "American creed," see Schlesinger (1991), and Huntingdon (1996).

16. *Afroyim v Rusk* US 253 (1967) 387.

17. The Supreme Court hardly qualifies as a body that can "represent" the American people in such a decision. Its representative "integrity" so to speak, is compromised by the same structural flaws as the office of the President, and both Houses of Congress, since it is appointed and confirmed by an officer elected by an "aggregated" but politically splintered electorate. See Bybee (2000) on the representative function of the Supreme Court.

18. "All persons born or naturalized in the United States, and subject to the jurisdiction thereof, are citizens of the United States and of the State wherein they reside," U.S. Constitution, Amendment XIV, §1.

19. Brubaker (1992, 32) says, "Every state ascribes its citizenship to certain persons at birth. The vast majority of persons acquire their citizenship in this way.... [Ascriptive citizenship] is difficult to reconcile with a central claim – perhaps the central claim – of liberal political theory: the idea that political membership ought to be founded on individual consent."

20. Art. I, §2 (qualification for Representatives); id., §3 (qualifications for Senators); Art. II, § 1 (qualification for President); cf. Art. I, §8 (power of Congress to regulate naturalization). See Tribe 2000, 1298.

21. See Berlin 1974, and Morris 1996 for discussions of the law and practices regarding freedmen and slaves before the war.

22. "Thus it is that in the United States the prejudice rejecting the Negroes seems to increase in proportion to their emancipation, and inequality cuts deep into mores as it is effaced from the laws." (Tocqueville 1969, 344)

23. The authoritative texts on this period are Foner 1988, Fredrickson 1991, 1997, 1998; Kousser 1999, DuBois 1935, 1979, Higginbotham 1996, Marable 1991. See also Wang 1996 and Finkleman 1993 for in-depth legal scholarship on the legal and political trajectory of black voting rights during Reconstruction.

24. Each regime has its own particular conception of justice, which refers to the distribution of offices and 'honors' among the citizens. Therefore the notion

of justice is explicitly contextual, and "political," rather than absolute or moral. "The good in the sphere of politics is justice; and justice consists in what tends to promote the common interest. General opinion makes it consist in some sort of equality...Justice involves two factors – things, and the persons to whom things are assigned – and it considers that persons who are equal should have assigned to them equal things. But here there arises a question that must not be overlooked. Equals and unequals – yes; but equals and unequals *in what?*" (III, 12)

25. A constitution (or polity) may be defined as "the organization of a polis, in respect of its offices generally, but especially in respect of that particular office which is sovereign in all issues. The civic body, [the *politeuma*, or body of persons established in power by the polity] is everywhere the sovereign of the state; in fact the civic body is the polity (or constitution) itself. In democratic states...the people [or demos] is sovereign." (1278b)

26. See Table 1 for current felon disenfranchisement provisions by state.

27. This claim will be analyzed and substantiated in a subsequent chapter on the politics of "crime" and prosecutorial discretion.

28. Dahl (1963) ch.3.

29. Based on U.S. Constitution, I, 2: "The House of Representatives shall be composed of Members chosen every second Year by the People of the several States, and the Electors in each State shall have the Qualifications requisite for Electors of the most numerous Branch of the State Legislature."

30. U.S. Constitution, IV,4.

31. OED.

32. This is actually an etymological contradiction in terms, since "franchise" and "freedom" originally meant the same thing. In the seven American states that currently disenfranchise ex-felons for life, this "disequilibrium" of political rights obtains. See Foner 1999, ch.1 for the connection in early American thought between freedom and the franchise. "In the popular language of politics, if not in law, freedom and the suffrage had become inter-changeable. "How can a Man be said to [be] free and independent," asked residents of Lenox, Massachusetts in 1778, "when he has not a voice allowed him" in elections? Henceforth, political freedom – the right to self-government – would mean not only, as in the past, a people's right to be ruled by their chosen representatives, but an individual's right to political participation." (18-19) Conversely, of course, the condition of slavery was synonymous with the lack of political rights, and even emancipated slaves were thought by most to be unfit to exercise political rights. See Patterson 1982 for the connection between freedom and honor and slavery and dishonor.

33. See Pitkin (1972), chapter 9 and Wolin 1960, p. 9: "The words 'public,' 'common,' and 'general' have a long tradition of usage which has made them synonyms for what is political...From its very beginnings in Greece, the Western political tradition has looked upon the political order as a

common order created to deal with those concerns in which all of the members of society have some interest."

34. See also Mahoney 2000 for analysis of path dependence in historical sociology.

35. The authoritative texts on early American citizenship regimes are Bailyn 1967, Wood 1969, Pocock 1975, Kettner 1978, Sinopli 1992, Hyneman 1994, and Smith 1997.

36. See Arendt 1963, esp. pp 127-35 on "public happiness."

37. The original self-appointed citizen bodies in the colonies were mixtures of aristocrats, merchants and religious dissidents who emigrated from the "Old Word" to make fortunes and new lives. Many who were subsequently incorporated into the citizen "elites" had originally come over as prisoners: "In 1717, the British Parliament formally designated the American colonies as England's penal colony. The first prisoners had been shipped in 1650. By 1776 there had been an estimated 100,000 prisoners shipped in chains to the American colonies...Prisons were seen as the substitute for banishment and capital punishment." (Fox , 1972, 11) Hughes (1986, 2) calls the American colonies a "fresco of repression": "After 1717, transportation was stepped up and rendered fully official by a new act, 4 Geo. I, c.11, which provided that minor offenders could be transported for seven years to America instead of being flogged or branded, while men on commuted capital sentences (recipients of the King's Mercy) might be sent for fourteen...For the next sixty years, about 40,000 people suffered this thinly disguised form of slavery: 30,000 men and women from Great Britain, 10,000 from Ireland. Virginia Colony was originally settled by convicts sent to work on the plantations. "All offenders out of the common gaols condemned to die should be sent for three years to the Colony." (40-42)

38. See Steinfeld, 1989, and Cogan 1997.

39. See Keyssar 2000 and Narr 1889, 1995 for detailed discussion and historical tabulation of voter qualifications in the states since the founding.

40. The powerful theoretical exposition of the concept of "whiteness as property" is Harris 1993, whose analysis is based on DuBois 1939: "The hyper-exploitation of Black labor was accomplished by treating Black people themselves as objects of property. Race and property were thus conflated by establishing a form of property contingent on race – only Blacks were subjugated as slaves and treated as property. Similarly, the conquest, removal, and extermination of Native American life and culture were ratified by conferring and acknowledging the property rights of whites in Native American land. Only white possession and occupation of land was validated and therefore privileged as a basis for property rights. These distinct forms of exploitation each contributed in various ways to the construction of whiteness as property."(1716). See also DuBois, 1935,1979: 700-101.

41. The Constitution and all branches of the federal government protected the institution of slavery until the Thirteenth Amendment was passed in 1865.

42. "Many theorists have traditionally conceptualized property to include the exclusive rights of use, disposition, and possession, with possession embracing the absolute right to exclude. The right to exclude was the central principle, too, of whiteness as identity, for mainly whiteness has been characterized, not by a unifying characteristic, but by the exclusion of others deemed "not white." The possessors of whiteness were granted the legal right to exclude others from the privileges inhering in whiteness; whiteness became an exclusive club whose membership was closely and grudgingly guarded. The courts played an active role in enforcing this right to exclude – determining who was or was not white enough to enjoy the privileges accompanying whiteness. In this sense, the courts protected whiteness as any other form of property." (Harris 1993, 1736.)

43. See, e.g., Locke, *Second Treatise of Government* § 149 (people retain supreme power to alter legislative acts when government acts contrary to ends for which government established); id. at § 222 (people reserve to themselves the choice of representatives). See generally W. Everdell, *The End of Kings* (1983) (tracing the history of the republican tradition from its Homeric and Biblical beginnings to the present day).

44. See also Amar 1994 for detailed discussion of the meaning of "republican" government, statements of the founders, and political conflicts over the meaning of "republican" government during the Civil War period.

45. *The Federalist* No. 39, see also *The Federalist* No. 10, at 62 (J. Madison) (A republic is characterized by "the delegation of the Government...to a small number of citizens elected by the rest..."); *The Federalist* No. 37, at 234 (J. Madison) ("The genius of Republican liberty, seems to demand on one side, not only that all power should be derived from the people; but, that those entrusted with it should be kept in dependence on the people...").

46. *The Federalist* No. 22, at 139 (A. Hamilton); see also *The Federalist* No. 57, at 384 (J. Madison or A. Hamilton) ("The elective mode of obtaining rulers is the characteristic policy of republican government.").

47. *Debates in the Several State Conventions on the Adoption of the Federal Constitution* 328 (J. Elliot ed. 1881); see also *Elliot's Debates* (statement by Patrick Henry to Virginia's ratifying convention. "The delegation of power to an adequate number of representatives, and an unimpeded reversion of it back to the people, at short periods, form the principal traits of a republican government."

48. First Inaugural Address by President Thomas Jefferson (Mar. 4, 1801), reprinted in *The Founders' Constitution*, 140, 141; see also *Van Sickle v. Shanahan*, 212 Kan. 426, 443, 511 P.2d 223, 237 (1973). The Framers spent relatively little time discussing "the elements of a republican form of government" because "there existed no substantial disagreement between the Founding Fathers as to the republican concepts upon which the government was to be patterned".

49. *Buchanan v. Rhodes*, 249 F. Supp. 860, 865 (N.D. Ohio), appeal dismissed, 385 U.S. 3 (1966), vacated and remanded to convene three-judge court, 400 F.2d 882 (6th Cir.), cert. denied, 393 U.S. 839 (1968).

50. *Harris v Shanahan*, 192 Kan. 183, 204, 387 P.2d 771, 789 (1963); accord *Baker v Carr*, 369 U.S. 186, 242 (1962) (Douglas, J., concurring); *Downes v Bidwell*, 182 U.S. 244, 279 (1901); *W.E. Tucker Oil Co. v Portland Bank*, 285 Ark. 453, 455, 688 S.W.2d 293, 294 (1985); *Eckerson v City of Des Moines*, 137 Iowa 452, 461, 115 N.W. 177, 181 (1908).
51. Montesquieu, *The Spirit of Laws* book 2, ch. 2 .
52. *The Federalist* No. 52, at 354 (J. Madison).
53. 360 U.S. 45 (1959).
54. *Id* at 50.
55. *Id* at 51.
56. 400 U.S. 112 (1970).
57. *Id* at 125 (Black, J., announcing judgments of the Court in an opinion expressing his own views).
58. *Id* at 294 (Stewart, J., joined by Burger, C.J., and Blackmun, J.; concurring in part and dissenting in part) (quoting opinion of Black, J., id. at 125); see also id. at 201 (Harlan, J., concurring in part and dissenting in part) ("The power to set state voting qualifications was neither surrendered nor delegated" to the national government under the original Constitution, "except to the extent that the guarantee of a republican form of government may be thought to require a certain minimum distribution of political power."). Even the Justices who voted to uphold federal regulation of the minimum voting age in state and local elections expressed some discomfort with widespread federal control over state voting qualifications. "It is important at the outset," Justice Brennan wrote: "to recognize what is not involved in these cases. We are not faced with an assertion of congressional power to regulate any and all aspects of state and federal elections, or even to make general rules for the determination of voter qualifications."
59. See also, for example Kaczorowski 1986, 884: "The Reconstruction Amendments and the statutes enacted to enforce them were the Northern Republican controlled Congress's translation of the North's Civil War victory into law. Through these amendments and statutes Northern Unionists imposed upon the nation their view of national supremacy: sovereignty centered in the nation, the primacy of citizens' allegiance to the nation, the primacy of national citizenship, and the primacy of national authority to secure and enforce the civil rights of the United States." Chief Justice Warren cited *The Philadelphia American* in his *Reynolds v Simms* ruling: "If there is one lesson written in bloody letters by the war, it is that national citizenship must be paramount to State..." (n. 82) See also Kettner (1978) at 334-51, Amar (1998) and Fletcher (2001). Fletcher briefly discusses the practice of felon disenfranchisement, but like many legal commentators on the issue treats it as an anachronism and an anomaly in an otherwise modern democratic America. I believe this approach fails to apprehend the theoretical underpinnings of the structure of dual citizenship entailed by the federal polity.
60. Indeed, in *Yick Wo v Hopkins* (118 U.S. 356) the Supreme Court referred to "the political franchise of voting "as a fundamental political right, because

preservative of all rights," a phrase repeated by the Chief Justice in *Reynolds*, but contradicted by his use of the phrase "qualified voters." Analysis of this contradiction will be taken up in the next chapter.

61. See Pangle 1990, on the "reinvention" of classical republicanism by the American founders, and the open-ended meaning of the Guarantee Clause.

62. Indeed, Aristotle, in an uncharacteristic display of democratic goodwill declared that there is a "combination of qualities to be found in the people – provided, that is to say, that they are not debased in character. Each individual may indeed, be a worse judge than the experts; but all, when they meet together, are either better than experts or at any rate no worse." (*Politics, III*, ix, 1282a) His use of a word such as "experts" reveals a similar preoccupation with learning.

63. " 'The method of consent' is said to consist in a procedure that 'leaves open to every sane, non-criminal adult the opportunity to discuss, criticize, and vote for or against the government.' This approach makes it possible to include all citizens, whether or not they exercise their right to vote, within the scope of consent." Gewirth (1962) quoted in Pateman 1979, 84. See also Christiano 1996, Ch. 2 for a discussion of the correspondence between the idea of *justice* and the equal distribution of political resources in a democracy. See also Pateman for discussion of the vote as a representation of *consent*.

64. Dewey's (1988) critique of democracy as a "mechanism" is apposite: "…the depth of the present crisis is due in considerable part to the fact that for a long period we acted as if our democracy were something that perpetuated itself automatically; as if our ancestors had succeeded in setting up a machine that solved the problem of perpetual motion in politics. We acted as if democracy were something that took place mainly at Washington and Albany or some other state capital – under the impetus of what happened when men and women went to the polls once a year or so – which is a somewhat extreme way of saying that we have had the habit of thinking of democracy as a kind of political mechanism that will work as long as citizens were reasonably faithful in performing political duties." 225

65. The meaning of "equal access" in a democracy is clearly a key issue for minorities and "cultural groups" whose distinctive "voices" and particular interests are drowned out by majoritarian democratic processes. See Kymlicka (1995, 1996), Guinier (1995), Young (1990,2000). Rather than address theories of group rights, or deliberative democracy, this section attempts to "reach underneath" them, to their normative foundations, in order to critique the practice of felon disenfranchisement. My definition of "democracy" takes for granted, though, Sartori's qualification that "To maintain democracy as an ongoing process requires us to ensure that *all* citizens (majority plus minority) possess the rights that are necessary to the method by which democracy operates." (34)

66. The lesson they may "learn" is a negative or punitive one, concerning what *not* to do in order to retain political rights. What I have in mind is a more positive type of learning, concerning development of public policies that

enrich the lives of citizens—policies whose long term goals are to reduce exclusion, 'alienation' and the 'repeat victimization' that characterizes the contemporary criminal justice system.

67. Clearly, as the civil rights movement and the woman suffrage movement demonstrated, though, citizens may be excluded from the political process because they do not enjoy political rights, but in the struggle to achieve them may be actively engaged as political "outsiders" in what can be described as "pedagogical" activities vis-à-vis the majority.

68. Du Bois (1935, 1979), Foner (1988), Tourgée (1989), Wells (1900).

69. The most recent (national) estimates of African-American disenfranchisement for crime are troubling: "Thirteen percent of all adult black men – 1.4 million—are disenfranchised, representing one-third of the total disenfranchised population and reflecting a rate of disenfranchisement that is seven times the national average. Election voting statistics offer an approximation of the political importance of black disenfranchisement: 1.4 million black men are disenfranchised compared to 4.6 million black men who voted in 1996." (Sentencing Project and Human Rights Watch)

70. "Power needs no justification, being inherent in the very existence of political communities; what it does need is legitimacy. The common treatment of these two words as synonyms is no less misleading and confusing than the current equation of obedience and support. Power springs up whenever people get together and act in concert, but it derives its legitimacy from the initial getting together rather than from any action that then may follow. Violence can be justifiable, but it will never be legitimate. Its justification loses in plausibility the further its intended end recedes into the future." (52)

71. Contrast this definition of what a polity should *not* be with Schmitt's (1996) definition of the "political": "The specific political distinction to which political actions and motives can be reduced is that between friend and enemy...The political enemy need not be morally evil or aesthetically ugly; he need not appear as an economic competitor, and it may even be advantageous to engage with him in business transactions. But he is, nevertheless, the other, the stranger; and it is sufficient for his nature that he is, in a specially intense way, existentially something different and alien, so that in the extreme case conflicts with him are not possible." (27)

72. "Just as the sailor is a member of an association (...) so too is a citizen. Sailors differ from one another in virtue of the different capacities in which they act: one is a rower, another a pilot, another a look-out man; and others again will have other names the same sort of way. This being the case, it is clear that (...) safety in navigation is the common end which all must serve and the object at which each must aim. What is true of sailors is also true of citizens. Though they differ in the capacities in which they act, they all have a common object; the end which they all serve is safety in the working of their association; and this association consists in the constitution." (*Politics*, IV, i 1276b) The conception of justice in the ideal polity is "self-

sufficiency" and "the good life," neither of which can be had in an atmosphere of political instability or *stasis*.

73. "Voters pursue their individual interest by making demands on the political system in proportion to the intensity of their feelings. Politicians, also pursing their own interests, adopt policies that buy them votes, thus ensuring accountability. In order to stay in office, politicians act like entrepreneurs and brokers, looking for formulas that satisfy as many, and alienate as few, interests as possible. From the interchange between self-interested voters and self-interested brokers emerge decisions that come as close as possible to a balanced aggregation of individual interests." Mansbridge (1980, 17) For classical critiques of this model see Schattschneider 1960, Lukes 1970, Lowi 1969, Gaventa 1980, Bachrach and Baratz 1962, Macpherson 1977. For more recent critiques see also Barber 1984, Christiano 1996, Mansbridge 1980, Dahl 1989, Benhabib 1996, Fraser 1993, Young 1990, 2000.

74. This is the classical definition of democracy, which is grouped with oligarchy and tyranny as "perverted" regimes where one class or person rules in their own interest. Aristotle, *Politics* 1279b. Book III.vii-viii. Also, see Walzer, 1970, Shapiro 1999, chapter 3, and Sen 1999, chapter 6, for a discussion of the crucial role of opposition in democracy.

75. "Political liberty in a citizen is that tranquility of spirit which comes from the opinion each one has of his security, and in order for him to have this liberty the government must be such that one citizen cannot fear another citizen." (Montesequieu, 1989)

76. I will develop this idea of "democratic individuality" in this chapter. The term is George Kateb's, based on his reading of the Emersonians and analyzed in *The Inner Ocean* (1992).

77. "The method of looking to the bottom is analogous to, but different from the method of legal philosophers such as Rawls and Ackerman, who have proposed moral theories that call for special attention to the needs of the least advantaged. (…) The technique of imagining oneself black and poor in some hypothetical world is less effective than studying the actual experience of black poverty and listening to those who have done so. When notions of right and wrong, justice and injustice, are examined not from an abstract position, but from the position of groups who have suffered through history, moral relativism recedes and identifiable normative priorities emerge." (Matsuda 1995, 63)

78. The impersonal individual aims to acquire an indefatigable capacity to know and love impersonally. The view of all three writers is that a democratic society is best justified as a preparation for this individuality and is indeed justifiable as the only society in which such individuality can exist as a possibility for all (96). See White 2000, chapter 2, for an interesting discussion and critique of the ontology of democratic individuality.

79. For an excellent and interesting argument on the "matrix of contempt" see Kim 1999. Kim defines contempt as "a sense of offense toward an object or target in virtue of perceived base and infectiously debasing qualities of that

target, accompanied by a drive to effect an elevated distance. The target of contempt is an individual who is positioned below the contemptuous agent due to features of the target that register on the low end of some scale valued by the agent."

80. The translation of this essay leaves much to be desired. I believe Lefort means to say "to replace the notion of a regime governed by laws, of a legitimate power, *with*" rather than *by* "the notion of a regime governed by legitimate laws."

81. See Lewis 1998 for a history of the development of this idea and the praxis that developed out of it. See also Dyson 2000, Chapter Six, for an analysis of Rev. Dr. Martin Luther King Jr.'s religious radicalism, which resembles Emerson's.

82. See Hochschild 1988, Gutmann 1988, 1989.

83. Marable 1983, Pettigrew 1985, and Wilson 1987, 1996 on capitalism, globalization, and institutionalized racism.

Chapter 3:

1. *Politics*,1278b.

2. Carl Schmitt would argue that this "crisis"... "Springs from the consequences of modern mass democracy and in the final analysis from the contradiction of a liberal individualism burdened by moral pathos and a democratic sentiment governed essentially by political ideals. It is, in its depths, the inescapable contradiction of liberal individualism and democratic homogeneity." (1992, 17) The "liberal individualism" is institutionalized in the nominally equal citizenship of *all* Americans ("the People") who are represented by the elected President and comprise the basis of representation of the U.S. House of Representatives and the Electoral College; the "democratic homogeneity" is institutionalized in the majoritarian governments and laws of the several states, whose diversity of felon disenfranchisement provisions create the plethora of citizenship regimes that determine who may actually *vote*.

3. "Laws must relate to the nature and the principle of the government that is established or that one wants to establish, whether those laws form it as do political laws, or maintain it as do civil laws. They should be related to the *physical aspect* of the country...to the way of life of the peoples...to the degree of liberty that the constitution can sustain; (...) finally, the laws are related to one another, to their origin, to the purpose of the legislator, and to the order of things on which they are established." (Montesquieu 1989 I.3) "The one clear fact is that laws must be constituted in accordance with constitutions (regimes); and if this is the case, it follows that laws which are in accordance with right constitutions must necessarily be just, and laws which are in accordance with wrong or perverted constitutions must be unjust." *Politics* 1282b

4. Madison is arguing that the ancient republics were familiar with the concept of representation. He claimed, however, that "The true distinction between [the ancient constitutions] and the American governments lies in *the total*

exclusion of the people in their collective capacity, from any share in the latter, *and not in the total exclusion of the representatives of the people* from the administration of the former." *Federalist* 63, Rossiter, p. 387 (italics in original.)

5. *Richardson v Ramirez* 418 U.S. 24.

6. Marshall was citing *Byers v Sun Savings Bank,* 41 Okla. 728, 731(1914).

7. The American system of punishment will be reviewed in the next chapter.

8. I am not claiming that felon disenfranchisement is always institutionalized and used as a tool of party competition. In this chapter I will show how, structurally speaking, it can and historically has been explicitly used as such. The unintended consequences of institutionalizing the practice for reasons unrelated to party competition, however, such as "expressive punishment" (Hampton 1988) still have, as I will show in Section 4 below, system-wide effects on the norms of equality and security.

9. The majority ruling in *Richardson v Ramirez* 418 U.S. 24, which represents the contemporary Supreme Court position on felon disenfranchisement, left it up to the states to retain or dispense with the practice.

10. As James Madison observed, "the difference most relied on between the American and other republics consists in the principle of representation, which is the pivot on which the former moves, and which is supposed to have been unknown in the latter." Federalist Papers #63. Bybee footnotes this passage as follows: "To be precise, Madison actually conceded the existence of representation in the ancient world, but he claimed that American government was unique because it entirely removed the people from all positions of direct legislative power." 33, n12.

11. See Hansen 1999, ch. 6; particularly 159-60.

12. Hansen translates *isegoria* as "the equal right to address the Assembly."

13. For an interesting couple of essays on *isegoria* generally, and the relationship between *isegoria* and freedom of speech see Hansen 1996 and Wood 1996 in Ober and Hedrick. Martha Minnow (1990, 297) makes the point that the equality of modern "rights discourse" embodies "an equality of *attention.* The rights tradition in this country sustains the call that makes those in power at least *listen.*" (italics in original)

14. See Urbinati 2000 for arguments about the normative value of "indirectness" in modern representative democracy: "the intermediary network of communication that fills the gap between speaking/hearing and rectifying/voting. Such communication can reunite the *actual* dimension (parliament) and the *deferred* dimension (voters) so that representative democracy might enjoy what made Athenian democracy exceptional – the simultaneity of "standing" and "acting." (766)

15. See Pitkin 1967, ch. 9 for a discussion of the representation of interests; see Aldrich 1995, particularly chs.1-4 on theories of party formation and function in the American system.

16. See Woodward 1951, ch. 12 for a discussion of the Populist Party and competition for black votes in the South during the post-Reconstruction period. Woodward argues that the disenfranchising conventions of the 1890s

were triggered in part by *white* competition for blacks' votes, which according to the political rhetoric of the time was the cause of rampant election corruption and fraud. The solution reached by competing factions of whites, was to disenfranchise blacks so that whites could compete freely amongst themselves as they had in the former citizenship regime. As Woodward notes, while the scheme succeeded in disenfranchising almost all blacks in the Southern states that adopted measures such as the poll tax, literacy clauses, and felon disenfranchisement, as well as many poor whites, the same states reverted to one-party rule for the next one-half century at least, so there was no competition to speak of.

17. "Between 1890 and 1910, many Southern states tailored their criminal disenfranchisement laws, along with other voting qualifications, to increase the effect of these laws on black citizens." (Shapiro 1993) Crimes that triggered disenfranchisement were written to include crimes blacks supposedly committed more frequently than whites and to exclude crimes whites were believed to commit more frequently. For example, in South Carolina, "among the disqualifying crimes were those to which [the Negro] was especially prone: thievery, adultery, arson, wife-beating, housebreaking, and attempted rape. Such crimes as murder and fighting, to which the white man was as disposed as the Negro, were significantly omitted from the list. In 1901 Alabama lawmakers – who openly stated that their goal was to establish white supremacy – included a provision in the state constitution that made conviction of crimes of "moral turpitude" the basis for disenfranchisement. The Supreme Court overruled this section of the Alabama constitution in *Hunter v Underwood* 471 U.S. 222 (1985) because plaintiffs were able to prove discriminatory intent. Until 2003, Alabama was one of 13 American states that disenfranchised ex-felons for life. It is now possible for ex-felons to apply for restoration of their voting rights.

18. For detailed analyses of the disenfranchising conventions see in particular Kousser 1974, 1999; Woodward 1951, Fredrickson, 1988.

19. This is Manin's (1997) point about "retrospective voting." "The central mechanism whereby voters influence governmental decisions results from the incentives that representative systems create for those in office: representatives who are subject to reelection have an incentive to *anticipate* the future judgment of the electorate on the policies they pursue....Voters thus influence public decisions through the *retrospective* judgment that representatives anticipate voters will make." (178-9. Emphasis in original.) Elected majorities that shrink the electorate by means of opportunistic deployment of institutions such as felon disenfranchisement bypass this key mechanism that confers structural accountability on representatives.

20. "When the states one acquires by conquest are accustomed to living under their own laws and in freedom, there are three policies one can follow in order to hold onto them: The first is to lay them to waste; the second to go and live there in person; the third is to let them continue to live under their own laws, make them pay you, and create there an administrative and

political elite who will remain loyal to you. (…) Neither the passage of time nor good treatment will make its citizens forget their previous liberty. In former republics there is more vitality, more hatred, more desire for revenge. The memory of their former freedom gives them no rest, no peace. So the best thing to do is to demolish them or go and live there oneself."

21. See Gerteis 1973 for details of the Union confiscations and military plantations farmed by contrabands and freedmen, lands that were then restored to their former owners. On May 21, 1865, President Johnson granted amnesty to all but the top military and civil leaders of the confederacy. Only a few were ever imprisoned, and then only for a few months. The sole confederate to be executed was Henry Wurtz, commandant of the Andersonville, Georgia prison camp where 13,000 Union soldiers died. See Kennedy 1995, p.21. See also Foner 1988, ch.5.

22. Among the authoritative texts are DuBois 1935, 1979; Gillette 1979, Foner 1988, Smith 1997, Kousser 1999, Brandwein 1999. A Machiavellian explanation for the failure of Reconstruction would attribute it to the North's weakness and inconsistency. As Albion Tourgée said in *A Fool's Errand*, "The North lacks virility." This cowardly shirking of responsibility, this pandering to sentimental whimsicalities, this snuffling whine about peace and conciliation is sheer weakness. The North is simply a conqueror; and, if the results she fought for are to be secured, she must rule as a conqueror."
The North could not rule as a conqueror, though, because The Prince (Lincoln) was dead, and the new Prince (Johnson, a Southerner) had no desire to punish the former Confederacy.

23. See Gillette 1965 for extensive analysis of the debates and the national, state, and Congressional elections during the 1860s and 1870s.

24. The law in American slave states defined slaves as "chattel," and the federal constitution, as well as federal statutes, protected slaveholders' property in their slaves. Slaves had no moral personality, and were reduced to the status of "beasts of the field." "While the impact of the law did not and could not completely wipe out the fact that the Negro slave was human, it raised a sufficient barrier to make the humanity of the Negro difficult to recognize and legally almost impossible to provide for. This legal definition carried its own moral consequences and made the ultimate redefinition of the Negro as a moral person most difficult." Tannenbaum 1946, 1992, 103. Tannenbaum's thesis is that the ease of manumission in the Latin American slave system compared to the relative impossibility of manumission in the U.S. and British slave systems accounts for the "crucial differences" between the character and outcome of the two slave systems. "The principle of manumission encrusted the social structure in the Southern states and left no escape except by revolution, which in this case took the form of a civil war." (110) "The Civil War gave the Negro legal equality with his former master, but it could not and did not give him either the experience in the exercise of freedom or the moral status in the sight of his white fellow citizens to make the freedom of the Negro an acceptable and workable

relationship for them. The endowing of the Negro with a legal equality left a moral vacuum that remained to be filled in. In Latin America the Negro achieved complete legal equality slowly, through manumission, over centuries, and after he had gained moral personality. In the United States he was given his freedom suddenly, and before the white community credited him with moral status." (112) See Fehrenbacher 1978, 2001 for the authoritative discussion of the Dred Scott case and the meaning of Taney's ruling for free blacks.

25. See Amar 1994 on the debate during the 39th Congress on the constitutional meaning of "republican" government and the issue of African-American citizenship. See Kaczorowski, 1986, for a detailed analysis of the framing of the Thirteenth Amendment and the presumption of the "natural rights of citizens" it entailed.

26. See Amar 1994 for constitutional interpretation.

27. "Citizenship is not simply a legal formula; it is an increasingly salient social and cultural fact. As a powerful instrument of social closure, citizenship occupies a central place in the administrative structure and political culture of the modern nation-state system... But while the practice of closure varies across demographic, economic, political, and cultural contexts, the principle and the administrative apparatus of closure are *essential to the modern state and its project of territorial rule.*" (Brubaker 1992, 23-24. My italics.)

28. See Arendt 1968, Ch. 5.

29. See Foner 1988, 57, Gerteis, 1973.

30. Justice Miller in Slaughter-House 83 U.S. (16 Wall) 36 (1873). Ironically, while citing the Black Codes and the post-Emancipation situation of the freedpeople as the primary motivation for the framing and passage of the Fourteenth Amendment, Justice Miller ruled in *Slaughter-House* that national citizenship did not trump state's rights, and that the Fourteenth Amendment had not extended the Bill of Rights to the States. This was a highly contested ruling whose legacy is felt to the present day. See Brandwein 1999 for detailed analysis of the two strands of post-Emancipation jurisprudence, one of which favored "state's rights," the other federal intervention on behalf of minorities.

31. Cited in Brandwein 1999, 53.

32. See Fehrenbacher 1978.

33. "I think that the bitterness was greater toward the Negro after his enfranchisement than it would have been if there was no disenfranchisement of whites. The beginning of bitterness in our country was the disenfranchisement of whites...this coupled with Negro suffrage was the origin of the difficulty." KKK Report to Congress. Alabama testimony. Statement of governor R.B. Lindsay, cited in Fleming 1950, and "Not only the sting of defeat, but the shame of punishment without its terror combined to induce those who had cast all their hopes of honor and success upon the confederate cause to lend themselves to anything that would tend to humiliate the power which, in addition to the fact of conquest, had endeavored to impose upon them the stigma of treason. There is no doubt

that the disfranchisement of those who had engaged in rebellion – or a "war for secession," as they prefer that it should be termed – was almost universally deemed an insult and an outrage only second in infamy to the enfranchisement of the colored man, which was contemporaneous with it." (Tourgée 1989, 132) These rounds of disenfranchisement would have been characterized by the Athenian theorists as *staseis*. See Chapter One, *supra*.

34. The Guarantee clause is inherently paradoxical, as Amar (1994) points out, because of the "denominator" problem. Who counts as the "people" from which the "majority" that rules is elected? A "republican" form of government based on majority rule may mean Jim Crow law, and be "guaranteed" to the states that encode it, if blacks don't count among "the people" of the polity. However, if "republican" government means that "the majority of the free male citizens in every State shall have the political power." a polity based on jim crow laws does not qualify. The restored Southern states got around the paradox by accepting the formal constitutional requirements of the 13th, 14th, and 15th amendments, but disenfranchising in a variety of "color-blind" ways that passed federal judicial scrutiny.

35. Gillette 1965, Foner 1988, Wang 1996.

36. Hirshson 1962, 52. Although Blaine's statement was made in the context of Redeemer violence that disenfranchised freedmen who were attempting to vote in South Carolina, the theoretical point holds. See also Kousser 1999, 37: "By denying the suffrage to most [blacks and white oppositionists] Democrats diluted its value for all individual members. Thus, suffrage restriction exposed the distinction between group and individual rights as unreal. If voting preferences are correlated with race, then the value of an individual's right depends on how her group is treated."

37. See Gillette 1979, ch.1; James (1965), particularly ch. 3; Fredrickson 1995, Ch. 1 Fredrickson attributes the radical democratic methods of Reconstruction to the "extraordinary challenge of reconstructing the Union on a permanent basis and insuring the future success of the Union-saving Republican party... [This] required measures that in other circumstances they would have deemed unwise or unjustified." Republican leaders were not radical democrats or firm believers in racial equality. "They were conventional nineteenth-century liberals and moderate white supremacists."

38. Kousser 1999, Woodward 1966, Foner 1988, Shapiro 1993.

39. Valleley's (1995) thesis is that an intense commitment of Republican Party resources in the South could not be sustained after the 1890s because the costs of party competition in that region were too great relative to the benefits. "The new state-level rules restricted the electorate to a pool of white conservative Democrats that Republicans could never mobilize. The disenfranchising conventions and the southern legislatures had devised rules that shrank the legal registrant pool. Under *Yarborough* only national regulation of national elections was protected: states could pretty much do what they wanted. But what point was there to national regulation of national elections if the registrant pool was miniscule, white, and strongly

Democratic? Only a massive new commitment – a true "second Reconstruction" – could cope with this problem." (206) "The costs of a southern policy were now very high indeed, and the benefits were nil. Both a resurgence of strength in historic Republican areas [the Northeast and Midwest] and new strength in the West made the South superfluous to Republican capacity to achieve unified government." (209)

40. See for example Lieberman 1995 for an analysis of the influence of the Southern Congressional delegation in the development of the New Deal policies of the welfare state, and the exclusion of domestic and agricultural workers from Old Age Insurance.

41. See Maveety 1991, esp. chs. 1-3 for the evolution of theories of representation endorsed by different courts.

42. "To this strange Doctrine, *viz. That in the State of Nature, every one has the Executive Power* of the Law of Nature, I doubt not that it will be objected, That it is unreasonable for Men to be Judges in their own Cases, that Self-love will make Men partial to themselves and their Friends. And on the other side, that Ill Nature, Passion and Revenge will carry them too far in punishing others. And hence nothing but Confusion and Disorder will follow, and that therefore God hath certainly appointed Government to restrain the partiality and violence of Men. I easily grant that *Civil Government* is the proper Remedy for the Inconveniences of the state of Nature, which must certainly be Great where Men may be Judges in their own Case since 'tis easily imagined that he who was so unjust as to do his Brother an Injury, will scarce be so just as to condemn himself for it." Locke SC II, §13, 276 (Emphasis in original)

43. For the details of trial procedures see Hansen 1999 and for an interesting comparative study of ancient and modern juries see Allen 200, Introduction.

44. Pamela Karlan argues that modern American ex-offender disenfranchise-ment is unconstitutionally punitive rather than regulative, but I believe the argument misses the point. The contemporary practice may well be punitive, but the central point of the practice is political, to dilute the voting power of citizens who would vote for a particular party or candidate. After Reconstruction, the Republican Party was the target. At the present time, it is the Democratic Party. See the recent scholarship of Uggins and Manza on vote dilution and felon disenfranchisement.

45. "Eleventhly, to the Soveraign is committed the Power of Rewarding with riches, or honour; and of Punishing with corporall, or pecuniary punishment, or with ignominy every Subject according to the Law he hath formerly made..." *Leviathan*, Ch. 18. On the "republican' side of social contract theory, Rousseau argues in Chapter VII of *The Social Contract* that in a legitimate polity, each person "places himself and all his power in common under the supreme direction of the general will. (...) For since each person gives himself whole and entire, the condition is equal for everyone; and since the condition is equal for everyone, no one has an interest in making it burdensome for others."

46. Judge William Quinlan of Wisconsin, cited in Jacoby 1980, 34.

47. See Jacoby 1980 for comparative evolution of all three offices. See also Baker 1992 for historical analysis. Misner 1996 for details of constitutional and statutory provisions regarding elections of district attorneys: "More than 95% of chief prosecutors are elected locally; about three-fourths of the prosecutor's offices represented jurisdictions with less than 65,000 people (…) Prosecutors are usually white males – 70% of the prosecutors are male and 88% are white, non-Hispanic."

48. Baker, Newman and Earl DeLong in *Journal of Criminal Law and Criminology*, cited in Jacoby 1980, 33.

49. This state of affairs existed in Athenian democracy prior to the revision of the laws after the "reconciliation" at the end of the fifth century See Ostwald 1986, in particular, Chapter Ten. It is beyond the scope of this book to compare the postwar period following the deposition of the Thirty Tyrants in Athens, and the Reconstruction in the U.S. Suffice to say that the Athenians elected a commission to conduct a minute revision of *all* the laws of Athens in order to ensure that they were consistent with the postwar political "reconciliation" between the democracy and the oligarchy, which had altered the citizenship requirements. It would be an interesting counterfactual exercise to speculate whether, had the Reconstruction Congresses commissioned a similar review of state laws, the powers of the criminal justice system to charge, prosecute, incarcerate, and disenfranchise would have remained the same under the new citizenship regime.

50. See Morris 1996 and Higginbothman 1978 for detailed treatment of legal codes under slavery.

51. The Fourteenth and Fifteenth Amendments, appearances notwithstanding, did *not* give blacks, or anyone for that matter, the right to vote. The Constitution contains no affirmative right to vote.

52. Indeed, the Ku Klux Klan could be construed as a "self-help" organization that defended the rights of white citizens vis-à-vis Radical Reconstruction. And *that* self-help organization had effective impunity, just as did the Athenian citizens who were legally allowed to persecute the *atimos*. See Fleming 1950 for texts of KKK documents.

53. *United States v Cruikshank* 92, U.S. 542 (1876); *United States v Reese*, 92 U.S. 214 (1875). In the former case, the Supreme Court "shrouded the gruesome events that led to the indictments in constitutional theory." *Cruikshank* involved a Ku Klux Klan led massacre of sixty freedmen in Louisiana following a disputed gubernatorial election. The counts in the indictment alleged a conspiracy to deprive African Americans "of their respective several lives and liberty of person without due process of law." Chief Justice Waite asserted that "[s]overeignty, for this purpose, rests alone with the States. It is no more the duty or within the power of the United States to punish for a conspiracy to falsely imprison or murder within a State, than it would be to punish for false imprisonment or murder itself." (Higginbotham 1996, 89) In the latter case, the Supreme Court voided two sections of the Enforcement Act of 1870 as beyond congressional powers to enforce the Fifteenth Amendment. The case involved an indictment under

the Act "against two of the inspectors of a municipal election in the State of Kentucky, for refusing to receive and count at such election the vote of William Garner, and African-American." (Ibid. 235 n.47.) This is not to say that there was *no* enforcement or criminal prosecution under the Enforcement Act of 1870 and the Federal Elections Act of 1871. For a period between 1870 and 1877 "besides the frequent military interventions and deployment of federal troops initiated by the President or on his authority, the Department of Justice launched a total of 3,635 criminal cases." (Valleley 1995, 196)

54. Mills' theory is discussed in detail in Chapter Five.

55. This has historically been the case for politically disempowered (disenfranchised) groups: women, children, people of color, prisoners, homosexuals, and the mentally and physically "disabled." Charges are not filed, or juries will not convict (or charges are not filed simply because the DA knows a jury will not convict) when the perpetrator of a crime is a member of what Weber called a "protected law community." Members of a vulnerable community that are unprotected by the "representative" legal system are materially equivalent to *atimoi*. The situation of prisoners and members of minority communities that are the targets of police violence in the United States will be reviewed in the following chapters.

56. My analysis here is indebted to Hannah Arendt's key text *On Violence* (1972) as well as Giorgio Agambin's (1998) philosophical exegesis of the concept of *homo sacer*.

57. I am not making the claim that this is the *intention* of all contemporary state felon disenfranchisement policies, as it was during the post-Reconstruction period, only that this is now their *effect*. Contemporary criminal justice and felonization policies are the subject of the next chapter. See Uggens and Manza 2000, and 2003 for studies of how felon disenfranchisement may have affected the outcomes of some close political races.

58. See Ides and May (1998, ch. 7) for detailed exposition of the jurisprudential concepts of vote denial, and individual and group vote dilution.

59. *Reynolds v Simms*, 377 U.S. 533, 568 (1964).

60. *Id* At 577.

61. *Id.*

62. As Justices Harlan and Frankfurter pointed out in their dissents in *Baker v Carr* 396 U.S. 186, fundamental choices concerning political philosophy are at issue in the concept of vote dilution. Martin Shapiro (1964) argued at the time, the Court's failure to grapple with the complex philosophical and theoretical issues that lie behind the notion of constitutional democracy led it away from the delicate and tentative adjustments that our peculiar form of democracy requires and into the formulation of appealing slogans. The "one man, one vote" slogan, in equating the whole of democracy with majority-rule elections represents naïve political philosophy, bad political theory, and no political science. See Phillips 1995 for theoretical and empirical analysis of the problems it spawned. Phillips' claim concerns racial vote dilution and the injustice suffered by minorities under the new rule. Schwartz 1993

points out that [Warren] "did not sacrifice good sense for the syllogism. Nor was he one of 'those who think more of symmetry and logic in the development of legal rules than of practical adaptation to the attainment of a just result.' When symmetry and logic were balanced against considerations of equity and fairness, he normally found the latter to be the weightier." (275) Warren characterized the reapportionment cases as the most important cases decided by the Court during his tenure. [He] had no doubts about the correctness of the reapportionment decisions. He maintained that if the "one person, one vote" principle had been laid down years earlier, many of the nation's legal sores would never have festered. According to Warren, 'many of our problems would have been solved a long time ago if everyone had the right to vote, and his vote counted the same as everybody else's. Most of these problems could have been solved through the political process rather than through the courts. But as it was, the Court had to decide." 279.

63. Citing *Gomillion v Lightfoot* 364 U.S. at 347.
64. *Reynolds v Sims.*
65. Warren's ruling in *Reynolds.*
66. Cited in Justice Harlan's dissent in *Reynolds v Simms* (449).
67. As Valleley (1995) points out in his argument about the Reconstruction-era contest between the major political parties, [The Democratic presidential platform for 1892] made the Elections Bill and, by implication, the very idea of a federal electoral-regulatory system its first objects of attack. Both in its printed material for public circulation and in the themes chosen by Democratic speakers touring the country, the Democratic campaign made electoral regulation the party's most important – its first and paramount – issue. ...In 1893 and 1894 Congressional Democrats repealed twenty-eight of the sections in the United States Statutes under the title of "elective Franchise" and ten of the sections, and a part of an eleventh, under the title of "crimes." (203)
68. See Amar 1998 for a discussion of the "incorporation" theory of the Bill of Rights.
69. "The equality of the Greek *polis*, its isonomy, was an attribute of the *polis* and not of men, who received their equality by virtue of citizenship, not by virtue of birth. Neither equality nor freedom was understood as a quality inherent in human nature, they were not given by nature; they were conventional and artificial, the products of human effort and qualities of the man-made world." *On Revolution,* 31.
70. 396 U.S. 186, 330.
71. Harlan's dissent in *Reynolds,* 545.
72. "In reaching what he considered the just result, the Chief Justice was not deterred by the demands of stare decisis. For Warren, principle was more compelling than precedent." (Schwartz 1993, 284)
73. *Reynolds,* 612.
74. Harlan's dissent in *Carrington v Rash* 380 U.S. 89; 85 S.Ct. 775 (1965).
75. *Reynolds,* 625.
76. *Wesberry v Sanders, Oregon v Mitchell.*

77. "The theory of law as the general Will (a will that is valuable as such because of its general character, in contrast to every particular will) ... can be understood as an expression of the concept of law in a Rechstaat." (Schmitt 1992, 44)

78. *Wesberry v Sanders, Oregon v Mitchell*

79. As noted in the Introduction to Chapter Two, *supra*, the vast majority of scholarly articles on felon disenfranchisement argue that the practice results in *minority* vote dilution as per the Voting Rights Act.

80. "The smaller the society, the fewer probably will be the distinct parties and interests composing it, the more frequently will a majority be found of the same party; and the smaller number of individuals composing a majority, and the smaller the compass within which they are placed, the more easily they will concert and execute their plans of oppression. Extend the sphere and you take in a greater variety of parties and interests; you make it less probable that a majority of the whole will have a common motive to invade the rights of other citizens." *Federalist* 10.

81. As opposed to the perspective of "abstract justice" derided by Justice Harlan in all the apportionment cases. Although Harlan was in the (vehemently) dissenting minority in all these cases, his perspective was unremittingly "political" if "unjust" by modern "universalist" standards.

82. Indeed, following Schattschneider, felon disenfranchisement can be seen as a way of using the criminal justice system to privatize or shrink the sphere of conflict rather than socializing conflict through a more inclusive political system. The moral, or normative conception of democratic citizenship that I presented in the previous chapter is more congruent with Schattschneider's view of democracy as "made for the people, not the people for democracy. Democracy is something for ordinary people, a political system designed to be sensitive to ordinary people regardless of whether or not the pendants approve of them." (132) "The socialization of conflict is the essential democratic process."(138)

83. I.e., in the Preamble, and the Ninth and Tenth Amendments.

84. 372 U.S. 368 (1963), 379-380.

85. *Id* at 380.

86. 376 U.S. 1 (1964).

87. *Id.* The average Congressional district in the U.S. contains 580,000 people.

88. *Id.*

89. *Garza v County of Los Angeles* U.S. Court of Appeals for the Ninth Court, 918 F.2d 763, Dissent by Kozinski at 51. The plaintiffs in *Garza* alleged that the Hispanic vote in Los Angeles County had been impermissibly diluted by the way the Board of Supervisors had drawn district lines. What is interesting for my purposes is that the defendants (LA County) alleged that the large population of undocumented and non-citizen Hispanic aliens in the proposed (equipopulous) majority Hispanic district, would dilute the votes of "legitimate" Angelino citizens. They were claiming, in other words, that inclusion of the non-voting, disenfranchised Hispanics in a majority-minority district diluted the votes of white citizens in the other districts. The

9th Circuit Court rejected this argument, and directed the Board to create the majority Hispanic district, but did not address the vote dilution issue. Judge Kozinski analyzed the theoretical problems, but interestingly enough, none of the justices proposed solving the problem by *enfranchising the disenfranchised*!

90. *Id* at 50.
91. *Id* at 52.
92. 384 U.S. 73.
93. See Hench 1998, Harvey 1994, Shapiro 1993, Demleitner 2000
94. Vote dilution could be claimed between congressional districts in the same state if one district had more disenfranchised felons than another. For example, New York City compared to upstate, predominantly suburban districts.
95. We saw this in Florida during the 2000 Presidential election. Twenty-four percent of the black males in Florida were unable to vote because of felony convictions. According to Fletcher (2001, 243) "If they had been able to vote, there is little doubt about who would have won the election (90% of blacks voted for Gore in 2000.)
96. This was a deliberate "anti-democratic" choice of "the Founders" and was not adjusted when the American citizenship regime was "re-founded" during the Reconstruction Congresses.
97. See Smith 1998 for a very interesting proposal to create Senate districts in order to counteract minority vote dilution and "preserve" the Second Reconstruction.
98. See O'Sullivan 1992, Anglim 1993, and Harvard Note 2001 for analysis of the Electoral College and proposals for reform.
99. The presence of other "disenfranchised citizens" besides convicted felons within the basis of apportionment – such as children and the mentally incompetent – is irrelevant to my argument that vote dilution results from different felon disenfranchisement laws distorting the electorate of states with identical apportionment bases. The rules disqualifying minors and the insane are uniform for all state electorates. There is a qualitative difference that has theoretical significance between the population of disenfranchised felons in the apportionment base, and that of minors and the insane. Disenfranchised felons are not randomly distributed among the states: their (negative) political status is a function of positive law. Populations of minors and the mentally incompetent *are* randomly distributed, and while their exclusion is certainly *intentional*, their political status is a uniform one within the national citizen body, which as we have seen, does not correspond with the national electorate. See Bennett 2000 for an interesting proposal "to give parents extra votes on account of their children."
100. Similar comparison may be made between other sets of states with equal numbers of Electoral College votes such as Idaho and Maine, each of which is entitled to four presidential electors. Idaho disenfranchises convicted felons in prison, on probation and on parole, whereas Maine allows prisoners to vote. The votes of citizens in Maine are therefore diluted

relative to those in Idaho, where the enfranchised population is smaller, relative to an identical basis of apportionment (1.2 million residents for both states.)

101. See e.g. Hench 1998, Harvey 1994, Shapiro 1993 for the argument about minority vote dilution and felon disenfranchisement.

102. This is because the conception of justice in the national regime is not based on the democratic political principle of "equality of equals and the will of those who belong to the equals" (Schmitt 1992, 15-16) but on the principle of natural human equality, which is "a certain kind of liberalism, not a state form but an individualistic-humanitarian ethic and *Weltanschauung*." (ibid. 11) See Kaczorowski 1986 for discussion of the "natural law" principles inscribed in the Reconstruction Amendments that institutionalized the sovereignty of the national regime.

103. *Yick Wo v. Hopkins* 118 U.S. 356 (1886)

104. *Wesberry v Sanders* 376 U.S. 1 (1964)

105. *Reynolds v Simms* 377 U.S. 533 (1964)

106. *Ibid.*

107. "In a 1985 interview [Chief Justice Rehnquist] noted that he joined the Court with a desire to counteract the Warren Court decisions. 'I came to the court,' Rehnquist said, 'sensing...that there were some excesses in terms of constitutional adjudication during the era of the so-called Warren Court." (Schwartz 1993, 365)

108. 9 Cal. 3d 199, 216-17, 507 P.2d 1345, 1357 (1973).

109. "Representatives shall be apportioned among the several States according to their respective numbers, counting the whole number of persons in each State, excluding Indians not taxed. But when the right to vote at any election for the choice of electors for President and Vice-President of the United States, Representatives in Congress, the Executive and Judicial Officers of a state or the members of the Legislatures thereof, is denied to any of the male inhabitants of such State, being twenty-one years of age and citizens of the United States, or in any way abridged *except for participation in rebellion or other crime*, the basis of representation therein shall be reduced in proportion which the number of such male citizens shall bear to the whole number of male citizens twenty-one years of age in such State." (Italics added.)

110. States used criminal justice system, poll taxes, and literacy clauses to shape the electorate to their "republican" requirements and reduce black political participation. See Kousser 1974.

111. "I ___ do solemnly swear (or affirm) in the presence of Almighty God, that I am a citizen of the State of ___; that I have resided in the state for ___ months next preceding this day, and ___ parish. That I am a twenty-one year old; that I have not been disfranchised for participation in any rebellion or civil war against the United States, nor for felony committed against the laws of any state or of the U.S." See Fleming (1950) p. 408.

112. *Murphy v Ramsey*, 114 U.S. 15 (1885) and *Davis v Beason* 133 U.S. 333 (1890).

113. *Dillenburg v Kramer*, 469 F.2d 1222, 1226.
114. *Reynolds v Simms* 377 U.S. at 555.
115. See *Green v Board of Elections* 380 F.2d 445, 451.
116. *Cipriano v City of Houma*, 395 U.S. at 705-706; Communist Party of Indiana v Whitcomb, 414 U.S. 441.
117. 380 U.S. at 94.
118. "In the post-Reconstruction period, both parties renewed their previous Reconstruction-era struggle over electoral rules and institutions. Both remained cohesive with regard to electoral regulatory policy. The Republicans preferred national rules developed ruing the Reconstruction; the Democrats opposed such rules, preferring regional or local rules." (Valleley 1995, 191)
119. Indeed, this is the recommendation of the report of the National Commission on Federal Election Reform, entitled "To Assure Pride and Confidence in the Electoral Process" (August 2001): "Each state should allow for restoration of voting rights to otherwise eligible citizens who have been convicted of a felony once they have fully served their sentence, including any term of probation or parole."

Chapter 4:

1. See Uggen and Manza 2002 for an interesting counterfactual argument on how felon disenfranchisement may have affected certain presidential and senatorial races. The authors claim that, were felons not disenfranchised in particular states, the outcome of some of the races would have been different, favoring the Democratic Party.
2. Again, this is what happened in California when the California Supreme Court held that the constitutional and statutory provisions disenfranchising felons violated the Fourteenth Amendment, triggering the appeal by a county clerk and registrar of voters that resulted in the *Richardson* ruling. A case is now pending in U.S. District Court in Florida challenging the constitutionality of the Florida practice of disenfranchising ex-felons: *Thomas Johnson et al. v Jeb Bush, Katherine Harris, et al.* U.S. District Court, Southern District of Florida 2000. Felons' voting rights are being reviewed by courts all over the country as this book goes to press.
3. Although Utah and Massachusetts, both states that until recently allowed even prisoners to vote, recently enacted laws disenfranchising prisoners for the period of their incarceration. In Massachusetts, the law was changed in 2001 by popular referendum, following a campaign persuading citizens in predominantly white districts hosting prisons whose inmates were from the cities, that the "prisoner vote" in those districts would have a distorting effect on elections. See Conn 2003 for analysis of state partisan politics.
4. Between 1980 and 1997, the number of women in prison increased from 12,300 to 82, 800, a rise of 573%. Drug offenses accounted for half (49%) of the rise of the number of women incarcerated in state prisons, compared to one-third (32%) for men. Minority women (black and Hispanic) represent a disproportionate share of the women sentenced to prison for a drug

offense. (*Gender and Justice: Women, Drugs and Sentencing Policy*, The Sentencing Project, November 1999) An earlier report stated, "Although research on women of color in the criminal justice system is limited, existing data and research suggest that it is the combination of race and sex effects that is at the root of the trends that appear in our data." (Mauer and Huling 1995).

5. See Fletcher 2000 on the argument that disenfranchised felons constitute a "caste."

6. I use the term "non-convicted" rather than non-criminal, because it is conviction that triggers disenfranchisement, not any inherent "criminality" in the act or the person. See Pinaire et al. on public attitudes towards felons and voting rights.

7. My use of the concept of a "continuum" is slightly different from Foucault's "carceral network" or "archipelago" to describe all the mechanisms and institutions of discipline in modern society. Foucault uses the term "carceral continuum" to describe "the communication between the power of discipline and the power of the law [which] extends without interruption from the smallest coercions to the longest penal detention." (1977, 393)

8. This is particularly true in the case of drug crime. According to Human Rights Watch report on incarceration in the US, Blacks make up about 13% of regular drug users in the US, but 62.7% of all drug offenders admitted to prison. While there are 5 times as many white drug users as black drug users, black men are admitted to state prison for drug offenses at a rate that is 13.4 times greater than that of white men. This drives an overall black incarceration rate that is 8.2 times higher than the white incarceration rate. The category of felony drug offenses includes both sale and possession. There are generally three times as many arrests for possession as for sale of both marijuana and heroin/cocaine. Furthermore, "The participation of African Americans in the drug trade is not greater than that of whites. Although statistics do not analyze drug dealers by race before they are arrested, former DEA chief Robert Bonner has argued that it is 'probably safe to say that whites themselves would be in the majority of traffickers.'" Cited in Bertram 1996, 38.

   In seven states, blacks constitute 80 to 90% of all drug offenders sent to prison. In 15 states, black men are admitted to state prison for drug charges at a rate that is 20 to 57 times the white male rate." Cited in "Poor Prescriptions: The Costs of Imprisoning Drug Offenders in the United States." (Website of the Justice Policy Institute: www.cjcj.org/drug /pp.html.) The other kind of "crime" that is "punished" much more lightly than drug crime, if at all, is "white collar crime," which I do not analyze in this book. The authoritative texts on the different criminological approaches to "street" and "suite" crimes are Currie 1998, Rieman 1996, Cole 1999, Brown 2001, and Mustard, 2001.

9. "The problem with most official records of who commits crime is that they are really statistics on who gets arrested and convicted....Some social scientists, suspicious of the bias built into official records, have tried to

devise other methods of determining who has committed a crime. The President's Crime Commission conducted a survey of 10,000 households and discovered that "91 percent of all Americans have violated laws that could have subjected them to a term of imprisonment at one time in their lives." A number of other studies support the conclusion that serious criminal behavior is widespread among middle- and upper-class individuals, although these individuals are rarely, if ever, arrested. Some of these studies show that there are no significant differences between economic classes in the incidence of criminal behavior." (Reiman 1995, 96)

10. See Hampton 1998 for a particularly interesting argument supporting disenfranchisement of prisoners who are convicted of rape and other crimes against women. See also the Justice Gauthier's dissent in the recent Canadian case *Sauve v Canada*, that allowed the enfranchisement of felons serving more than two years. The Canadian case is interestingly different from the American case, since it acknowledges the rights of the Canadian states to disenfranchise imprisoned felons for crime.

11. See Karlan 2003 citing Johnson v Bush 214 F. Supp. 2d 1333 (S.D. Fla.2002) and Farrakhan v Locke, 2000 U.S. Dist. LEXIS 22212 (E.D. Wash 2000).

12. The State of New York disenfranchises felons for the period of their imprisonment, probation, and parole.

13. Judge Friendly in *Green v Board of Elections* 380 F. 2d 445 (2d. Cir. 1967) *cert denied*, 389 U.S. 1048 (1968).

14. "The early exclusion of felons from the franchise by many states could well have rested on Locke's concept, so influential at the time, that by entering into society every man "authorizes the society, or which is all one, the legislature thereof, to make laws for him as the public good of the society shall require, to the execution whereof his own assistance (as to his own decrees) is due." Judge Friendly quoting Locke: *An Essay Concerning the True Original, Extent and End of Civil Government* (1698), 380 F. 2d 445 (1967).

15. *Beacham v Braterman* 300 F. Supp. 182 (S.D. Fla), aff'd mem., 396 U.S. 12 (1969) and *Kronland v Honstein* 327 F. Supp. 71 (N.D. Ga. 1971).

16. A "serious crime" in New York under the "Rockefeller Drug Laws" can be defined as possession of a small amount of marijuana, and earn the citizen twenty years in the penitentiary, disenfranchising him during his sentence, and thereafter until his parole is up. These laws are currently being challenged both in court and in the legislature. Moreover, the "three strikes" laws popular during the 1990s sentenced citizens to life imprisonment for relatively trivial offenses such as the theft of a pizza, or other small ticket items, effectively disenfranchising the citizens for life. The "seriousness" of the crime lay in the cumulative pattern of petty criminality of the offender rather than in the dimensions of the crime itself. Meanwhile, as this book goes to press, the Rockefeller Laws are being debated in Albany and the Supreme Court has effectively struck down mandatory minimum sentencing.

17. "A contention that the equal protection clause requires New York to allow convicted mafiosi to vote for district attorneys or judges would not only be without merit but as obviously so as anything can be." *Green v Board of Elections, 380* F.2d 445, 451-52 (2d. Cir. 1967).
18. *Carrington v Rash*, 380 U.S. 89 (1965).
19. See Urbinati 2000 on the virtues of "indirect" democracy, particularly deliberation and advocacy between elections.
20. Indeed, the journalistic reports on the issue of felon disenfranchisement in many states in the wake of the Florida election have told the stories of such ex-offenders who exhibit all the traditional characteristics of civic virtue. See The Sentencing Project website for journalistic as well as scholarly coverage of the issue.
21. Within the republican tradition, according to Philip Pettit (1993, 315) "It is understandable why (..) the antonym of liberty should have been slavery or subjection or vulnerability. The aim of republican theorists was to identify the characteristics of a society in virtue of which its citizens – its citizens as distinct from residents who do not enjoy citizenship – are marked off from those who are the victims of despotic rule, corrupt officialdom, external control of the like. They used the concept of liberty to serve this purpose of demarcation and so it is no surprise that they should have conceived of liberty as the antithesis of slavery or subjection. The approach is clearly in place, for example, in the eighteenth century republican tract *Cato's Letters*. 'Liberty is, to live upon one's own terms; slavery is, to live at the mere mercy of another; and a life of slavery is, to those who can bear it, a continual state of uncertainty and wretchedness, often an apprehension of violence, often the lingering dread of a violent death.' (Trenchard and Gordon 1971, Vol.2, 249-50) The lives of convicted felons incarcerated in contemporary prisons and "free" in urban ghettoes resembles such a "continual state of uncertainty and wretchedness."
22. The first two references are from Whitman's *Song of Myself* (Shambala 1998), the last one from *Song For Occupations*, cited in Kateb 1992, 250. Kateb comments, "The individual demands to share the goods, the suffering, the fate of the stranger, and does so by imagining the stranger's life as a life he or she could lead and never feel out of place. As Whitman says in his earliest Notebook, 'A man is only interested in anything when he identifies himself with it.' Whitman wants to coax us into thinking that we can identify with anything if we try, and that if we try we show not presumption, but democratic honesty." (250)
23. The history of the framing of felon disenfranchisement provisions in the post-Reconstruction constitutional conventions is unequivocal: they were explicitly framed to discriminate against the new African-American citizens. (See Shapiro 1993 for documentary evidence. See also *Hunter v Underwood*). So (even hypothetical) consent to such laws would be irrational on the part of blacks today. If they have consented to anything, it would have to be to the Voting Rights Act in its original and amended versions, and as Shapiro (1993), Hensch (1998) and others have argued,

since contemporary state felon disenfranchisement practices have racially discriminatory results, they are unconstitutional under the Section 2 of the Amended Act.

24. I formulate the term anti-consent, to distinguish it from active non-consent or civil disobedience.

25. The other "traditional" justifications of punishment are rehabilitation, retribution, and incapacitation. Incapacitation – political incapacitation – is the only explanation of felon disenfranchisement, unless the offense is election fraud, which would make disenfranchisement explicitly retributive,

26. "A man who breaks the laws he has authorized his agent to make for his own governance could fairly have been thought to have abandoned the right to participate in further administering the compact. (...) It can scarcely be deemed unreasonable for a state to decide that perpetrators of serious crimes shall not take part in electing the legislators who make laws, the executives who enforce these, the prosecutors who must try them for further violations, or the judges who are to consider the cases."

27. "Some of the acts of episodic citizenship – say civil disobedience in the 1960s – derived in part from the spirit of representative democracy and in part from its failures. Civil disobedience is the child of representative democracy: faithful in rebellion, faithful because rebellious." (Kateb 1993, 51)

28. With regard to the stability of the polity, Aristotle thought that the existence of such a group was a bad idea: "It would thus seem possible to solve, by the considerations we have advanced, both the problem raised in the previous chapter 'what body of *persons* should be sovereign?' and the further problem which follows upon it, 'What are the *matters* over which freedmen, or the general body of citizens – men of the sort who neither have wealth nor can make any claim on the ground of goodness —should properly exercise sovereignty?' It may be argued, from one point of view, that it is dangerous for men of this sort to share in the highest offices, as injustice may lead them into wrongdoing, and thoughtlessness into error. But it may also be argued, from another point of view, that there is serious risk in not letting them have *some* share in the enjoyment of power; for a state with a body of disenfranchised citizens who are numerous and poor must necessarily be a state which is full of enemies." *Politics* III, xi.(1281b)

29. See Harvard Note (1989) 1300

30. But see Furman 1997 for a critique of the Rawlsian position in *Political Liberalism* that can justify felon disenfranchisement.

31. *Ibid*, 1306

32. The U.S. Supreme Court has upheld this argument about the basic nature of the right to vote in a series of cases, as we saw in Chapter Three, yet makes an "exception" for felon disenfranchisement, because it apparently has "affirmative constitutional sanction" in Section 2 of the Fourteenth Amendment. Furman calls the Supreme Court jurisprudence on voting rights "paradoxical and contradictory," arguing that it mirrors the ambivalence in Rawls' theory of justice. Rawls argues on the one hand for the maintenance

of consensus (those who violate the terms of social cooperation are excluded or contained so as not to threaten the "consensus" of the others), and on the other hand, for a commitment to radical toleration in the allocation of political liberties.

33. "If a citizen disclaim the lawful Government of the Country he was born in, he must also quit the Right that belong'd to him by the Laws of it…" Locke, *Second Treatise*. And "Every offender who attacks the social right becomes through his crimes a rebel and a traitor to his homeland; he ceases to be one of its members by violating its laws, and he even wages war against it…He has broken the social treaty, and consequently is no longer a member of the state." Rousseau, SC.

34. *Trop v Dulles*, 356 U.S. 86 (1958) at 92-101.

35. "The removal of felons' voting rights violates the Lockean principle that each transgression from the social contract should be "punished to that degree, and with so much severity, as will suffice to make it an ill bargain to the offender, give him cause to repent, and terrify others from doing the like." Accordingly, "[d]isenfranchisement for life fails to meet this standard [since] permanent exclusion from the political community is imposed equally on all felons" regardless of degree of severity of their crimes." Harvard Note

36. The contrast with the classical practice of *atimia*, discussed in Chapters One and Three, is instructive, since disenfranchisement was used selectively to punish only certain crimes directly related to the institution of citizenship, which was an honorific status. It was not a consequence of conviction for *all* felonies, as is the case in many U.S. states, where citizenship is a universally distributed, non-honorific status. As I argued in those chapters, *atimia* was a just institution in the context of the classical citizenship regimes, but not in a modern one. Challenges to state felon disenfranchisement practices on the basis of their "irrationality" – the fact that they classify all convictions for crime, from trivial to grave, as felonies – have had only sporadic success in the lower courts. See, for instance, *Otsuka v Hite* 51 Ca. Rptr. 284, 414 P. 2d 412 (1966); *Stephens v Yeomans*, 327 F. Supp. 1182 (D.N.J. 1970); *Ramirez v Brown*, 9 Cal. Reptr. 137, 507 P. 2d 1345 (1973).

37. The annual cost of the U.S. criminal justice system is around \$150 billion (Dyer 2000, 2).

38. For analysis of the prison industry, the including the corporations that profit from crime, many of which are publicly traded, and "owned" by American citizens through mutual fund portfolios, see Dyer 2000.

39. See in particular Hallinan 2001.

40. According to one "minority" sociologist, "the problem of controlling crime in the ghetto is primarily one of changing the conditions that tend to breed widespread violence rather than one of reforming the individual criminal. An apt analogy might be to compare ghetto pathology to an epidemic. To prevent epidemics, necessary public health and sanitation measures are taken; one does not attempt to control the epidemic through the impossible

task of trying to control individuals. Yet the tendency has been, in terms of ghetto crimes, to concentrate on imprisonment of individuals, rather than to seek to destroy the community roots of crime itself." (Clark 1989, 109)

41. More theoretically speaking, "If all *individuals* are responsible citizens, punished as a matter of justice and right, then there is no need to recognize that *this* citizen was poor, unemployed, brought up in deprivation, or the product of a broken family. Fault resides in the individual, not in the system (Norrie 1993, 26).

42. "Here in the richest nation in the world, where more crime is committed than in any other nation, we are told that the answer to this problem is to reduce our poverty. This isn't the answer...*Government's function is to protect society from the criminal*, not the other way around" (emphasis added) and "[I]t is abundantly clear that much of our crime problem was provoked by a social philosophy that saw man as primarily a creature of his material environment. The same liberal philosophy that saw an era of prosperity and virtue ushered in by changing man's environment through massive Federal spending programs also viewed criminals as the unfortunate products of poor socio-economic conditions or an underprivileged upbringing. Society, not the individual, they said, was at fault for criminal wrongdoing. We were to blame. Well, today, a new political consensus utterly rejects this point of view."

43. See in particular Kennedy 1987. See also Bertram 1996, on Rep. Charlie Rangel's approach to the war on drugs. Representative John Conyers, joined by the Congressional Black Caucus, has sponsored a bill (HR 906 in the 106th Congress) "To Secure the Voting Rights of Persons Who Have been Released from Incarceration." Section 2 C of the Bill claims that "state disenfranchisement laws disproportionately impact ethnic minorities." And Section 6 states that "Thirteen percent of the African American adult male population, or 1,400,000 million African American men are disenfranchised. Given current rates of incarceration, three in ten of the next generation of black men will be disenfranchised at some point in their lifetime....These discrepancies should be addressed by Congress." Congressman Conyer's bill has not made it out of Committee.

44. See Bertram et al. on the negative social (including health and economic) consequences of incarceration for black communities. See also the Vera Institute of Justice Report on "Unintended Consequences of the Drug War."

45. For critical analyses of contract theory from the perspective of historically oppressed status groups, see Pateman 1988 and Mills 1997. The final chapter of this book will analyze the American "incarceration polity" from the perspectives of contract and postcolonial theory.

46. The critical scholarly literature on felon disenfranchisement focuses largely on the racially discriminatory effects of the practice, seen as "collateral damage" of the American "wars" on crime and drugs that began in earnest in the 1970s. See, for example, Hensch 1998, Harvey 1994, Shapiro 1993, Demleitner 2000, specifically on disenfranchisement, and Parenti 1999, Christianson 1998, Cole 1999, Hallinan 2001, Mauer 1999, Tonry 1994,

Donziger, Gordon 1993, James 2000, Conover 2001, on the racial demography of incarceration. See Baum 1996, J. Miller 1996, R. Miller 1996, Gray 1998, Lusanne 1991, Duke and Gross 1993, on the "war on drugs." See Howe 1994, Collins 1997, and Mauer 1999 on the combination of race-gender-class with incarceration.

47. See *Richardson v Ramirez*, 418 U.S. 24, 79 (1974), Marshall, J. dissenting.

48. *Kronland v Honstein*, 327 F. Supp., 71 (N.D. Ga. 1971).

49. Mead, *The Psychology of Punitive Justice*, 23 Am. J. Soc. 591 (1918). Mead further observed that "the price paid for this solidarity of feeling is great and at times disastrous."

50. See also Erikson 1966. [Confrontations between offenders and the criminal justice system] act as boundary-maintaining devices in the sense that they demonstrate to whatever audience is concerned where the line is drawn between behavior that belongs in the special universe of the group and behavior that does not." Reiman (1995, 36) comments that "not only does unacceptable behavior *but that it positively needs unacceptable behavior.*" (Italics in original.)

51. "The endeavor of a normal state consists above all in assuring total peace within the state and its territory. To create tranquility, security, and order and thereby establish the normal situation is the prerequisite for legal norms to be valid. Every norm presupposes a normal situation, and no norm can be valid in an entirely abnormal situation. As long as the state is a political entity, this requirement for internal peace compels it in critical situations to decide also upon the domestic enemy. Every state provides, therefore, some kind of formula for the declaration of an internal enemy." (Schmitt 1996, 46)

52. Michelman, *Law's Republic*, 97 Yale L.J. 1493, 1495 (1988)

53. This assumption is, of course, a basic "republican" assumption, present in both Aristotle and Arendt, among others.

54. For effects of a felony conviction on employment see Street 2002, citing Freeman, and Western. In New York state, for example, a convicted felon, even after he is released from prison, may not live in a public housing project, even if his family is living there. See Burton et al.(1987) for a comprehensive survey of all the collateral consequences of a felony conviction. These include loss of the right to remain married, to have custody of children, to serve on a jury, to own firearms, and to hold public employment.

55. The reason for separating political rights from civil rights in the Fourteenth Amendment was discussed in Chapter Three, *supra*. There was no national consensus during the period of Reconstruction that African-Americans should have the vote. Hence, Section 2 of the Amendment, which reduced representation in those states that disenfranchised Blacks for anything other than "participation in rebellion or other crime."

56. This statistic is generous. In some states, such as Mississippi and Alabama, and some cities, such as Baltimore and Washington DC, more than one-quarter of the black population is disenfranchised.

57. This is because for Democrats who do not represent 'high crime' areas, felon disenfranchisement simply is not an issue in their constituency, and raising it would generate the perception that they are 'soft' on crime elsewhere. In districts having significant numbers of disenfranchised felons, such as in Florida and Maryland, representatives whose party could benefit from changes in the law support proposed legislation restoring political rights to the convicted. It is fair to say that, until the 2000 election, little or no mainstream political or journalistic attention was paid to the issue of felon disenfranchisement, and the effect that it might have on particular races. The fact that the numbers, however shocking in some districts, are still marginal, combined with the moral stigma attaching to the status of 'convicted felon' is a disincentive to (rational) politicians seeking to change the law on felon disenfranchisement. Politicians seeking to mobilize votes, to build coalitions in order to capture the elusive "political center" attempt to attract public attention with popular issues, not to draw attention to their support for unpopular or stigmatized minorities whose electoral support would be minimal at best. For a most interesting study of the state politics of felon disenfranchisement, see Conn 2003.

58. In November 2001, a Democrat won the Virginia governor's race, despite the fact that a quarter of a million citizens, mostly African-American, presumably "safe" Democratic voters, were permanently disenfranchised.

59. Ironically, Virginia was originally settled as a British penal colony. Robert Hughes, in *The Fatal Shore* (Knopf, NY 1986) states that "After 1717, transportation was stepped up and rendered fully official by a new act, 4 Geo. I, c.11, which provided that minor offenders could be transported for seven years to America instead of being flogged or branded, while men on commuted capital sentences (recipients of the King's Mercy) might be sent for fourteen...For the next sixty years, about 40,000 people suffered this thinly disguised form of slavery: 30,000 men and women from Great Britain, 10,000 from Ireland. Virginia Colony was originally settled by convicts sent to work on the plantations. "All offenders out of the common gaols condemned to die should be sent for three years to the Colony." (40-42) These felons where white, of course, and now in the twenty-first century, there are almost three million (permanently) disenfranchised felons in Virginia, over one million of whom are African-American, representing more than one-quarter of the black men in the state as a whole.

60. Clegg, cited in "Once a Felon, Never a Voter?", Megan Twohey, *The National Journal*, 1/6/01

61. Cited in "The Daily Progress" an online newspaper based in Charlottesville, VA. 10/03/01. It is interesting that Clegg believes that society must pay attention to the "history of the individual" at the point of the criminal justice continuum concerned with disenfranchisement, since mandatory sentencing guidelines prevent judges from considering the history of the individual when sentencing them to long prison terms.

62. Cited in "A vengeful cloud hangs over Florida" by Joe Davidson, http://www.msnbc.com/news 11/16/2000

63. See "Public Attitudes Toward Felon Disenfranchisement in the United States." Briefing sheet by Jeff Manza, Christopher Brooks and Jeff Uggen. At the Sentencing Project website.

64. See Gordon 1994 on the contemporary resurrection of the "dangerous classes" by American politicians.

65. See in particular, Gest 2001, Windlesham 1998, and Beckett 1997 for histories of the "war on crime" and the use of crime as a campaign issue for candidates of both parties. See Bertram 1996 on the war on drugs and the moral climate of electoral politics created by the "punishment paradigm."

66. Reider, "The Rise of the Silent Majority" in *The Rise and Fall of the New Deal Order, 1930-1980*, ed. Steven Fraser and Gary Gerstle (Princeton University Press)

67. Beckett (1997, 42) citing Edsall, Thomas Byrne and Mary Edsall, *Chain Reaction: The Impact of Rights, Race, and Taxes on American Politics* (New York: Norton and Co. 1991)

68. This formulation might seem peculiar to readers who believe that the continuum begins with the offense, but as my analysis of the *theory* of crime and punishment in Chapter Five will show, the concept of an offense, and therefore the decision to charge, is contingent rather than substantive. Felon disenfranchisement is a substantive penalty that is the endpoint of a continuum whose "front-end" is entirely discretionary.

69. I am using Habermas' (1987) framework of lifeworld and system to distinguish the two perspectives involved. See generally Vol. 2, ch. VI of *Theory of Communicative Action*.

70. According to Emile Durkheim (1893; 1984, 39), "an act is criminal when it offends the strong, well-defined states of the collective consciousness." Durkheim defines the "collective consciousness" as "the totality of beliefs and sentiments common to the average members of a society." These form "a determinate system with a life of its own." The collective consciousness is "the entire social consciousness, that is co-terminus with the psychological life of society, whereas, particularly in the higher societies, it constitutes only a very limited part of it. Judicial, governmental, scientific or industrial functions appertain to the psychological order, but "they clearly lie outside the common consciousness." What characterizes a crime is that it determines the punishment. "Thus if our own definition of crime is exact it must account for all the characteristics of punishment." (44)

71. "The judicial authorities and legislators are interpreters of the collective sentiments in modern societies, contrasted with ancient ones where the people themselves passed judgment. For repressive law to define crime, the collective sentiments must be deeply written. They are in no way mere halting, superficial caprices of the will, but emotions and dispositions strongly rooted within us." (Feinberg 1965)

72. The number of adults under the supervision of federal, state and local authorities was 6,288,600 at the beginning of the millennium, according to Bureau of Justice Statistics, about three percent of all the adults in the United States. The percentage of the adult population under correctional

supervision has tripled since 1980. See "Population Supervised by Authorities Rose in '99" *New York Times*, July 25, 2000.

73. Clearly political rights can only be "lost" once they have been gained. Many more African-American, female, Native, and immigrant citizens were *without* political rights for centuries than have "lost" them now, but those political rights hadn't been gained during those centuries of "*un*enfranchisement." An estimated four million Americans, or one in fifty adults, currently cannot vote as a result of a felony conviction. Women represent about a half million of this total. Thirteen percent of the African-American adult male population, or 1,400,000 African-American men are disenfranchised. Given current rates of incarceration, three in ten of the next generation of black men will be disenfranchised at some point during their lifetime, possibly permanently, depending on their state of residence. Hispanic citizens are also disproportionately disenfranchised, since they are disproportionately represented in the criminal justice system.

74. For recent scholarly analyses of the role of felon disenfranchisement in the Florida race, see Fletcher 2001; Behrens, Uggen and Manza (2003), Manza, Brooks and Uggen (2003). For statistics and legal arguments see Johnson v Bush F.3d (11th Circ. 2003) (2003 U.S. App. LEXIS 25859).

75. Doubts about this should be put to rest by the fact that the outcome of the 2000 Presidential election in Florida *possibly* hinged on fraudulent interpretations of Florida state law concerning the disenfranchisement of felons convicted in other states. See Gregory Pallast "Florida's 'Disappeared Voters': Disfranchised by the GOP." *The Nation*, February 5, 2001. Thirty-one percent of the state's black men are permanently prohibited from voting, and approximately 500,000 citizens of Florida of all races are disenfranchised. See Uggen and Manza (2001, 2002, 2003) for the political significance of felon disenfranchisement in other races.

76. Woodward (1951, 348) discussing the disenfranchising movement in the South at the turn of the century, quoted a participant in the Alabama Convention of 1901 as saying "Elections under [the new system] would turn not primarily upon the will of the people but upon the partisan or factional allegiance of the registrars."

77. For instance, the practices of "zero-tolerance policing" and "racial profiling" are usually the result of informal decision-making processes among law-enforcement personnel that are distinct from formal law making processes resulting in statutes. Nonetheless, they have a profound impact on the "front end" of the continuum of the criminal justice system that culminates in disenfranchisement. See Thompson (2001) for analysis of the effects of "zero-tolerance policing" in New York City. See also Cole 1999 on profiling and discretion of police officers and prosecutors as well as Harris 2002 on racial profiling.

78. State and federal mandatory minimum sentencing laws passed by many state legislatures have removed sentencing discretion from judges, to the despair of many on the bench, and have resulted in a dramatic increase of commitments to prison, particularly of blacks. For one judge's account of its

impact, see Forer 1994. See Bertram 1996, Mauer 1999, and Gest 2000 on the history of mandatory minimum sentencing.

79. "In theory, ex-offenders can regain the right to vote. In practice, this possibility is usually illusory. In eight states, a pardon or order from the governor is required; in two states, the ex-felons must obtain action by the parole or pardons board. Released ex-felons are not routinely informed about the steps necessary to regain the vote and often believe – incorrectly – that they can never vote again. Moreover, even if they seek to have the vote restored, few have the financial and political resources needed to succeed." *Losing the Vote: The Impact of Felon disenfranchisement Laws in the United States* (Human Rights Watch and The Sentencing Project 1988. See also recent documents on the Sentencing Project website.)

80. For example: "*We* are a nation both afraid of and obsessed with crime...*We* have fought a war on drugs. Annual expenditures on police have increased from $5 billion to $27 billion over the past two decades. We have built more prisons to lock up more people than almost every country in the world...Yet *Americans* in record numbers still report that they feel unsafe in their streets and homes." (Donziger, ed. 1996, 1. Emphasis added.) "Three findings about race, crime, and punishment stand out concerning blacks. First, at every criminal justice system stage from arrest to incarceration, blacks are present in numbers greatly out of proportion to their presence in the general population....Between 1979 and 1990, for example, the percentage of blacks among persons admitted to state and federal prisons grew from 39 to 53 percent. By contrast, 44.1 percent of violent crime arrests in 1979 were of blacks, virtually the same as the 1992 figures." (Tonry 1995, 49).

81. What follows is an example of urban arrest data from various cities that constitutes what one critic calls a pattern: "The collateral effects of this war on minority communities were devastating. Some of the most striking evidence can be found in Baltimore. Again, remember that African-Americans and whites were using drugs at roughly the same rate all across the country. Of 12, 956 arrests in that city for "drug abuse violations" in 1991, 11,107 were of African-Americans. In Columbus, Ohio, African-Americans accounted for 90 percent of drug arrests despite comprising only 8 percent of the population. In New York City, 92 percent of drug arrests were of African-Americans or Hispanics. In St. Paul, African-Americans were 26 times as likely to be arrested on drug charges as whites. *USA Today* found that in some cities African-Americans were arrested at as much as 50 times the rate of whites for drug offenses. This pattern was repeated in cities throughout the country.

This pattern helps explain the exploding rates of incarceration among African-Americans. In 1979, only 6 percent of state inmates and 25 percent of federal inmates had been convicted of drug offenses. In 1991, the proportion of state inmates convicted of drug offenses had nearly quadrupled to 21 percent, while the proportion federal inmates had more than doubled to 58 percent. The overwhelming majority of those new prison admissions for drug offenses were minority men, because that is who the drug war targeted." (Donziger 1996, 117) Other texts that reflect this type of critique include Duke and Gross 1993, Gordon 1994, Baum 1996, Gray, Bertram et al. 1996, Currie 1998, Rieman 1996, Christianson 1998, Mauer 1999, Parenti 1999, Cole 1999, Dyer 2000.

82. See Conn 2003 on attempts in Congress to change federal voting rights of American citizens.

83. According to Aristotle's analysis in *The Politics*, each regime has its own particular conception of justice, which refers to the distribution of offices and 'honors' among the citizens. Therefore the notion of justice is explicitly contextual, and "political," rather than absolute or moral.

Chapter 5:

1. Sartre, from "Introduction" to *Wretched of the Earth* (20).

2. Extensive lack of awareness on the part of the enfranchised would seem to dash Alexander Hamilton's hope, articulated in *The Federalist Papers*, that Americans have the responsibility of deciding before the world if it is possible to found a good government "from reflection and choice."

3. The ancient taxonomy given by Plato, Aristotle, and Polybius among others included oligarchy, aristocracy, timarchy, tyranny, democracy, and combinations thereof. All of these regimes comprehended a multitude of legal statuses, including citizen, slave, metic, etc. In *The Politics*, Aristotle identified regimes in terms of who was a "citizen proper." I identify the American regime in terms of who is *not* a citizen proper. A modern taxonomy comprehends only one legal status: citizen, yet the practice of felon disenfranchisement denotes the presence of a status group who are not "citizens proper."

4. This is up from 600 per 100,000 population in 1995, and compares to a range of 55-120 per 100,000 in the other industrialized countries. (Currie 1996, 15)

5. The historian William Wiecek (1977) has listed the following direct and indirect accommodations to slavery contained in the Constitution: Article I, §2, §8, §9, §10; Article IV, §2, §4; Article V, Provisions of Article 1, §9, clauses 1 and 4 (pertaining to the slave trade and direct taxes) were made unamendable. (Cited in Thomas 1999, n. 109)

6. Works of critical criminology and sociology include Rusche and Kirchheimer 1939, Quinney 1977, Greenberg 1993, Blomberg and Cohen 1995, Garland 1999, Howe 1994, James 1998, 2000, Davis 1971, Doyle 1997, Young 1996, Rosenblatt 1996, Gordon 1997.

7. See Manent 1995 for an account of Machiavelli as one of the intellectual founders of liberalism, who did not shrink from describing the founding of the state as a violent moment.

8. Some of these prisons, like the one Malcolm X was imprisoned in (Norfolk Colony, MA), are even called "colonies."

9. But see Allen 1969, who "views black America as a domestic colony of white America;" Bell (2001) says "we cannot escape the burden of Allen's analysis, nor should we wish to." Clark 1966 and 1989, claimed, "In the age

of decolonization, it may be fruitful to regard the problem of the American Negro as a unique case of colonialism, an instance of internal imperialism, and underdeveloped people in our very midst;" and Ture and Hamilton 1967, 1992 argued: "To put it another way, there is no 'American dilemma' because black people in this country form a colony, and it is not in the interest of the colonial power to liberate them. Black people are legal citizens of the United States, with for the most part, the same *legal* rights as other citizens, yet they stand as colonial subjects in relation to white society. Thus institutional racism has another name: colonialism."

10. See Bittker 1973 for detailed legal analysis of why African-Americans should be compensated for the period of legalized segregation and discrimination, and possible remedies; and see Westley 1988 for a comparative legal analysis of Jewish and Japanese (American) reparations, and the case for compensation of African-Americans for slavery. See also *Transafrica Forum* 2000 "The Case for Black Reparations" a roundtable discussion chaired by Randall Robinson for informal remarks on reparations by Robinson, Rep. John Conyers, Dr. Ronald Walters, Dr. Westley, Dr. Ali Mazrui, Dr. Ogletree, Adjoa AiYetoro, Professor Richard America, Dr. Marie Matsuda, Dr. Henderson, and Dr. Height.

11. The obvious comparison is to Nuremberg and Tokyo, when the Allies took it upon themselves to assemble a coherent theory of punishment that would justify their trials of Nazi and Japanese prisoners of war, because their theories of punishment were insufficient. "Following the Second World War, jurisprudential thinking generally moved towards a theoretical interest in natural law justifications. If the Nuremberg trials with their accompanying charges of 'Crimes against Humanity' were to have theoretical foundation, then one needed a radically different account of the nature of law from that proposed by the then reigning theory, legal positivism. Legal positivism, in many ways, had not advanced beyond the catchy phrase of Justinian's code—'What pleases the prince has the force of law!' Legal positivism did not offer theoretical grounds to warrant claims like 'Crimes against Humanity' which were needed to provide justification for the war crimes trials." (Lisska 1996, 8-9) It was not until the year 2001 that the American enslavement of Africans was labeled a "crime against humanity" in an official international forum.

12. "The cancellation [*Aufheben*] of crime is *retribution* in so far as the latter, by its concept, is an infringement of an infringement, and in so far as crime, by its existence [*Dasein*] has a determinate qualitative and quantitative magnitude, so that its negation, as existent, also has a determinate magnitude. But his identity [of crime and retribution], which is based on the concept, is not an *equality* in the specific character of the infringement, but in its character *in itself* – i.e. in terms of its *value*." (Hegel 1991, 126 italics in original)

13. The attempt, through affirmative action law and jurisprudence to "remedy the effects of *past* discrimination" does not come close to the type of acknowledgment and accounting I am suggesting was called for. See

Thomas 1999 for an analysis of the history of American (racial and gender) affirmative action discourse and Westley 1998 for the deficiencies of affirmative action remedies in the context of the unrepaired legacy of slavery.

14. "Memorializing injustices committed in the past is not only an obviously important way of preventing those same injustices from occurring in the future; it also provides public recognition of suffering, a chance for victims and their ancestors to mourn their loss in a social space that symbolizes respect, and a constant reminder to potential aggressors or the destructively indifferent that history will not overlook grievous abuses of human dignity." (Westley 1988, 452)

15. Pierre Van den Berghe 1978 coined the term *herrenvolk* democracies to refer to the white settler states such as South Africa, Rhodesia, Australia and New Zealand, which institutionalized democracy for the settlers, but not for the "native" populations. Van den Berghe discusses the "competitive" model of race relations, which he believes corresponds to the American situation. "The political system often takes the form of a *Herrenvolk* democracy" that is a parliamentary regime in which the exercise of power and suffrage is restricted, de facto, and often de jure, to the dominant group." (132) See also Mills 1997, 1998, 2000, Fredrickson 1981, and Smith 1997 for use of the concept in American political analysis.

16. See Manaugh 1999 for an interesting analysis, based on Robert Cover's concept of the narrativity of law, of the jeremiadic tradition that began in early America, and is currently finding expression in the war on drugs.

17. *Transafrica Forum* 2000, Remarks of Dr. Ronald Walters, Distinguished Leadership Scholar, James MacGregor Burns Academy of Leadership, University of Maryland.

18. Scholars of the ante-bellum, Reconstruction, and post-Reconstruction periods have pointed out how laws curtailing the freedoms of blacks, and restricting blacks' rights, reciprocally harmed and curtailed the rights of all whites to associate with blacks. See Bittker 1973, Kaczorowski 1986, Westley 1998, Brandwein 1999.

19. "In a social condition in which there are neither magistrates nor laws, punishment always takes the form of revenge; this remains inadequate inasmuch as it is the action of a subjective will, and thus out of keeping with the content. It is true that the members of a tribunal are also persons, but their will is the universal will of the law, and they do not seek to include in the punishment anything but what is naturally present in the matter in hand...Among uncivilized peoples revenge is undying...There is still a residue of revenge in several legal codes in use today, as in those cases where it is left to individuals to decide whether they wish to bring an offense to court or not." PR, 102.

20. Deterrence theories such as Hobbes' and Locke's are also legitimated by contract.

21. "It is the desire that the offender be forced to recognize his equality as a person with his victim, not the desire for suffering itself, that constitutes what is rational in the desire for revenge." (Reiman 1990, 195)

22. "An injury is a purely negative thing for the particular will of the injured party and of others. The *positive existence of the injury* consists solely in the *particular will of the criminal*. Thus, an injury to the latter as an existent will is the cancellation [*Aufheben*] of crime, *which would otherwise be regarded as valid*, and the restoration of right. "(PR,124) Kant (1991, 156) also insists on the "categorical imperative" of retributive punishment: "Even if civil society were to dissolve itself with the consent of all its members (for example if a people who inhabited an island decided to separate and to disperse to other parts of the world), the last murderer in prison would first have to be executed in order that each should receive his deserts and that the people should not bear the guilt of a capital crime through failing to insist on its punishment; for if they do not do so, they can be regarded as accomplices in the public violation of justice."

23. See Morris 1996, and Higginbotham 1978, as well as the discussion in Chapter One of the "dual system of law" under slavery.

24. The same argument can also be applied to segregation, which until *Brown v Board* was legal. See Bittker (1973) for legal arguments on reparations for the harms of segregation.

25. "The state is by no means a contract, and its substantial essence does not consist unconditionally in the *protection* and *safeguarding* of the lives and property of individuals as such. The state is rather that higher instance which may even itself lay claim to the lives and property of individuals... Furthermore the *action* of the criminal involves not only the *concept* of crime, its rationality *in and for itself* which the state must enforce *with* or *without* the consent of individuals, but also the formal rationality of the *individual's volition*. In so far as the punishment which this entails is seen as embodying the *criminal's own right*, the criminal is *honored* as a rational being. He is denied this honor if the concept and criterion of his punishment are not derived from his own act..." PR §100 (italics in original).

26. "The intellectual focus is now much more upon *retribution* – whether as a Kantian requirement of justice or as a means of communicating community values. Utilitarian argument and reformative purposes have given way to an emphasis on desert, denunciation, and punishment. And although much of this retributive theorizing emerged as a liberal reaction to the excesses of the therapeutic state, the new respectability it has lent to 'punishment' would seem to have encouraged more punitive government discourses and policies. What was originally intended as a liberal critique of modernist reasoning in favor of classic Enlightenment restraints has been taken up by a more punitive anti-modernism, which emphasizes the importance of punishment as a symbol of sovereign power and social authority. " (Garland 1990)

27. See Pestritto 2000 on the intellectual origins of American penological thought.

28. For a practical review of actual rehabilitation programs within prisons and a more pragmatic approach to "what works" see Lin 2000.
29. For the "default" justification of punishment as incapacitation, see Zimring and Hawkins 1995.
30. Nietzsche 1967, 190 ("The Dawn" 236).
31. A major American Revolutionary era thinker, signer of the Declaration of Independence, and founder of the first penitentiary and lunatic asylum.
32. Note I use the term "citizen." Both Plato and Rush thought and wrote in the context of "slave societies" (Finley), and their subject was appropriate punishment for *citizens*. Entirely different legal codes governed slave punishments in both Athens and the American colonies and U.S. states.
33. *Laws*, IV 718.
34. Quoted in Colvin 1997, 52.
35. The theological cornerstone of these arguments is troubling given my tentative suggestion about the Dewey/Emersonian theories of democratic individuality and the theoretical requirement of transcendental assumptions in Chapter 2.
36. My main criticism of Dumm's very interesting book is that its "subject" is the free white male. Women and minorities have never been permitted to "constitute themselves" as "self-controlled" rather than "other-controlled", and have historically been oppressed by those who *have* so constituted themselves. Dumm at no point identifies gender and race as a structural component of criminal justice policy. The liberal democratic citizen he discusses is a white male, and constituted as a disciplined subject, according to his thesis. The most interesting implication, therefore, which is never argued for, is that *he* must constitute women and people of color in the same way in the 'second generation' of citizenship, as it were.
37. "To say that Tocqueville saw U.S. society through the prism of punishment would be to overstate the case. But a careful reading of his theory of democratic despotism, and the materials from which it was derived, reveals that he understood the absolute despotism of the penitentiary and the more ordinary despotism of the democratic majority to have common ground." (Dumm 1987, 128)
38. "Mixing treatment with coercion in the penal system not only lengthens sentences and increases the suffering and sense of injustice, it also vitiates the treatment programs that are its justifications....Beyond the special problems of effecting "treatment" in prisons, is it possible to coerce people into "treatment" in any setting? Is the necessary therapeutic relationship between the helper and the helped possible if the person to be helped is forced into the relationship." AFSC *Struggle for Justice* 1971.
39. See Gest 2000 for detailed analysis of the politics of this transition in penology.
40. The reappearance of retributivism in legal philosophy circles (see Von Hirsch 1976, 1985 in particular) corresponds with a change in political regimes that has been variously characterized as 'neoliberal' or neoclassical, reflecting the resurgence of interest in Hayekian themes in that it claims pre-

welfare state 'traditional' American values of individual 'freedom' and 'rights.' These are clearly antithetical to a paternalist state that would spend public resources to 'rehabilitate' criminals.

41. According to David Garland, "a theoretical point, which is nowhere explicitly stated in Rusche and Kirschheimer's text, although it is in fact crucial to their analyses, is that penal institutions are to be viewed in their interrelationship with other institutions, and with non-penal aspects of social policy. In effect, penal policy is taken to be one element within a wider strategy of controlling the poor, in which factories, workhouses, the poor law, and of course the labor-market, all play corresponding parts. In his 1933 essay, George Rusche remarked that '...the criminal law and the daily work of the criminal courts are directed almost exclusively against those people whose class background, poverty, neglected education, or demoralization drove them to crime.' (Georg Rusche, "Labor Market and Penal Sanction: Thoughts on the Sociology of Criminal Justice" (orig. pub.1939) trans. and reproduced in T. Platt and P. Takagi (eds) *Punishment and Penal Discipline* (Berkeley, CA, 1980) p.11.

42. The OED example of usage of "impunity" quotes Coke, saying "This unlimited power of doing anything with impunity, will only beget a confidence in kings of doing what they list."

43. "The initial use of coercion, as force employed by a free agent in such a way as to infringe the existence [*Dasein*] of freedom in its *concrete* sense – i.e. to infringe right as right – is *crime*. This constitutes a *negatively infinite judgment* in its complete sense...whereby not only the particular – i.e. the subsumption of a thing [*Sache*] under my will – is negated, but also the universal and infinite element in the predicate 'mine' – i.e. my *capacity for rights*...This is the sphere of penal law." (Emphasis in original) See *Philosophy of Right*, esp. §90-103.

44. "A Crime, is a sinne, consisting in the Committing (by Deed, or Word) of that which the Law forbiddeth, or the Omission of what it hath commanded. So that every Crime is a sinne; but not every sinne is a Crime. (...) A Sinne, is not onely a Transgression of a Law, but also any Contempt of the Legislator. For such Contempt, is a breach of all his Lawes at once." *Leviathan*, Ch. XXVII

45. Locke defines "crime" indirectly in terms of the right of the Community to punish "those Offenses which any Member has committed against the Society, with such Penalties as the Law has established." ST, §87.

46. "We have seen what the true measure of crimes is, namely, *harm to society*. This is one of those palpable truths which, though they call for neither quadrants nor telescopes to be discovered, but are within the grasp of the average intelligence, nevertheless, have, by a curious conjunction of circumstances, only been firmly recognized by a few thinkers in every nation and in every century....Some crimes directly destroy society or its representative. Some undermine the personal security of a citizen by attacking his life, goods or honor. Others still are actions contrary to what

each citizen, in view of the public good, is obliged by law to do or not to do."

47. Locke, *Second Treatise* (ST§135; emphasis in original).

48. Hegel, however, explicitly referred to slavery as a crime that infringes "the will's existence and determinacy throughout its entire extent." PR §96. He declines, however, to condemn slavery outright, saying "the wrong of slavery is the fault not only of those who enslave or subjugate people, but of the slaves who subjugated themselves. Slavery occurs in the transitional phase between natural human existence and the truly ethical condition; it occurs in a world where wrong is still right." (§57, Addition)

49. For the critiques of the historical sociology of crime, see Rusche and Kirchheimer 1939, Rothman 1971, Ignatieff 1978, Colvin 1997, Meranze 1996, Gordon 1994, Friedman 1993, and of course Foucault 1997.

50. See Habermas 1996, Cohen 1989, Mansbridge 1992, Gutmann and Thompson 1996, Christiano 1996, Young 2000 etc. for theories of deliberative democracy.

51. *Plessy v Ferguson*, 163 U.S. 537, 551 (1866).

52. This, of course, is the implication of rejecting reform as a justification for punishment, and applying "just deserts" and incapacitation ("lock 'em up and throw away the key") penology, which is the "social science" analog of law-and-order politics. See Zimring and Hawkins 1995 for an account of the development of the incapacitation justification. See also Zimring, Hawkins and Kamin 2001 for an account of the emergence of the "three strikes and you're out" policy in California.

53. "We affirm that slavery, particularly of Africans and their descendants, and especially the transatlantic slave trade, was a unique and appalling tragedy in the history of humanity and a crime against humanity, not only because of its abhorrent barbarism, but also in terms of its enormous magnitude, its institutionalized nature, its transnational dimension and especially its negation of the very essence of the human nature of its victims" Third Session Draft Declaration presented at the 2001 U.N. Conference Against Racism, Racial Discrimination, Xenophobia, and Related Intolerance, Durban, SA.

54. On the issue of reparations and the contemporary political climate see Robinson 2000, ch.9. See also Bittker 1973 on "the case for black reparations" for slavery.

55. It's difficult to put this point better than Aimé Césaire did in 1955: "First we must study how colonization works to *decivilize* the colonizer, to *brutalize* him in the true sense of the word, to degrade him, to awaken him to buried instincts, to covetousness, violence, race hatred, and moral relativism; we must show that each time a head is cut off or an eye put out in Vietnam and in France they accept the fact, each time a little girl is raped and in France they accept the fact, each time a Madagascan is tortured and in France they accept the fact, civilization acquires another dead weight, a universal regression takes place, a gangrene sets in, a center of infection begins to spread; and that at the end of all these treaties that have been violated, all

these lies that have been propagated, all these punitive expeditions that have been tolerated, all these prisoners who have been tied up and "interrogated," all these patriots who have been tortured, at the end of all the racial pride that has been encouraged, all the boastfulness that has been displayed, a poison has been instilled into the veins of Europe and, slowly but surely, the continent proceeds toward *savagery*." (Césaire 1955, 1972: 13. Italics in original.)

56. "The radicalness of the prerequisites for the full undoing of the racial contract is ultimately manifested in nothing less than the reshaping of ourselves as human beings. Especially in its Rousseauian version, contract is about the constitution and reconstitution of people, their transformation from one kind of entity to another. Since the domination contract involves the creation of an oppressive social ontology, an ontology of persons and sub-persons, undoing it requires a metamorphosis of the self as well as social structures. And ultimately the aim would be the abolition of whiteness itself." (Mills 2000, 459)

57. "[O]*ur criminal justice system affirmatively depends on inequality*. Absent race and class disparities, the privileged among us could not enjoy as much constitutional protection of our liberties as we do; and without these disparities, we could not afford the policy of mass incarceration that we have pursued over the past two decades." (Cole 1995, 5. Italics in original.)

58. And in a 1968 letter to his mother about the decline of the black family: "Our change in status from an article of moveable property to untrained misfits on the labor market was not as most think a change to freedom from slavery but merely to a *different kind of slavery*." (Jackson 1994, 146, 174). Postcolonial theorist Stuart Hall corroborates this point in "Race, Articulation, and Societies structured in Dominance" in Sociological Theories, Race and Colonialism (Paris, UNESCO 1980) "Capitalism does not simply erase pre-capitalist formations such as slavery. It is in the interest of capitalism that certain older social older structures *not* be totally transformed, and certain older forms of exploitation based on racial and ethnic hierarchies continue to make available cheap labor." Hall describes this as 'an articulation between different modes of production, structured in some relation of dominance.'

59. "That a crime committed in society should appear greater and yet be punished leniently is an apparent contradiction. But whereas it would be impossible for society to leave a crime unpunished – since the crime would then be posited as right – the fact that society is sure of itself means that crime, in comparison, is always of a purely individual character, an unstable and isolated phenomenon." (Hegel: PR 218, Addition H.)

60. "The bottom line, the ultimate payoff from structuring the polity around a racial axis, is what W.E.B. Du Bois once called "the wages of whiteness." Particularly in the United States, usually viewed as a Lockean polity, a polity of proprietors, whiteness is, as Derrick Bell, Cheryl Harris, George Lipsitz, and others have pointed out, *property*, differential entitlement. The racial polity is by definition exploitative. Whiteness is not merely full

personhood, first-class citizenship, ownership of the aesthetically normative body, membership in the recognized culture; it is also material benefit, entitlement to differential moral/legal/social treatment, and differential rational expectations of economic success. For a *Herrenvolk* Lockeanism, whites' full self-ownership translates not merely into proprietorship of their own bodies and labor but also includes a share in the benefits resulting from the *qualified* self-ownership of the non-white population. The racial contract between whites is in effect an agreement to divide among themselves (as common white property) the proceeds of nonwhite subordination." (Mills 1998, 135)

61. "The simple central innovation is to posit a group domination contract which is exclusionary rather than genuinely inclusive, and then to rethink everything from that perspective (...) By bringing in groups as the key players rather than individuals, it is then possible to recuperate the insights of radical oppositional theory within a framework still in some sense 'contractarian.'" (2000, 446)

62. "Race Prejudice as Sense of Group Position," *Pacific Sociological Review I*, no. 1 (spring 1958) 3-4.

63. Mills 1999, 28.

64. "Part of what it means to be constructed as 'white' (the metamorphosis of the sociopolitical contract) part of what it requires to achieve Whiteness, successfully to become a white person...is a cognitive model that precludes self-transparency and genuine understanding of social realities. (...) As a general rule, *white misunderstanding, misrepresentation, evasion, and self-deception on matters related to race* are among the most pervasive mental phenomena of the past few hundred years, a cognitive and moral economy psychically required for conquest, colonization, and enslavement." (Mills 1997, 18-19)

65. " 'Ghetto' was the name for the Jewish quarter in sixteenth-century Venice. Later, it came to mean any section of the city which Jews were confined. America has contributed to the concept of the ghetto the restriction of persons to a special area and the limiting of their freedom of choice on the basis of skin color. The dark ghetto's invisible walls have been erected by the white society, by those who have power, both to confine those who have *no* power and to perpetuate their powerlessness. The dark ghettos are social, political, educational, and—above all—economic colonies. Their inhabi-tants are subject peoples, victims of the greed, cruelty, insensitivity, guilt, and fear of their masters." (Clark, 1989, 11)

66. "What is the effect of focusing on individual guilt? Not only does this divert our attention from the possible evils in our institutions but it puts forth half the problem of justice as if it were the *whole* problem. To focus on individual guilt is to ask whether the individual citizen has fulfilled his or her obligations to his or her fellow citizens. *It is to look away from the issue of whether the fellow citizens have fulfilled their obligations to him or her.* To look only at individual responsibility is to look away from social responsibility." (Reiman 1995, 142. Italics in original.)

67. See Habermas 1996, especially Chapter 3, for a discussion of how law is legitimized and 'positivized.'
68. Mills 1997, 1998, 2000. See Childs and Williams 1997, Worsham 1999, Chambers and Kurti 1996, Loomba 1998and Gandhi 1998 for introductory reviews of the debates about what 'postcolonial' or 'post-colonial' mean, and how the terms are being used.
69. Mills (1997) explicitly says that the "Racial Contract ("the theory as against the Racial Contract itself")…is intended a conceptual bridge between two areas largely segregated from each other: on the one hand the world of mainstream (i.e. 'white') ethics and political philosophy, preoccupied with discussions of justice and right in the abstract, on the other hand, the world of Native American, African American, and Third and Fourth World political though, historically focused on issues of conquest, imperialism, colonialism, white settlement, land rights, racism and slavery, jim crow, reparations, apartheid, cultural authenticity, national identity, *indegismo*, Afrocentrism, etc." (4)
70. Alabama and Mississippi.
71. See Eltis 2000 for a very recent account of the evolution of the Atlantic slave trade, and its relation to the rise of 'freedom' in the new European nations. For a classical treatment, see Davis (1966).
72. See Churchill (1977) for this type of documentation.
73. See DuBois (1939) and Foner (1988).
74. See Barnett, Ida Wells (1995).
75. See Cockburn (1999) on the international drug trade, CIA involvement, and official complicity in domestic supply.
76. See Hodgkins 1969.
77. Cited in Jacobs 1996:33-35.
78. See Jordan 1999, Cockburn and St. Clair 1998, and Levine 1993 for the international dimensions of the domestic drug war.
79. "The argument is not that, thereafter [the Enlightenment] everything has remained the same – colonisation [*sic*] repeating itself in perpetuity to the end of time. It is, rather, that colonisation so refigured the terrain that, ever since, the very idea of a world of separate identities, of isolated or separable and self-sufficient cultures and economies, has been obliged to yield to a variety of paradigms designed to capture these different but related forms of relationship, interconnection and discontinuity. This was the distinctive form of dissemination-and-condensation which colonisation set into play. It is in privileging this missing or downgraded dimension in the official narrative of 'colonisation' that the discourse of 'postcolonial' is conceptually distinctive. Although colonisation's particular forms of inscription and subjection varied in almost every other respect from one part of the globe to another, its general effects also require to be crudely but decisively marked, theoretically alongside its pluralities and multiplicities. That, in my view, is what the anomalous signifier 'colonial' is doing in the concept of the 'post-colonial.'" (Hall 1996, 252-253)

80. "Songlines" or "yiri" in the Walpiri language are tracks across the landscape created by Mythical Aboriginal ancestors when they rose out of the dark Earth and traveled, creating mountains, valleys, waterholes and all the physical features of the land. I am using the term "songlines" symbolically, rather than literally as the Aboriginal people, believing that the land was "sung" into existence by the ancestors, do. I envision the original creation of the colonial system, and the development of the modern American polity in terms of the tracks taken across the oceans by captive Africans, slavers, colonists, and convicts who first settled the American colonies. The international drug trade digs new tracks or songlines, as it brings in opiates from all over the globe; still newer tracks are marked by the route between inner-cities and rural prisons, as family members visit inmates, and inmates return to their communities.

81. After introducing the subject of the disciplines, the scale of control, the object of control, and the modality in Part Three of *Discipline and Punish*, Foucault comments "These methods, which made possible the meticulous control of the operations of the body, which assured the constant subjection of its forces and imposed upon them a relation of docility-utility, might be called 'disciplines.' Many disciplinary methods had long been in existence – in monasteries, armies, workshops. But in the course of the seventeenth and eighteenth centuries the disciplines became general formulas of domination." (137) "In the first instance, discipline proceeds from the distribution of individuals in space. To achieve this end, it employs several techniques. Discipline sometimes requires enclosure, the specification of a place heterogeneous to all others and closed in upon its self. It is the protected place of disciplinary monotony." (141)

82. In the sense of not bifurcated by the metropolis/periphery dichotomy I am proposing. Clearly it is a federal nation-state, but it is legally unified by the constitution, and therefore is seen to have a unitary, rather than dual system of law. See Chapter One, particularly for discussion of the distinction.

83. See Wallerstein 1980 on the imperatives of the "world system." The longevity and unconscious reproduction of gender, another constructed hegemonic binary, is usually taken for granted.

84. A sample of the evidence of "othering" in the literature would include de Tocqueville 1969, Myrdal 1962,Sniderman and Piazza 1993, Hacker 1995, Kinder and Sanders 1996, Bobo and Ryan, Gross and Kinder 2000, Bobo et al. 2000.

85. Fanon, *Wretched of the Earth*.

86. Hegel comments on how the inward "instability" of a society leads to harsh penal policies, whereas "in a society that is internally stable, the positedness of crime is so weak that cancellation [*Aufheben*] of this positedness must itself assume similar proportions." (PR: §218, Addition H)

87. Smith calls citizenship laws "an institutionalized response to one of the most elemental necessities for organizing and conducting an associated enterprise, in this case a political societies. Before all else, political associations need members. Would-be political leaders need a people to

lead, a collection of persons that generally understand themselves and are understood by others as forming one political society."

88. This is due to the fact that the institutions of the criminal justice system are largely staffed by elected representatives. See Chapter Three, *supra*, for a discussion of this problem.

89. See Bell 1999, 14 on Allen: "Robert Allen explains the limits of the club. He views black America as a domestic colony of white America. Colonial rule, Allen claims, is predicated upon an alliance between the occupying power and indigenous forces of conservatism and tradition. Allen finds aspects of this policy in American slavery, where divisions were created between field hands and house hands. "Uncle Tom" is the term used to describe the collaborator torn, with conflicting loyalties, between his people and the foreign rulers."

90. On the term "underclass" see Wilson 1987, 1996; Gordon 1994. Gunnar Myrdal notes heritage from slavery in *Time* article (8/27/77) popularizing the term "underclass" "though its members come from all races and live in many places, the underclass is made up mostly of impoverished urban blacks, who still suffer from the heritage of slavery and discrimination... Their bleak environment nurtures values that are often at radical odds with those of the majority – even the majority of the poor. Thus the underclass minority produces a highly disproportionate number of the nations' juvenile delinquents, school dropouts, drug addicts, and welfare mothers, and much of the adult crime, family disruption, urban decay and demand for social expenditure." (Quoted in Clark 1989, xix)

91. See Chapter Four, *supra*, for detailed discussion of Beckett's argument. See also Carter 1995, Glazer 1996 for the political trajectory of the 1960s to the present.

92. A paradigmatic example of this was the Reconstruction Era offer promoted by Thaddeus Stevens, followed by its withdrawal, of "40 acres and a mule" for all freed slaves. This withdrawal was accompanied by the return of previously redistributed Confederate plantations to their former owners, a policy that forced legions of emancipated slaves into sharecropping and peonage. (DuBois 1939, Foner 1988, Smith 1997). This era saw large increases in the felonization and disenfranchisement of the newly enfranchised blacks, and the racialization of convict labor systems in the South (Waldrep 1998, Myers 1998, Davis 1991). A further example is the Depression/New Deal policy that excluded African-Americans and Hispanics from national insurance, benefits and credit policies that subsidized *white* farmers and homeowners. This was a policy that continues today, and is the target of class action lawsuits challenging "redlining." (Lipsitz 1998, Sugrue 1996, Hill 1985, Lieberman, Pettigrew 1985, Massey and Denton 1993.) A final example is the welfare reform policy initiated by Congress in the context of a post-industrial globalizing economy during the 1990s. On the socio-economic effects of these policies in the "inner cities" and structural links to the "incarceration polity" see Wilson 1987, 1996; Katz 2001.

93. Sartre, Introduction to Fanon's *Wretched of the Earth*. It is interesting that St. Augustine also referred to those who have impunity from prosecution as a "gang." In the context of the Roman empire, foreshadowing modern European colonialism he asked: "Remove justice, and what are kingdoms but gangs of criminals on a large scale? What are criminal gangs but petty kingdoms? A gang is a group of men under the command of a leader, bound by a compact of association, in which the plunder is divided according to an agreed convention. If this villainy wins so many recruits from the ranks of the demoralized that it acquires territory, establishes a base, captures cities and subdues peoples, it then openly arrogates to itself the title of kingdom, which is conferred on it in the eyes of the world, not by the renouncing of aggression but by the attainment of impunity. Indeed, that was an apt and true reply which was given to Alexander the Great by a pirate who had been seized. For when the king had asked the man what he meant by keeping hostile possession of the sea, he answered with bold pride, "What thou meanest by seizing the whole earth; but because I do it with a petty ship, I am called a robber, whilst thou who dost it with a great fleet art styled emperor." *City of God*, 139. Book IV, Ch. 5.4.

94. According to Ralf Dahrendorf (1994) "The problem of the underclass, is not one of class, or even of "ordinary status." The universe of stratification is a universe of gradations and of mobility. The position of the underclass is one beyond the threshold of basic opportunities of access. It is a problem of entitlements, and thus of citizenship. It therefore touches on our most basic values – in that sense, the moral texture – of our societies. Tolerating an underclass is economically feasible and politically riskless. But it betrays a readiness to suspend the basic values of citizenship – equal rights of participation for all – for one category of people, which by the same token weakens the intrinsically universal claims of these values." (15)

References

Ackerman, Bruce (1991) *We The People* Vol. 1 (Cambridge University Press)

Adriaansens, Hans (1994) "Citizenship, Work and Welfare" in van Steenbergen, ed.

Agambin, Giorgio (1998) *Homo Sacer: Sovereign Power and Bare Life* (Stanford University Press)

Aldrich John H. (1995) *Why Parties? The Origin and Transformation of Party Politics in America* (University of Chicago Press)

Allen Danielle (2000) *The World of Prometheus: the politics of punishing in democratic Athens* (Princeton University Press)

Allen, Robert L. (1969) *Black Awakening in Capitalist America: An Analytic History* (New York: Anchor)

Amar, Akhil 1994 "Guaranteeing a Republican Form of Government: The Central Meaning of Republican Government: Popular Sovereignty, Majority Rule, and the Denominator Problem" 65 *University of Colorado Law Review* 749

— (1998) *The Bill of Rights* (Yale University Press)

Anderson, Benedict (1983, 1991) *Imagined Communities* (Verso)

Anglim, Christopher 1993 "A Selective, Annotated Bibliography on the Electoral College, Its Creation, History, and Prospects for Reform." 85 *Law Library Journal* 297

Arendt, Hannah (1963) *On Revolution* (Penguin Twentieth Century Classics)

— (1969, 1972) *On Violence* (Harcourt, Brace and Co.)

(1968) *Imperialism:* Part II of *The Origins of Totalitarianism* (Harcourt Brace and Company: New York)

Aristotle (1958) *Politics,* Translated by Ernest Barker (Oxford University Press)

— *Magna Moralia* , cited in Martha Nussbaum (1980) 417, "Shame, Separateness and Political Unity" in Amelie Oksenberg Rorty *Essays on Aristotle's Ethics* (University of California Press

Babbitt, Susan and Sue Campbell (eds.) (1999) *Racism and Philosophy* (Cornell University Press)

Bachrach, Peter and Baratz, Morton S. (1962) "Two Faces of Power" *American Political Science Review* 56, No.4: 947-52

Bailyn, Bernard (1967) *The Ideological Origins of the American Revolution* (Harvard University Press)

Baker, Nancy V. (1992) *Conflicting Loyalties: law and politics in the attorney general's office, 1789-1990* (University of Press of Kansas)

Baldwin, James (1963) "Many Thousands Gone" in *Notes of a Native Son*

Balibar, Etienne (1998) *Spinoza and Politics* (Verso: London and New York)

Barbelet, J.M. (1988) *Citizenship: Rights, Struggle, and Class Inequality* (University of Minnesota Press)

Barber, Benjamin (1998) *A Passion for Democracy* (Princeton University Press)

Barker, Ernest (1958) *The Politics of Aristotle* (Oxford University Press)

Bauman, Richard A. (1996) *Crime and Punishment in Ancient Rome* (Routledge: London and New York)

Beaumont, Gustave de, and Alexis de Tocqueville (1883) *On the Penitentiary System of the United States and Its Application in France.* Translated by Francis Lieber. (Philadelphia: Carey, Lea and Blanchard)

Beckett, Katherine (1997) *Making Crime Pay: Law and Order in Contemporary American Politics* (Oxford University Press)

Behrens, Angela, Christopher Uggen and Jeff Manza, "Ballot Manipulation and the 'Menace of Negro Domination': Racial Threat and Felon Disenfranchisement in the United States, 1850-2002, 109 Am. J. Soc. 559

Bell, Derrick (1999) "Here Come de Judge: The Role of Faith in Progressive Decision-making" 51 *Hastings Law Journal*

— (2001) "Tribute: Judge A. Leon Higginbotham Jr.'s Legacy" 53 *Rutgers Law Review* 627

Beiner, Ronald, ed. (1995) *Theorizing Citizenship* (State University of New York Press)

Benhabib, Seyla (1987), The generalized and concrete other: the Kohlberg-Gilligan controversy and feminist theory" in Seyla Benhabib and Drucilla Cornell, eds. *Feminism as Critique: on the politics of gender* (University of Minnesota Press)

— (1996) *Democracy and Difference* (Princeton University Press)

Benjamin, Walter (1973) *Illuminations* (London: Fontana)

Bennett, Robert W. (2000) "Should Parents be Given Extra Votes on Account of their Children? Toward a Conversational Understanding of American Democracy" *Northwestern University Law Review* 94 (Winter)

Bennett, William, John DiIulio, Walters (1996): *Body Count: Moral Poverty...and How to Win America's War against Crime and Drugs* (New York: Simon & Schuster)

Bentham, Jeremy (1988) *The Principles of Morals and Legislation* (New York: Prometheus Books)

Berlin, Ira (1974) *Slaves Without Masters* (The New Press: New York)

Bertram, Eva, Morrris Blachman, Kenneth Sharpe, and Peter Andreas (1996) *Drug War Politics: the price of denial* (University of California Press)

Bessler, John (1994) "The Public Interest and the Unconstitutionality of Private Prosecutors" 47 *Arkansas Law Review* 511

Bhahba, Homi (1994) *The Location of Culture* (London: Routledge)

Bittker, Boris L. (1973) *The Case for Black Reparations* (New York: Vintage)

Blauner, Robert (1969) 'Internal colonization and ghetto revolt' *Social Problems* 16, 4

Blumberg, Thomas G. and Stanley Cohen, eds. (1995) *Punishment and Social Control* (New York: Aldine de Gruyter)

Bobbio, Norberto (1987) *The Future of Democracy: in defense of the rules of the game* (University of Minnesota Press)

Bobo, Lawrence D. and Ryan A. Smith "From Jim Crow Racism to Laissez-Faire Racism: The Transformation of Racial Attitudes"

— Jim Sidanius and David O. Sears (2000) *Racialized Politics* (University of Chicago Press)

Bourdieu, Pierre (1977) *Outline of a Theory of Practice* (Cambridge University Press)

(1980) *The Logic of Practice* (Trans. Richard Nuce) Stanford University Press

(1989) *The State Nobility* (Stanford University Press)

(1998) *Practical Reason* (Stanford University Press)

Brandwein, Pamela (1999) Reconstructing Reconstruction: The Supreme Court and the Production of Historical Truth (Duke University Press)

Brock, W.R. 1963, *An American Crisis: Congress and Reconstruction 1865-1867* (London: McMillan & Co.)

Brook, Thomas (1997), ed. *Plessy v. Ferguson: a brief history with documents* (Boston: Bedford Books)

Brown, Darryl K. (2001) "Street Crime, Corporate Crime, and the Contingency of Criminal Liability" 149 *U. Pa. Law Rev.* 1295

Brown, Wendy (1988) *Manhood and Politics: A Feminist Reading in Political Theory* (Rowman and Littlefied: New Jersey)

Brubaker, Rogers (1992) *Citizenship and Nationhood in France and Germany* (Harvard University Press)

Burdick, Charles K. (1929) *The Law of the American Constitution; its Origin and Development* (New York and London: Putnam)

Bybee, Keith J. (2000) *Mistaken Identity: The Supreme Court and the Politics of Minority Representation* (Princeton University Press)

Cain, Bruce E. (1999) "Election Law as Its Own Field of Study: Election Law as a Field: A Political Scientist's Perspective" 32 *Loyola L.A. Law Review* 1105

Camus, Albert (1956) *The Fall* (Vintage International: New York)

Carter, Dan T. (1995) *The Politics of Rage: George Wallace, The Origins of the new conservatism, and the transformation of American Politics* (Louisiana State University Press)

— (1996) *From George Wallace to Newt Gingrich: Race in the conservative counterrevolution* (Louisiana State University Press)

Césaire, Aimé (1955, 1971) *Discourse on Colonialism,* Translated by Joan Pinkham, (New York: Monthly Review Press)

Chambers, Iain and Lidia Curti, eds. (1996) *The Post-Colonial Question: Common skies, divided horizons* (London: Routledge)

Childs, Peter and Patrick Williams (1997) *An Introduction to Post-Colonial Theory* (Prentice-Hall Europe)

Christiano, Thomas (1996) *The Rule of the Many: Fundamental issues in democratic theory* (Boulder: Westview Press)

Christianson, Scott (1998) *With Liberty for Some: 500 Years of Imprisonment in America* (Northeastern University Press)

Churchill, Ward (1997) *A Little Matter of Genocide: Holocaust and Denial in the Americas 1492 to the Present* (City Lights Books: San Francisco)

Cicero (1959) (trans. C.W. Keyes) *De Re Publica* (Heinemann: London, and Cambridge, MA: Harvard University Press)

Clark, Kenneth B and I.F. Stone (1966) "White Power, The colonial situation" *NY Review of Books*, 8/18/66

— (1989, 1965) *Dark Ghetto: Dilemmas of Social Power*, 2nd. Ed. (Wesleyan Paperback)

Cockburn, Alexander and Dennis St. Clair (1998) *Whiteout: The CIA, Drugs, and the Press* (Verso)

Cogan, Jacob Katz (1997) "The Look Within: Property, Capacity and Suffrage in Nineteenth Century America" *The Yale Law Journal:* 107: 427

Cohen, David (1991) *Law, Sexuality and Society: the enforcement of morals in classical Athens* (Cambridge University Press)

— (1995) *Law, Violence and Community in Classical Athens* (Cambridge)

Cohen, Joshua (1989) "Deliberation and Democratic Legitimacy" in Alan Hamlin and Philip Pettit (eds.) *The Good Polity* (London: Blackwell)

Cole, David (1999) *No Equal Justice: Race and Class in the American Criminal Justice System* (The New Press)

Collins, Catherine Fisher (1997) *The Imprisonment of African-American Women: Causes, Conditions, and Future Implications* (Jefferson, NC and London: McFarland and Co.)

Colvin, Mark (1997) *Penitentiaries, Reformatories, and Chain Gangs: Social Theory and the History of Punishment in Nineteenth-century America* (St.Martin's Press, New York)

Conn, Jason Belmont (2003) *Excerpts from the Partisan Politics of Ex-Felon Disenfranchisement Laws,* (Unpublished Thesis, Cornell University, available at htt://www.thesentencing project.org.)

Crenshaw, Kimberlé, Neil Gotanda, Gary Peller and Kendall Thomas, eds. (1995) *Critical Race Theory: the key writings that formed the movement* (New York: The New Press)

Crozier, Michel J., Samuel P. Huntington, and Jojo Watanuki (1975) *The Crisis of Democracy: Report on the Governability of Democracies to the Trilateral Commission* (New York University Press)

Currie, Elliot (1998) *Crime and Punishment in America: Why the Solutions to America's most Stubborn Social Crisis have not worked, and what will* (New York: Metropolitan Books)

Dahl, Robert (1963) *A Preface to Democratic Theory* (University of Chicago Press)

__ (1971) *Polyarchy: Participation and Opposition.* New Haven (Yale University Press)

— (1989) *Democracy and Its Critics* (Yale University Press)

— (1998) *On Democracy* (Yale University Press)

Dahrendorf, Ralf (1994) "The Changing Quality of Citizenship" in Van Steenbergen (ed.)

Davis, Angela (1971) *If They Come in the Morning* (New York: Signet)

— (1997) "Race and Criminalization: Black Americans and the Punishment Industry" in Wahneema Lubiano *The House that Race Built* (New York: Pantheon)

— (1991) "From the Prison of Slavery to the Slavery of Prison: Frederick Douglass and the Convict Lease System" in James, 1998.

Davis, David Brion (1975)*The Problem of Slavery in the Age of Revolution, 1770-1823* (Cornell University Press)

Demleitner, Nora V. (2000) "Continuing Payment on One's Debt to Society: The German Model of Felon Disenfranchisement as an Alternative" *Minnesota Law Review* [Vol. 84:753]

Dewey, John (1988) *The Later Works: 1925-1953,* vol. 14, ed. Jo Ann Boydston (Southern Illinois University Press)

DiIulio, John (1994) "The Question of Black Crime" *The Public Interest* 117 (Fall)

(1995) "White Lies About Black Crime" *The Public Interest* 118 (Winter)

— (1996) "My Black Crime Problem" *City Journal* 6 (Spring 1996)

Donziger, Steven R., ed. *The Real War on Crime: The Report of the National Criminal Justice Commission* (Harper Perennial)

Doyle, James F. (1997) *"A Radical Critique of Criminal Punishment"* in Stephen M. Griffin and Robert C.L. Moffat, eds. *Radical Critiques of the Law* (University of Kansas Press)

DuBois, W.E.B. (1935,1979) *Black Reconstruction: 1860-1880* (New York: Atheneum)

Dumm, Thomas L. (1987) *Democracy and Punishment: Disciplinary Origins of the United States* (University of Wisconsin Press).

Durkheim, Emile (1984, 1933) *The Division of Labor in Society* (New York: The Free Press)

Dyer, Joel (2000) *The Perpetual Prisoner Machine: How America Profits from Crime* (Westview)

Dyson, Michael Eric (2000) *I May Not Get There With You: the true Martin Luther King Jr.* (New York: The Free Press)

Elazar, Daniel J. (1972) *Federalism, A view from the states* (New York: Thomas Y. Crowell Company)

Elster, Jon (1990) "Norms of Revenge" *Ethics* 100: 862-85

(1999) *Alchemies of the Mind: Rationality and the Emotions* (Cambridge University Press)

Eltis, Stanley (2000) *The Rise of African Slavery in the Americas* (Cambridge University Press)

Erikson, Kai T. (1966) *Wayward Puritans* (New York: Wiley)

Euben, J. Peter, John R. Wallach, and Josiah Ober (1994) *Athenian Political Thought and the Reconstruction of American Democracy* (Cornell University Press)

Fanon, Franz (1963) *Wretched of the Earth* (New York: Grove Press)

Fehrenbacher, Don E. (1978, 2001) *The Dred Scott case: Its significance in American law and politics* (Oxford University Press)

Feinberg, Joel (1965) "The Expressive Function of Punishment" *Monist,* 49 (3), 297-408

Finkleman, Paul (1993) "The Crime of Color" *Tulane Law Review,* Vol. 67

Finley, Moses "Freedom of the Citizen"

Fleming, Walter D. (1950) *Documentary History of Reconstruction: Political, Military, Social, Religious, Education and Industrial. 1865- the present time.* (New York: Peter Smith)

Fletcher, George P. (1999) "Symposium: Disenfranchisement as Punishment: Reflection on the Racial Uses of Infamia" 46 *UCLA Law Review,* 1895

— (2001) *Our Secret Constitution: How Lincoln Redefined American Democracy* (Oxford University Press)

Foner, Eric (1988) *Reconstruction: America's Unfinished Revolution 1863-1877* (New York: Harper and Row)

Forer, Lois G. (1994) *A Rage to Punish: The Unintended Consequences of Mandatory Sentencing* (W.W. Norton)

Foucault, Michel (1977, 1995) *Discipline and Punish: The Birth of the Prison* (Random House: New York)

Fox, Vernon (1972) *Introduction to Corrections,* (NJ: Prentice Hall)

Franklin, H. Bruce (1998) *Prison Writing in 20th Century America* (Penguin)

Fraser, Nancy (1993) 'Rethinking the Public Sphere: A Contribution to the critique of actually existing democracy' in Bruce Robbins (ed.) *The Phantom Public Sphere* (University of Minnesota Press)

Fraser, Nancy and Linda Gordon (1994) "Civil Citizenship Against Social Citizenship?" in van Steenbergen, ed. 1994.

Fredrickson, George (1971, 1987) Black Image in the White Mind: the debate on Afro-American character and destiny, 1817-1914 (Middletown, CT)

— (1981) *White Supremacy: A Comparative Study in American and South African History* (New York)

(1988) *The Arrogance of Race: historical perspectives on slavery, racism, and social inequality* (Wesleyan University Press)

— (1995) *Black Liberation*

Friedman, Lawrence M. (1993) *Crime and Punishment in American History* (New York: Basic Books)

Furman, Jesse (1997) "Political Illiberalism: the paradox of disenfranchisement and the ambivalences of Rawlsian justice" *The Yale Law Journal* 106: 1197)

Gandhi, Leela (1998) *Postcolonial Theory: A critical introduction* (Columbia University Press)

Garland, David (1990) *Punishment and Modern Society* (University of Chicago Press)

Garner, Richard (1987) *Law and Society at Classical Athens* (New York: St. Martin's Press)

Gaventa, John (1980) *Power and Powerlessness* (University of Illinois Press)

Gerteis, (1973) *From Contraband to Freedman: Federal Policy Toward Southern Blacks, 1861-1865* (Westport)

Gest, Ted (2001) *Crime and Politics: Big Government's Campaign for Law and Order* (Oxford University Press)

Gewirth, A. (1962) 'Political Justice' in R.B. Brandt (Ed.) *Social Justice* (Prentice-Hall)

Gibson, William (1994) *Warrior Dreams: Violence and Manhood in Post-Vietnam America* (Harper Collins: Canada)

Giddens, Anthony (1985) *The Nation State and Violence. Vol. II of A Contemporary Critique of Historical Materialism* (Macmillan: London)

— *The Consequences of Modernity* (Polity Press: Cambridge)

Gillette, William (1965, 1969) *The Right to Vote: Politics and Passage of the Fifteenth Amendment* (Johns Hopkins University Press)

— (1979) *Retreat from Reconstruction* (Baton Rouge: Louisiana State University Press)

Gilliam, F.D. and Shanto Iyengar (2000) "Prime Suspects: The influence of local television news on the viewing public" *American Journal of Political Science* 44 (3): 560-573 July.

Glazer James M. (1996) Race, Campaign Politics, & The Realignment of the South (Yale University Press)

Gonzales-Casanova, Pablo (1965) "Internal colonialism and national development" *Studies in Comparative International Development,* 1, 4

Gordon, Diana R. (1994) *The Return of the Dangerous Classes: Drug Prohibition and Policy Politics* (New York: Norton)

Greenberg, David F. ed. (1993) *Crime and Capitalism, Readings in Marxist Criminology* (Temple University Press)

Greenridge, A.H.J. (1894) *Infamia: its place in Roman Public and Private Law* (Oxford University Press)

Gross, Kimberly and Donald R. Kinder (2000) "Ethnocentrism Revisited: Explaining American Opinion on Crime and Punishment" (Unpublished paper presented at APSA 2000)

Guinier, Lani (1995) *Tyranny of the Majority* (New York: Free Press)

Gutmann, Amy (1988) "Public Education in a Democracy" in Gutmann, ed. *Democracy and the Welfare State* (Princeton University Press)

— (1989) "Undemocratic Education" in Rosenblum (ed.)

Gutmann, Amy and Dennis Thompson (1996) *Democracy and Disagreement* (Harvard University Press)

Habermas, Jurgen (1975) *Legitimation Crisis* (Beacon Press)

Habermas, Jurgen (1987) *Theory of Communicative Action. Vol. 1.Reason and the Rationalization of Society.* Vol. 2. *Lifeworld and System: A critique of Functionalist Reason* (MIT Press)

— (1994) "Citizenship and National Identity" in van Steenbergen

(1996) *Between Facts and Norms* (MIT Press)

Hacker, Andrew (1995) *Two Nations: Black and White, Separate, Hostile, Unequal* (New York: Ballantine)

Hall, Stuart 1996 "When Was the Post-Colonial"? Thinking at the Limit" in Chambers and Curti (eds.)

— , Chas Chritcher, Tony Hefferson, John Clarke, and Brian Roberts (1978) *Policing the Crisis: Mugging, the State and Law and Order* (New York: Holmesand Meier Publishers, Inc.)

Hale, Grace Elizabeth (1999) *Making Whiteness: The Culture of Segregation in the South, 1980-1940* (New York: Vintage)

Hallinan, Joseph T. (2001) *Going up the River: Travels in a Prison Nation* (Random House)

Hampton, Jean (1998) "Punishment, Feminism, and Political Identity: A Case Study in the Expressive Meaning of the Law" *Canadian Journal of Law and Jurisprudence*, Vol. XI, No. 1

Hansen, Mogens Herman (1976) *Apagoge, Endeixis and Ephegis against Kakourgoi, Atimoi and Pheugontes: A Study in the Athenian Administration of Justice in the Fourth century B.C.* (Odense University Press)

— (1996) "The Ancient Athenian and the modern Liberal View of Liberty as a Democratic Ideal" in Josiah Ober and Charles Hedrick (eds) *Demokratia: A Conversation on Democracies Ancient and Modern* (Princeton University Press)

— (1999) *The Athenian Democracy in the Age of Demosthenes* (University of Oklahoma Press)

Harris, Cheryl "Whiteness as Property" (1993) *Harvard Law Review (*106) 1707

Harris, David A. (2002) Profiles in Injustice: Why Racial Profiling Cannot Work (New York, The New Press)

Harrison, A.R.W. (1971) *The Law of Athens, Procedure* (Oxford: Clarendon press)

Harrison, Beverly Wildung (1985) *Making the Connections: Essays in feminist social ethics* (Boston: Beacon Press)

Hart, H.L.A. (1982) *Essays on Bentham: Jurisprudence and Political Theory* (Oxford University Press)

Harvard Law Review Note: (1989) "The Disenfranchisement of Ex-Felons: Citizenship, Criminality, and 'the purity of the ballot box.'" (Vol. 102, 1300)

Harvard Note (2001): Rethinking the Electoral College Debate: The Framers, Federalism, and One Person, One Vote. 114 *Harvard Law Rev.* 2526

Harvey, Alice E. (1994) "Ex-Felon Disenfranchisement" *University of Pennsylvania Law Review* (Vol. 142, 1145)

Hechter, Michael (1999) *Internal Colonialism: The Celtic Fringe in British National Development* (Transaction Publishers: New Brunswick and London)

Hedrick, Charles (1994) "The Zero Degree of Society" in Euben, Wallach and Ober *Athenian Political Thought and the Reconstruction of American Democracy.* (Cornell University Press: Ithica and London)

Hegel, G.W.F. (1821, 1991) *Elements of the Philosophy of Right,* ed. Allen W. Wood (Cambridge University Press)

Held, David (1989) *Political Theory and the Modern State: Essays on State, Power and Democracy* (Stanford University Press)
— (1991) *Political Theory Today* (Stanford University Press)
Hench, Virginia E. (1998) "The Death of Voting Rights: The Legal Disenfranchisement of Minority Voters" *Case Western Reserve Law Review,* Vol. 48, no.4
Higginbotham, A. Leon Jr. (1978) *In the matter of Color: race and the American legal process: the colonial period.*
— (1996) *Shades of Freedom: Racial politics and the presumptions of the American legal process* (New York: Oxford University Press)
Hill, Herbert (1985) *Black Labor and the American Legal System* (University of Wisconsin Press)
Hirschmann, Albert O. (1977) *The Passions and the Interests* (Princeton University Press)
Hirshson, Stanley P. (1962) *Farewell to the Bloody Shirt* (Chicago: Quadrangle Paperbacks)
Hochschild, Jennifer (1988) "Race, Class, and Power in the Welfare State" in Gutmann, (ed.)
Hodgkin, Thomas M.D. (1969; 1833) *An Inquiry into the Merits of the American Colonization Society and a Reply to the Charges Brought Against It. With An Account of the British African Colonization Society by* (Originally published in London by J.A. Arch, Cornhill, Harvey and Darton 1833. New Impression African Publication Society, London.)
Howe, Adrian (1994) *Punish and Critique: Toward a Feminist Analysis of Penality* (Routledge)
Hughes, Robert (1986) *The Fatal Shore* (NY: Knopf)
Huntingdon, Samuel P. (1996) *The Clash of Civilizations: Remaking of World Order*
Hyland, James L (1995) *Democratic Theory: the philosophical foundations* (Manchester University Press)
Hyneman, Charles S. (1994) *The American Founding Experience* (University of Illinois Press)
Ides, Allen and Christopher N. May (1998) *Constitutional Law and Individual Rights* (Aspen)
Igniateff, Michael (1978) *A Just Measure of Pain* (Pantheon)
Itzkowitz, Howard and Lauren Oldak (1973) "Note, Restoring the Ex-Offender's Right to Vote: Background and Developments" *American Criminal Law Review* (Vol. 11, 695)
Iyengar, Shanto (1991) *Is Anyone Responsible? How Television Frames Political Issues* (University of Chicago Press)
Jackson, George (1994) *Soledad Brother* (Lawrence Hill Books, Chicago 1994)
Jacobs, Jane M. (1996) *Edge of Empire: Postcolonialism and the City* (Routledge)
Jacoby, Joan E. (1980) *The American Prosecutor, A Search for Identity* (MA: Lexington Books)

James, Joseph B. (1965) *The Framing of the Fourteenth Amendment* (Urbana: University of Illinois Press)

James, Joy, ed. (1998) *The Angela Y. Davis Reader* (Blackwell)

Johnston, David (1994) *The Idea of a Liberal Theory: A Critique and Reconstruction* (Princeton University Press)

Jordan, David C. (1999) *Drug Politics: Dirty Money and Democracies* (Oklahoma University Press)

Kaczorowski, Robert J. (1986) "Revolutionary Constitutionalism in the Era of the Civil War and Reconstruction" *New York University Law Review,* 61 N.Y.U.L.Rev. 863

Kalimtzis, Kostas (2000) *Aristotle on Political Enmity and Disease: an inquiry into stasis* (SUNY Press)

Kant, Emmanuel (1991) *Political Writings,* ed. Hans Reiss Cambridge University Press)

Karlan, Pamela, S. (2004) "Convictions and Doubts: Retribution, Representation, and the Debate over Felon Disenfranchisement." Stanford Public Law and Legal Theory Working Paper Series.

Kateb, George (1989) "Democratic Individuality and the Meaning of Rights" in Rosenblum, (ed.)

— (1992) *The Inner Ocean* (Cornell University Press)

(1995) *Emerson and Self Reliance* , ed. Morton Schoolman (Sage Publications)

Katz, Michael B. (2001) *The Price of Citizenship: Redefining the American Welfare State* (New York: Metropolitan Books)

Kelsen, Hans (1953, 1995) *Introduction to the Problems of Legal Theory,* Trans. Bonnie Litschewski Paulson and Stanley L. Paulson (Oxford, Clarendon Paperbacks)

Kennedy, Randall (1987) *Race, Crime and the Law* (New York: Vintage)

Kennedy, Stetson (1995) *After Appomattox: How the South Won the War* (University Press of Florida)

Kettner, James H. (1978) *The Development of American Citizenship* (University of North Carolina Press)

Keyssar, Alexander (2000) *The Right to Vote: The Contested History of Democracy in the United States* (Basic Books: New York)

Kim, David Haekwon (1999) "Contempt and Ordinary Inequality" in Babbitt and Campbell, eds.

Kinder, Donald R. and Lynn M. Sanders (1996) *Divided by Color: Racial Politics and Democratic Ideals* (University of Chicago Press)

Kousser, J. Morgan (1974) *The Shaping of Southern Politics* (Yale University Press0

— (1992) "The Voting Rights Act and the Two Reconstructions" in Grofman, Bernard and Chandler Davidson, Eds. *Controversies in Minority Voting* (Brookings Institution)

— (1999) *Colorblind Injustice: Minority Voting Rights and the Second Reconstruction* (University of North Carolina Press)

Kymlicka, Will and Wayne Norman (1995) "Return of the Citizen" in Beiner op.cit.

— (1996) *Multicultural Citizenship* (Oxford University Press)

Laclau, Ernesto and Chantal Mouffe (1985) *Hegemony and Socialist Strategy* (London)

Lefort, Claude (1988) *Democracy and Political Theory* (University of Minnesota Press)

Levine, Michael (1993) *The Big White Lie* (New York: Thunders Mouth Press)

Lewis, John (1998) *Walking With the Wind* (Simon and Schuster)

Lieberman, Robert C. "Race and the Organization of Welfare Policy" in *Classifying by Race*, ed. P.E. Peterson (Princeton University Press)

Lin, Ann Chih (2000) *Reform in the Making: The Implementation of Social Policy in Prisoin* (Princeton University Press)

Lipsitz, George (1998) *The Possessive Investment in Whiteness* (Temple University Press)

Lisska, Anthony J. (1996) *Aquinas's Theory of Natural Law* (Oxford University Press: Clarendon Paperbacks)

Lock, Shmuel (1999) *Crime, Public Opinion and Civil Liberties: The Tolerant Public* (Westport: Praeger)

Locke, John (1960) *Two Treatises of Government* ed., Peter Laslitt (Cambridge University Press)

Loomba, Ania (1998) *Colonialism/Postocolonialism* (Routledge: London and New York)

Lopez, Ian F. Haney (1996) *White By Law: The Legal Construction of Race* (New York University Press)

Lowi, Theodore J. (1969) *The End of Liberalism* (New York: W.W. Norton)

Lowi, Theodore J. and Benjamin Ginzburg (1990) *American Government: Freedom and Power* (New York: Norton)

Lukes, Stephen (1970) *Power*

MacDowell, Douglas M. (1978) *The Law in Classical Athens* (London: Thames and Hudson)

— *Spartan Law* (Edinburgh: Scottish Academic Press)

Machiavelli, Niccolò (1970) *The Discourses* (Penguin)

MacIntyre, Alasdair (1981) *After Virtue* (University of Notre Dame Press)

— (1988) *Whose Justice? Which Rationality?* (University of Notre Dame Press)

MacPherson, C.B. (1977) *The Life and Times of Liberal Democracy* (Oxford University Press)

Mahoney, James (2000) "Uses of Path Dependence in Historical Sociology" *Theory and Society* (issue?)

Manaugh, Sara (1999) "An American Tragedy: The Jeremiadic Impulse of the War on Drugs" *Critical Sense*, Spring 1999, 11.

Manent, Pierre (1995) *An Intellectual History of Liberalism* (Princeton University Press)

Manin, Bernard (1997) *Principles of Representative Government* (Cambridge University Press)

Mansbridge, Jane (1980) *Beyond Adversary Democracy* (New York: Basic Books)

(1992) "A Deliberative Theory of Interest Representation" in Mark P. Patracca (ed.) *The Politics of Interest: Interest Groups Transformed* (Westview)

Manza, Jeff, Clem Brooks and Christopher Uggen (2003) "Civil Death" or Civil Rights? Public attitudes Towards Felon Disenfranchisement in the United States. Availaable at http://www.socsci.umn.edu/~uggenPOQ8.pdf.

Manville, Philip Brook (1990) *The Origins of Citizenship in Ancient Athens* (Princeton University Press)

Marable, Manning (1983) *How Capitalism Underdeveloped Black America*
— (1991) *Race, Reform and Rebellion: The Second Reconstruction in Black America, 1945-1990* (University Press of Mississippi)

Marshall, T.H. (1973) *Class, Citizenship and Social Development* (Greenwood Press: Westport, Conn.)

Massey, Douglas S. and Nancy A. Denton (1993) *American Apartheid: Segregation and the Making of the Underclass*

Matsuda, Marie (1995) "Looking to the Bottom: Critical Legal Studies and Reparations" in Crenshaw et al. (eds.)

Mauer, Mark and Tracy Huling (1995) *Young Black Americans and the Criminal Justice System: five Years Later* (Washington D.C.: The Sentencing Project)
— and The Sentencing Project (1999) *Race to Incarcerate* (The New Press)

Maveety, Nancy (1991) *Representation Rights and the Burger Years* (University of Michigan Press)

Mehta, Uday Singh (1999) *Liberalism and Empire: A Study in Nineteenth Century British Liberal Thought* (University of Chicago Press: Chicago and London)

Memmi, Albert (1991) *The Colonizer and the Colonized* (Boston: Beacon Press

Meranze, Michael (1996) *Laboratories of Virtue: Punishment, Revolution and Authority in Philadelphia, 1760-1835* (University of North Carolina Press, Chapel Hill and London)

Merritt, Deborah Jones (1988) Article: The Guarantee Clause and State Autonomy: Federalism for a Third Century, 88 *Columbia Law Review* 1

Michelman, Frank (1988) "Political Truth and the Rule of Law" *Tel Aviv University Studies in Law* 8, 283.
—— (1998a) "Law's Republic" *Yale Law Journal* Vol. 97, 8, 1493

Miller, Jerome (1996) *Search and Destroy: African-American Males in the Criminal Justice System* (Cambridge University Press)

Miller, Richard Lawrence (1996) *Drug Warriors and Their Prey: from police powers to police state* (Westport: Praeger)

Miller, William Ian (2000) "Honor," a review of Alchemies of the Mind: Rationality and the Emotions, by Jon Elster in *London Review of Books* Vol. 22, No. 15, 8/10/00 p. 36

Milligan, David and William Watts Miller, eds. (1992) *Liberalism, Citizenship, Autonomy* (Avebury: Hants)

Mills, Charles (1997) *The Racial Contract* (Cornell University Press)
— (1998) *Blackness Visible: Essays on Philosophy and Race* (Cornell University Press)

— (2000) "Race and the Social Contract Tradition" *Social Identities*, Vol. 6, No.4

Minow, Martha (1990) *Making All the Difference: Inclusion, Exclusion and American Law* (Cornell University Press)

Misner, Robert L. (1996) "Recasting Prosecutorial Discretion" 86 *Journal of Criminal Law and Criminology* 717, 734

Mohanram, Radhika (1999) *Black Body: Woman, Colonialism and Space* (University of Minnesota Press, Minneapolis and London)

Montesquieu, Charles Louis de Secondat (1989) *Spirit of the Laws* (Cambridge University Press)

Moran, Michael ((1991)"The Frontiers of Social Citizenship: The case of Health Care Entitlements" in Vogel and Moran

Morris, Thomas D. (1996) *Southern slavery and the Law: 1619-1860* (University of North Carolina Press)

Mouffe, Chantal (1993) *The Return of the Political* (Verso: London)

— (2000) *The Democratic Paradox* (Verso)

Murphy, Dennis L. (1991) "Case Comment: Garza v County of Los Angeles: The Dilemma over Using Elector Population as Opposed to Total Population in Legislative Apportionment" 41 *Case Western Reserve* 1013

Myers, Martha A. (1998) *Race, Labor and Punishment in the New South* (Ohio State University Press)

Myrdal, Gunnar (1962) *An American Dilemma* (New York: Harper and Row)

Mustard, David B. (2001) " Racial, Ethnic, and Gender Disparities in Sentencing: Evidence from U.S. Federal Courts 44 *Journal of Law and Economics* 285

Narr, M.D. (1880, 1985) *The Law of Suffrage and Elections* (Littleton, CO: Fred B. Rothman and Co.)

Nelson, Dana D. (1998) *National Manhood: Capitalist Citizenship and the Imagined Fraternity of White Men* (Duke University Press)

Nussbaum, Martha (1980) 417, "Shame, Separateness and Political Unity" in Amelie Oksenberg Rorty *Essays on Aristotle's Ethics* (University of California Press)

O'Sullivan, Michael J. (1992), "Note, Artificial Unit Voting and the Electoral College" 65 *Southern California Law Review* 2421

Ober, Josiah (1996) *The Athenian Revolution: Essays on Greek Democracy and Political Theory* (Princeton University Press)

Ober, Josiah and Hedrick, Charles Hedrick, eds. (1996) *Demokratia: A Conversation on Democracies Ancient and Modern* (Princeton University Press)

Offe, Claus (1996) *Modernity and the State: East, West* (MIT Press)

— and Ulrich K. Preuss (1991) "Democratic Institutions and Moral Resources" in Held, (ed.)

Oshinsky, David (1996) *Worse than Slavery* (New York: The Free Press)

Osterhammel, Jurgen (1995,1999) *Colonialism* (Markus Weiner Publishers)

Ostwald, Martin (1986) *From Popular Sovereignty to the Sovereignty of Law: Law, Society, and Politics in Fifth Century Athens* (Berkeley: University of California Press)

Pangle, Thomas L. (1990) "Symposium on Classical Philosophy and the American Constitutional Order: the Classical Challenge to the American Constitution. *Chicago-Kent Law Review 145*

Parenti, Christian (1999) *Lockdown America: Police and Prisons in the Age of Crisis* (Verso)

Parry, Geraint (1991) "Conclusion: Paths to Citizenship" in Vogel and Moran, eds.

Pashukanis, Evgeny B. (1978) *Law and Marxism: A General Theory* (Ink Links: London)

Pateman, Carole (1979) *The Problem of Political Obligation: A Critique of Liberal Theory* (University of California Press)

— (1988) *The Sexual Contract* (Stanford University Press)

Patterson, Orlando (1982) *Slavery and Social Death: A Comparative Study* (Harvard University Press)

— (1991) *Freedom in the Making of Western Culture*, vol. 1 of Freedom (New York: Basic Books

Peltason, J. W. (1988) *Understanding the Constitution* (University of California, Irvine)

Pestritto, Ronald J. (2000) *Founding the Criminal Law: Punishment and Political Thought in the Origins of America* (Northern Illinois University Press)

Peterson, Paul, ed. (1995) *Classifying By Race* (Princeton University Press)

Pettigrew, Thomas F. (1985) "New Patterns of Racism: The Different Worlds of 1984 and 1964" 37 *Rutgers Law Review* 674

Pettit, Philip (1993) *The Common Mind: An Essay on Psychology, Society, and Politics* (Oxford University Press)

Phillips, Barbara Y. (1995) "Reconsidering Reynolds v Sims: The Relevance of Its Basic Standard of Equality to Other Vote Dilution Claims." 38 *Howard Law Journal* 561.

Pierson, Paul (2000) "Increasing Returns, Path Dependence, and the Study of Politics" *AJPS,* Vol. 94, no.2

Pinaire. Briaan, Milton Heumann and Laura Bilotta, (2003) *"Public Attitudes Toward the Disenfranchisement of Felons,"* 30 Fordham Urb. L.J. 1519, 1540.

Pitkin, Hannah Fenichel (1967) *The Concept of Representation* (University of California Press)

— (1984) *Fortune is a Woman: Gender and Politics in the Thought of Niccolò Machiavelli* (University of California Press)

— *Wittgenstein and Justice* (University of California Press)

Plant, Raymond (1991) *Modern Political Thought* (Basil Blackwell: Cambridge, MA)

Pocock, J.G.A. (1975) *The Machiavellian Moment: Florentine Political Thought and the Atlantic Republican Tradition* (Princeton University Press)

(1995) "The Ideal of Citizenship Since Classical Times" in Beiner, ed.op.cit

Poole, J. R. (1978) *The Pursuit of Equality in American History* (University of California Press)

Quinney, Richard (1977) *Class, State, and Crime: on the theory and practice of criminal justice* (New York: Longman)

Rawls (1955) "Two Concepts of Rules" in H.B. Acton, ed. (1969) *The Philosophy of Punishment* (New York: St. Martin's Press)

(1971) *A Theory of Justice* (Harvard University Press)

— (1993) *Political Liberalism* (Columbia University Press)

Reback, Gary L. "Note, Disenfranchisement of Ex-felons: a Reassessment," 25 *Stanford Law Review.* 845

Reiman, Jeffrey (1990) *Justice and Modern Moral Philosophy* (Yale University Press)

— (1996) *And the Poor Get Prison: Economic Bias in Criminal Justice* (Simon and Schuster)

Reuter, Peter (1991) "On the Consequences of Toughness" in *Searching for Alternatives: Drug Control Policies in the United States* (Edited by Melvyn B. Krauss and Edward P. Lazear) (Hoover Institution Press)

Rigotti, Francesca (1998) *L'onore degli onesti* (Feltrinelli: Milan)

Riker, William H. (1964) *Federalism: Origin, Operation, Significance* (Little Brown)

Robinson, Randall (2000) *The Debt: What America Owes to Blacks* (New York: Dutton)

Rosenblatt, Elihu, ed. (1996) *Criminal Injustice: Confronting the Prison Crisis* (South End Press)

Rosenblum, Nancy (ed.) (1989) *Liberalism and the Moral Life* (Harvard University Press)

Rossiter, Clinton (ed.) (1961) *The Federalist Papers* (Penguin)

Rothman, David J. (1971) *The Discovery of the Asylum* (Little Brown and Co. 1971)

Rousseau, Jean Jacques (1987) *Basic Political Writings* (Hackett)

Rusche, Otto and Georg Kirchheimer (1939) *Punishment and Social Structure* (New York: Columbia University Press)

Said, Edward (1978) *Orientalism* (London: Routledge)

— (1993) *Culture and Imperialism* (Vintage)

Sampford, Charles and D.J. Galligan (1986) *Law, Rights, and the Welfare State* (Croom Helm: Kent)

Sandel, Michael (1996) *Democracy's Discontent* (Harvard University Press)

Schattschneider, E.E. (1960) *The Semi-Sovereign People* (The Dryden Press)

Schechter, Stephen L. (ed.) (1990) *Roots of the Republic: American Founding Documents Interpreted* (Madison: Madison House)

Schlesinger, Arthur M. Jr. (1991) *The Disuniting of America*

Schmitt, Carl (1992) *The Crisis of Parliamentary Democracy* (MIT Press)

— *The Concept of the Political* (University of Chicago Press)

Schwartz, Bernard (1993) *History of the Supreme Court* (Oxford University Press)

Scott, David (1999) *Refashioning Futures: Criticism After Postcoloniality* (Princeton University Press)

Sealey, Raphael *Women and Law in Classical Greece* (1990) University of North Carolina Press)

Sen, Amartya (1999) *Development as Freedom* (New York: Random House)

Sentencing Project and Human Rights Watch (1998) *Losing the Vote: The Impact of Felony Disenfranchisement Laws in the United States*

Shapiro, Andrew L. (1993) "Challenging Criminal Disenfranchisement Under the Voting Rights Act: A New Strategy" *The Yale Law Journal* (Vol. 103: 537)

Shapiro, Ian (1999) *Democratic Justice* (Yale University Press)

Shapiro, Martin (1964) *Law and Politics in the Supreme Court: New Approaches to Political Jurisprudence* (NY: Free Press of Glencoe)

Shklar, Judith N. (1991) *American Citizenship: the quest for inclusion* (Harvard University Press)

Simon, Thomas W. (1985) *Democracy and Social Injustice: Law, Politics, Philosophy* (Rowman and Littlefield: Lanham and London)

Sinoploi, Rirchard C. (1992) *The Foundations of American Citizenship: Liberalism, The Constitution, and Civic Virtue* (Oxford University Press)

Skinner, Quentin (1984) "The Idea of Negative Liberty: Philosophical and Historical Perspectives" in R. Rorty, J.B. Schneewind and Q. Skinner, *Philosophy in History* (Cambridge University Press)

Smith, Rogers (1997) *Civic Ideals: Conflicting Visions of Citizenship in U.S. History* (Princeton University Press)

Smith, Terry (1998) "Reinventing Black Politics: Senate Districts, Minority Vote Dilution and the Preservation of the Second Reconstruction." 25 *Hastings Constitutional Law Quarterly* 277

Sniderman, Paul M. and Thomas Piazza (1993) *The Scar of Race* (Harvard University Press)

Snyder, Steven B. "Let My People Run: The Rights of Voters and Candidates Under State Laws Barring Felons from Holding Elective Office" *Journal of Law and Politics*

Spinoza, Benedict de (1951) *A Theologico-Political Treatise* (Dover Publications: New York) also (1989) (Leiden: EJ Brill)

Spivak, Gyatri Chakravorti (1993) *Outside the Teaching Machine* (Routledge, 1993)

St. Augustine (1472, 1984) *City of God* (Penguin Books)

Stavenhagen, Rodolpho (1965) "Classes, colonialism and acculturation" *Studies in Comparative International Development* 1,6

Steinfeld, Robert J. (1989) "Property and Suffrage in the Early American Republic" *Stanford Law Review* 41:335

Street, Paul "Color Bind, Prisons and the New American Racism" (2001) *Dissent,* Summer 2001.

Sugrue, Thomas (1996) *The Origins of the Urban Crisis: race and inequality in postwar Detroit* (Princeton University Press)

Sundquist, James L. (1983) *Dynamics of the Party System* Revised Edition (Brookings; Washington D.C.)

Tannenbaum, Frank (1946, 1992) *Slave and Citizen* (Boston: Beacon Press)

Thernstron, Abigail and Stephan (1997) *America in Black and White* (New York: Simon and Schuster)

Thomas, Kendall (1999) "Constitutional Equality: The Political Economy of Recognition: Affirmative Action Discourse and Constitutional Equality in Germany and the USA" 5 *Columbia Journal of European Law*, 329

Thompson, J. Phillip (2001) "Has Liberalism Lost Its Mind? Race and Local Democracy" in John Mollenkopf, ed. *Rethinking the Urban Agenda: Reinvigorating the Liberal Tradition in New York City and Urban America* (Century Foundation)

Tilly, Charles (1996) *Citizenship, Identity, and Social History* (Cambridge: The University Press)

Tims, Douglas R. (1975) "The Disenfranchisement of Ex-Felons: A Cruelly Excessive Punishment" 7 *Southwestern University Law Review* 124

Tocqueville, Alexis de (1969) *Democracy in America*, translated by George Lawrence (Harper Perennial)

Tonry, Michael (1995) *Malign Neglect: Race, Crime, and Punishment in America* (Oxford University Press)

Tourgée, Albion Winegar (1989) *The Invisible Empire* (Louisiana State University Press)

Trattner, Walter I. (1994) *From Poor Law to Welfare State: A History of Social Welfare in America* (New York: The Free Press)

Tribe, Laurence H. (2000) *American Constitutional Law*, Third Edition Vol. 1 (New York: Foundation Press)

Tunick, Mark (1992) *Punishment* (University of California Press)

Ture, Kwame and Charles Hamilton (1992) *Black Power: The Politics of Liberation* (Vintage Books: New York) Original publication 1967.

Turner, Bryan S. ((1988) *Status* (University of Minnesota Press)

— (1993) *Citizenship and Social Theory* (Sage Publications)

Twine, Fred (1994) *Citizenship and Social Rights: The interdependence of Self and Society* (Sage Publications)

Uggen, Christopher and Jeff Manza (2002) "Democratic Contraction? The Political Consequences of Felon Disenfranchisement Laws in the United States", 67 Am. Soc. Rev. 777.

Urbinati, Nadia (2000) "Representation as Advocacy: A Study of Democratic Deliberation" *Political Theory*, Vol. 28, 6: 758-786

Valleley, R.M. (1995) "National Parties and Racial Disenfranchisement." In *Classifying by Race.* Ed. P.E. Peterson (Princeton University Press)

Van den Berghe, Pierre (1978) *Race and Racism: A Comparative Perspective,* 2nd ed.(New York: Wiley)

Van Steenbergen, Bart ed. (1994) *The Condition of Citizenship* (Sage Publications)

Viroli, Maurizio (1995) *For Love of Country* (Oxford University Press)

Vogel, Ursula and Michael Moran (1991) *The Frontiers of Citizenship* (Macmillan: London)

Von Bar, Ludwig (1916) *History of Continental Criminal Law* (Little Brown and Co: Boston) von Hayek, F.A. (1976) *Law, Legislation, and Liberty* (Routledge: London vol. 1 1973, vol2. 1976)

Von Hirsch, Andrew (1976) *Doing Justice: The Choice of Punishment* (New York: Hill and Wang)

— (1985) *Past or Future Crimes: Deservedness and Dangerousness in the Sentencing of Criminals* (Rutgers University Press)

Waldrep, Christopher (1998) *Roots of Disorder: Race and Criminal Justice in the American South (1817-80)* (University of Illinois Press)

Wallerstein, Emmanuel (1980) *The Modern World System II: Mercantilism and the Consolidation of the European World Economy 1600-1750* (Academic Press: New York and London)

Walzer, Michael (1970) *Obligations: Essays on Disobedience, War, and Citizenship* (Harvard University Press)

(1983) *Spheres of Justice* (Basic Books)

(1982) "Citizenship" in Ball, Farr, and Hanson (eds.) *Political Innovation and Conceptual Change* (Cambridge University Press)

(1996) *What it Means to be an American: Essays on the American Experience* (New York: Marsilio)

Wang, Xi (1996) "Black Suffrage and the Redefinition of American Freedom: 1860-1970" *Cardozo Law Review:* 17: 2153

Ward, Lee "Nobility and Necessity: The Problem of Courage in Aristotle's *Nichomachean Ethics" American Political Science Review*, Vol. 95, No. 1, March 2001

Watts, Michael J. (1991) "Mapping meaning, denoting difference, imagining identity: dialectical images and postmodern geographies," *Geografiska Annaler* 73B:7-16, cited in Jacobs (1996)

Weber, Max (1958a) *The Protestant Ethic and the Spirit of Capitalism*, trans. Talcott Parsons (Scribners: New York)

1958b "Bureaucracy" from *Max Weber: Essays in Sociology*, H.H. Gerth and C. Wright Mills (eds. And Translators) (New York: Galaxy Book Edition): Part 2, Ch. 8, pp. 214-15

— (1972) *From Max Weber*, eds. H.H. Gerth and C.W. Mills (Oxford University Press)

(1978) *Economy and Society, an Outline of Interpretive Sociology* ed. Guenther Roth and Claus Wittich (University of California Press)

Wells Barnett, Ida (1900) "Lynch Law in America" reprinted in Beverly Guy-Sheftall (ed.) *Words of Fire: an Anthology of African-American Feminist Thought* (New York: The New Press 1995)

Westley, Robert (1998) "Many Billions Gone: Is it Time to Reconsider the Case for Black Reparations?" 40 *Boston College Law Review* 429

Whelan, Frederick G. "Prologue: Democratic Theory and the Boundary Problem"

White, Stephen K. (2000) *Sustaining Affirmation: the strengths of weak ontology in political theory* (Princeton University Press)

Wiecek, William (1977) *Sources of Antislavery Constitutionalism in America, 1760-1848*

Wilson, James Q. (1975, 1983) *Thinking About Crime* (New York: Vintage)

Wilson, William Julius (1987) *The Truly Disadvantaged: The Inner City, The Underclass, and Public Policy* (University of Chicago Press)

— (1996) When Work Disappears: The World of the New Urban Poor (New York: Knopf)

Windlesham, David James George Hennesy, Lord (1998) *Politics, Punishment, and Populism* (Oxford University Press)

Windlesham, David James George Hennesy, Lord (1998) *Politics, Punishment, and Populism* (Oxford University Press)

Wolin, Shedon (1960) *Politics and Vision* (Boston: Little Brown and Co.)

— (1996) "The Liberal/ Democratic Divide: On Rawls' *Political Liberalism.*" *Political Theory* Vol 24, Number 1, February 1996. p. 97

Wood, Ellen Meiksins (1994) "Democracy, An Idea of Ambiguous Ancenstry" in Euben, Wallach and Ober *Athenian Political Thought and the Reconstruction of American Democracy.* (Cornell University Press: Ithica and London)

— (1996) "Demos versus "We the People": Freedom and Democracy, Ancient and Modern" in Ober and Hedrick 1996

Wood, Gordon S. (1969) *The Creation of the American Republic: 1776-1787* (University of North Carolina Press)

Woodward (1951) C.Vann. *Origins of the New South: 1877-1913* (Louisiana State University Press)

— (1966) *The Strange Career of Jim Crow* 2nd Revised Edition (Oxford University Press)

Wyatt-Brown, Bertram (1982) *Southern Honor: Ethics and Behavior in the Old South* (Oxford University Press)

Xenophon, *Constitution of the Lakedaimonians*, ix. 6.

Young, Alison (1996) *Imagining Crime: Textual Outlaws and Criminal Conversations* (London, Thousand Oaks: Sage)

Young, Iris Marion (1990) *Justice and the Politics of Difference* (Princeton University Press)

— (2000)*Inclusion and Democracy* (Oxford University Press)

Zimring, Frank E. and Gordon Hawkins (1995) *Incapacitation: Penal Confinement and the Restraint of Crime* (Oxford University Press)

— and Sam Kamin (2001) *Punishment and Democracy: Three Strikes and You're Out in California* (Oxford University Press)

Index